Peruvian Democracy under Economic Stress

AN ACCOUNT OF THE BELAÚNDE ADMINISTRATION, 1963-1968

Peruvian Democracy under Economic Stress

AN ACCOUNT OF THE BELAÚNDE
ADMINISTRATION, 1963-1968

Pedro-Pablo Kuczynski

PRINCETON UNIVERSITY PRESS
PRINCETON, NEW JERSEY

To J. C. K.
and
to the memory of my parents

Preface and Acknowledgments

This book is in part a memoir. During the late sixties, I had a unique opportunity, as Economic Adviser and as one of the *Gerentes* (managers or executive directors) of the Central Reserve Bank, to be near the center of much of economic policy-making in Peru. Much of the material used here is based on my own recollection of events as seen from the inside, buttressed where necessary with the public information available, which in the case of many events is rather scarce.

This book tries to give an account of economic policies—and their political context—during the Belaúnde administration in Peru, 1963-1968. It is not meant to be a comprehensive account of economic events during the Belaúnde administration.[1] Rather, I have tried to give an analytic account of the forces that shaped economic policy during the period, especially the years of crisis 1966-1968, and to explain why Peru, after a promising and energetic bout of growth in the period after 1960, was unable to come to grips with some of the basic problems of development in a democratic context. The narrative concentrates on the years

[1] Among the published commentary on the major events of Peruvian economic history in the second half of the 1960's, the following may be mentioned: Central Reserve Bank of Peru, periodic *Economic Survey* (published bimonthly or quarterly as *Reseña Económica y Financiera*); Banco Continental (formerly a Chase Manhattan affiliate and now a state-owned bank), *Quarterly Economic Report*; the *Peruvian Times*; UN Economic Commission for Latin America, *Annual Economic Survey of Latin America*. International financial institutions, principally the International Monetary Fund, the International Bank for Reconstruction and Development (the World Bank), and CIAP (the InterAmerican Committee for the Alliance for Progress), have closely followed developments, especially those of a fiscal and financial nature, in their economic reports, but these have a limited circulation.

1966-1968 and ends in 1968, but of necessity a substantial amount of background analysis has been necessary. This background is covered in Chapters I to IV.

Peru is not the first developing country that has experienced a sharp political change in recent years. In many instances, of course, the swing looks bigger than it is, as a result of exaggeratedly rosy pictures of what the past was like and of a darkened picture of today's problems. Governments, international institutions, and economists would like development to be a smooth process, but the history of the post-war years has shown, with very few exceptions, that this is not so. The desire to find cases where development proceeds smoothly has led some policy-makers to pin the label "show-case" with sometimes excessive haste on some countries, only to find a short time later that their hopes have been dashed.

Is Peru more than a special case? While each country obviously has its own features, several of the salient episodes of Peruvian economic history in the period covered in this book bring out clearly some of the problems that face the leadership of other countries at a similar level of development. Among these issues are the unsuitability of traditional political machinery to the task of development, the resulting heavy dependence of the fortunes of the nation on the strengths and weaknesses of a few central figures, and the concentration of decision-making upon issues of short-term importance while policies in basic areas—such as industrialization, taxation, income distribution, and employment—are often the result of circumstances rather than of clear direction.

The challenge of these problems does not always lead to failure, however. A rapid economic and social evolution took place in Peru during the period covered by this book, especially in the early years. It is probably still too early to judge the period, but at least a beginning can be made in giving a chronicle of the major events.

❊ ❊ ❊

I should explain why this book appears originally in English rather than Spanish. The reason is simply my belief (perhaps a wrong one) that the audience in North America and Britain, which has had before it a relative large quantity of commentary about recent events in Peru, might be interested in an account in a somewhat more historical perspective.

I would like to thank Tulio De Andrea, Carlos Rodriguez-Pastor, Fernando Schwalb, Richard Webb Duarte, and several other friends for their helpful comments on parts of the manuscript. The faults of this book, however, are exclusively my own, and the opinions in it are not in any way attributable to organizations with which I was or am at present connected.

I also wish to thank Mrs. Sadie Bahr, Miss Ana Ponce, and Miss Rosario Obispo for having typed the manuscript at its various stages and helped in many ways with the work of putting it together.

Finally, a word of appreciation to my family, who often sacrificed their leisure in order to let me finish this book.

Princeton, New Jersey
June, 1975

Contents

Preface and Acknowledgments vii

List of Tables xiii

I. The Economic and Social Setting 3

II. Dramatis Personae 24

III. The Early Belaúnde Years, 1963-1966
I: The Development Effort 38

IV. The Early Belaúnde Years, 1963-1966
II: The Financial Problem 75

V. Interlude: The IPC Issue and the
Question of U.S. Aid 106

VI. Crisis, January-September 1967: Devaluation 126

VII. The Battle for Taxes 174

VIII. Sixty Days 219

IX. Coup 259

X. Epilogue 277

Statistical Appendix 285

Bibliography 291

Index 295

Map 46

List of Tables

1. Value of Merchandise Exports, 1950-1968   6
2. Book Value of Outstanding U.S. Direct
   Investment in Peru   10
3. Trends in Agricultural and Manufacturing
   Output, 1957-1968   12
4. Size Distribution of Income Estimates:
   Peru and Other Countries   19
5. Estimated Distribution of Cropland Ownership:
   Peru and Other Countries, 1960   20
6. Peruvian Labor Force, 1950-1966   21
7. Summary of Central Government Revenues and
   Outlays, 1957-1961   43
8. Summary of Central Government Finances,
   1961-1963   48
9. Some Indicators of Aggregate Growth:
   Peru and Latin America, 1961-1966   50
10. Public Investment, 1960-1967   59
11. Shares of National Income, 1962-1966   72
12. Central Government Expenditures and Current
    Revenues in Relation to GNP, 1961-1967   80
13. Estimate of Duties Exempted on Locally
    Assembled Cars and Small Trucks,
    1966 and 1967   83
14. Import Taxation, 1962-1967   86
15. Trends in Profits and Income Taxes, 1963-1968   87
16. Composition of Central Government
    Expenditures, 1961-1967   90
17. Trends in Public Schoolteachers' Salaries,
    1963-1966   92
18. Financing the Deficit of the Central
    Government, 1962-1967   96
19. Price Increases, 1955-1968   102

20. Simplified Monetary Survey, 1963-1967   103
21. Commitments of U.S. AID Capital Assistance and
    Grants, and Commitments of the World Bank
    and the Inter-American Development Bank to
    Selected Latin American Countries,
    July 1964 to June 1968   125
22. Merchandise Export Indices, 1958-1968   128
23. Indices of Trends in the Exchange Rate,
    1959-1966   130
24. Net Merchandise Exports, 1962-1967   131
25. Merchandise Imports, 1962-1967   136
26. Summary of Foreign Exchange Flows, 1962-1966   137
27. Summary Central Government Budgetary Cash
    Operations, First Quarter 1966 and 1967   144
28. The Prospective 1967 Central Government
    Budget Deficit   148
29. Central Bank Foreign Exchange and Gold
    Reserves, December 1966 to August 1967   157
30. Central Government Expenditures and Current
    Revenues in Relation to GNP, 1965-1968   199
31. Principal Tax Measures Taken in June 1968
    under Law 17044   232
32. Summary Central Government Budgetary Cash
    Operations, April-September 1967-1968   235
33. Principal Decrees Issued under Law 17044   240
34. Trends in Peru's External Public Debt,
    1962-1969   255
35. Effect of the Partial Refinancing in 1968 of the
    External Public Debt   258

Statistical Annex: Summary of
National Accounts   285

Peruvian Democracy under Economic Stress

AN ACCOUNT OF THE BELAÚNDE ADMINISTRATION, 1963-1968

CHAPTER I

The Economic and Social Setting

MOST descriptions of the poorer (or "developing") countries generally begin by listing a low rate of savings and investment, the disparity of income levels, the instability of the economy due to its heavy dependence on a few exports, the low level of skills in both the private and public sector, and the difficulty of internal communications. Generally, but not always, the climate is said to be inhospitable. In some ways, Peru fits the stereotype of the developing countries at least in its general lines. The physical and cultural setting of Peru is, however, rather unusual. The sharp physical distinction between the coast and the Sierra is paralleled by an equally sharp distinction between the five million or so Indians in the Sierra—who are only slowly being integrated with the Spanish-speaking culture—and the urban mass in Lima and Callao.

The lack of water on the coastal strip has been a major problem for Peruvian agriculture: except for the river valleys in their last few miles before the sea, after they have precipitously tumbled down the Western slope of the Andes, the whole length of the 1,200 miles of coast is a complete desert. Beyond the Andes, after an as yet largely unexploited set of valleys on the eastern side, lies the Amazonian plain, almost entirely covered by jungle and large meandering rivers. The main city, Iquitos, a somnolent port of 150,000 inhabitants on the northern bank of the Amazon, has had its ups and downs with the rubber boom, the export of live jungle animals to the United States, and now the development of oil in the Amazonic region.

Most foreign visitors to Peru, even if they venture outside the normal tourist areas, would even today not fail to be impressed by the extent of the foreign presence. Billboards near a slum will tell the shopper to go to Sears, the handicraft store advertises that it accepts cards from Diners' Club, and El Skyroom and El Sheraton overlook Lima at night. Although in this respect Peru is different only in degree from similar countries, there is no doubt about the large extent of foreign participation in the Peruvian economy in the sixties. Although developments in the sixties tended to alter the economic setting of Peru as described in this chapter, the changes were, with a few exceptions, alterations in emphasis rather than in basic character. Of the larger South American countries, Peru, in 1968, was still more of an export and private enterprise economy than most of the other countries of the continent.

EXPORTS

Exports have in the past been the main dynamic force in the "modern sector" of the economy. Except for mining in the Sierra, export activity has left the interior largely untouched. The "modern sector" was and still is concentrated on the coast. The fortunes of Lima and the coast have depended heavily on one or two export products, although in the last twenty years the structure of exports has become somewhat more diversified than in most developing countries. Following the traditional pattern, export activity has tended to be liberal in its use of capital (land and equipment) and economical of employment. Whereas in the mid-sixties exports of goods and services accounted for 18-20 percent of Gross Domestic Output, direct employment was and still is much smaller: employment in mining, fishmeal, and major agricultural exports in the mid-sixties did not directly account for more than 7 percent of total employment.[1]

The role of exports is not a mere historical accident. With

[1] The proportion is in all likelihood lower today, partly because of the decline in fishmeal output.

4

almost half the population concentrated in the poor Sierra, domestic purchasing power has always been relatively low and has been concentrated on the coast, where most of the export agriculture has been within easy reach of seaports; even the mineral wealth of the Sierra has naturally enough had to go through the coast in order to reach export markets. In such a setting, foreign trade was bound to become a major activity. As in many of the poorer countries, the growth of foreign trade was in spurts, depending upon the exploitation of some new natural resource in high demand. Such was the case of guano—a natural fertilizer that accumulates on off-shore islands because of the large population of marine birds combined with the lack of rainfall—in the mid-nineteenth century;[2] of the development of lead, zinc, copper, and silver mining in the twenties; of the rapid expansion of cotton and sugar production after the Second World War; and of the fishmeal boom in the early sixties.

In the period of rapid economic growth of the fifties and sixties, Peruvian exports increased in volume and value at an unprecedented rate. The expansion of exports provided the foreign exchange for the fairly rapid industrialization of the sixties and for the increasing demands of the "middle" class, in reality the economic group just below the very top fraction of income recipients. The growth of exports took place on a broad front, so that Peru acquired a diversified export base—fishmeal, copper, silver, lead, zinc, cotton, sugar, and coffee, but the main thrust came from two sources: the extraordinary development of the fishing industry and of large-scale copper mining. (See Table 1.)

The history of the Peruvian fishmeal industry is one of the better-known economic "miracles" of recent history.[3]

[2] See Shane J. Hunt, *Growth and Guano in Nineteenth Century Peru*, Discussion Paper No. 34, Research Program in Economic Development, Woodrow Wilson School, Princeton University, February 1973.

[3] An account of the fishmeal industry in its heyday is found in Michael Roemer, *Fishing for Growth: Export-Led Development in Peru, 1950-67*, Harvard University Press, 1970.

TABLE 1. VALUE OF MERCHANDISE EXPORTS, 1950-1968
(f.o.b. values in millions of current U.S. dollars)

	1950	1955	1960	1965	1968
Fishmeal &
fish products	6	12	50	186	218
Copper	10	29	95	121	188
Lead and zinc	23	40	38	74	65
Silver	8	16	24	39	62
Iron ore	—	8	33	47	68
Cotton	68	68	73	87	61
Sugar	30	37	48	37	61
Coffee	1	8	19	29	30
Other	48	53	53	47	48
Total merchandise
Exports, f.o.b.	194	271	433	667	801

SOURCE: Central Bank, *Cuentas Nacionales*.

The cold Humboldt current that runs northward up the
Peruvian coast has caused a desert coast interrupted only
by occasional rivers and fertile valleys. Peru thus faces an
agricultural supply problem unless farm development can
take place in the thus far largely inaccessible areas east of
the Andes. On the other hand, the Humboldt current per-
mits a marine wealth not found at similar latitudes, and
indeed nowhere else. The desert coast is therefore in a sense
the price for the rich sea, a major factor in the decision of
successive Peruvian governments to uphold territorial
waters of up to 200 miles.[4] The main resource of the sea is
a tiny fish called the *anchoveta*—not an anchovy—which is
ideal because of its tiny size and special texture for the
making of fish flour or fishmeal, the animal feed with the
highest protein content that can be made economically.

The development of large-scale fishing and of the fishmeal industry has been largely a domestic Peruvian phenomenon. From 1958 on, production grew by leaps and

[4] Fishing, however, takes place nearer the coast, except perhaps for
whaling and tuna fishing.

bounds, from 130,000 tons of fishmeal to 1.4 million tons in 1964 and close to 2 million tons in 1967. Production in 1970 was over 2 million tons, with a fish catch of more than 10 million tons. The fishmeal boom of the early sixties was a pell-mell affair, with many middle-class Peruvians, including such professionals as doctors, lawyers, and others with no business experience, getting into debt to buy a stake in a fishmeal factory or in fishing vessels. Little equity was put in, and with long-term financing scarcely available, most of the fishmeal industry was erected with short-term debt. The complicated nature of the fishing business (due to the vagaries of the availability of fish and to government-imposed fishing bans, needed for purposes of conservation), the financial pressure under which most of the fishmeal producers operated, the fairly frequent fluctuation in world prices (influenced by the production of competing proteins such as soybean meal), turned fishmeal operators into an aggressive and vocal group. With a limited reliance on imported inputs—which amounted to no more than 40 percent of total costs—and a large component of wage costs, the fishing and fishmeal industry was and still is particularly sensitive to the exchange rate, a fact explained by economics but little understood by the press or by the majority of politicians. This fact, and the aggressive private enterprise attitude of many fishmeal producers, explain why the industry was so concerned with government policies during the period covered by this book.[5]

The mining industry stands in sharp contrast to the fishing industry. It was largely a foreign-owned and run operation, with a few large mines accounting for the bulk of the output. The spurt in mineral exports in the early sixties was the result of large well-planned investments, which contrasted sharply with the free-for-all growth of the fishmeal industry. The main investment, begun in 1955 and completed in 1959, was in the Toquepala copper mine in

[5] Early in 1973 the industry was nationalized, partly because of the difficulties caused by the virtual disappearance of the *anchoveta*.

the south. Developed by the Southern Peru Copper Corporation—a combination of American Smelting and Refining, Phelps Dodge, Cerro Corporation, and Newmont Mining—as a result of the introduction of the Mining Code and of an agreement with the Odría government, the Toquepala mine is the largest in Peru. Somewhat earlier, in 1953, the Marcona Mining Company, a consortium of Utah Construction and Cyprus Mines, had opened a large iron-ore mine. These two investments, totaling about U.S. $300 million, financed in large part with loans from the U.S. government-owned Export-Import Bank, propelled Peru from a backseat in the mining establishment of the world to the status of a major copper producer and a growing iron-ore exporter.

Peru has undeniable natural advantages for mining. In the course of its seventy years in Peru,[6] Cerro de Pasco Corporation, which was the largest and most diversified mining enterprise, either by itself or through others identified and measured copper deposits that form one of the largest single unexploited group of potential copper mines in the world. Although some of the deposits have a low ore content, the proximity of most of them to the sea, the development of advanced refining techniques, and the high cost of mining in the United States are making their exploitation progressively more feasible and financially attractive. On the basis of an agreement reached in 1969 with the military government, Southern Peru is at present developing the Cuajone deposit, the largest single unexploited mine waiting to be developed during the Belaúnde administration.

The attitude of international mining companies is in general conditioned by the long-term nature of their investments. Their main needs have been long-term tax agreements and guarantees about the availability of foreign

[6] Cerro began its operations in 1902. In January 1974, the government expropriated Cerro's local subsidiary, Cerro de Pasco Corporation, and in February 1974 signed an agreement with the U.S. government providing for compensation to Cerro and to several other U.S. investors.

8

exchange to repay their debts abroad and to remit their profits, and, if necessary, depreciation and depletion allowances. More than other investors, mining companies are willing to wait and negotiate for long periods of time until they obtain the best possible treatment, since the investments affected can have a life of twenty-five years or more.

The relations between the major foreign mining companies and the Peruvian government during the Belaúnde administration were somewhat distant but diplomatically maintained. The attitude of the companies was cautious, and they were generally scrupulous about paying their taxes.

At the time of the Belaúnde administration, the mining companies held the key to Peru's future prosperity.[7] Mining offered the only opportunity for the substantial growth in exports. The other export sectors, such as fishmeal and high-grade long-staple cotton, appeared to have limited possibilities because production depends on natural supply in the first case or on the availability of irrigated coastal lands in the latter; sugar and coffee faced limited markets. Although locally owned mining companies had shown drive and profits in the sixties, the major new investments required the presence of the foreign mining companies, whether alone or in conjunction with the Peruvian government. Since the Toquepala mine was opened in 1959, the companies had made only routine investments in Peru: opportunities elsewhere—as in Chile—were better from a tax point of view; a tax claim against Southern Peru Copper was pending until 1968, and it was not until then that Congress gave the executive authority to enter into the special agreements that the companies had continuously insisted upon. Mining output rose very slowly in the sixties, and it was only because the price of copper started a sharp rise in 1966 that the growth of export earnings kept up.

[7] The relative importance of mining may change somewhat because of the discovery of petroleum in commercial quantities in the Amazon basin.

The export boom that began in 1959 made it possible for Peru to maintain a stable exchange rate, without any exchange controls, for a much longer period than the increase in domestic costs would normally have allowed. Although the rise in the cost of living was very moderate in comparison with that in Chile, Argentina, or Brazil, the consumer price index—which probably underestimated the rise in domestic costs—was already rising at an annual rate of 6 percent from 1960 to 1963, and accelerated to over 10 percent in the three years to 1966, an increase of 70 percent in six years.

With its image as an economy with a stable and free exchange, rapid aggregate economic growth, and a reasonably stable government, Peru managed to attract a growing inflow of foreign investment, particularly from the United States. Although Peru had by the end of the sixties only 6 percent of total United States investment in Latin America, the increase was at a faster rate than into other Latin American countries, Mexico excepted. A growing and increasingly protected domestic market encouraged investment into manufacturing. (See Table 2.)

TABLE 2. BOOK VALUE OF OUTSTANDING U.S. DIRECT
INVESTMENT IN PERU
(millions of U.S. dollars)

	Total	Mining	Petro-leum	Manu-facturing	Utilities	Trade	Other
1961	436	242	71	37	20	43	23
1965	515	262	60	79	21	54	39
1967	605	340	38	98	22	54	53

SOURCE: U.S. Department of Commerce, *Survey of Current Business*.

AGRICULTURE AND MANUFACTURING

The export and foreign investment boom in the sixties continued the established export-induced pattern of development in Peru. At the same time, however, an accelerated shift from agriculture to manufacturing began taking place. Although Peru in the early sixties probably had a significantly lower level of protection than most other South American countries, protection increased sharply in the course of the decade as a result of two general import tariff increases and of the introduction in 1968 of various import prohibitions. Combined with higher purchasing power for consumer goods, protection inevitably provides a strong stimulus to manufacturing.

While manufacturing was thus more than shielded against the effects of a fixed exchange rate that increasingly encouraged imports, this was not the case with agriculture. The growing disadvantage of domestic agriculture in the face of food imports could have been offset through the aggressive use of existing tariff mechanisms, but this was not done, following the traditional policy of attempting to keep the price of basic foodstuffs down. This type of policy, practiced since the thirties in Peru, is a well-known feature of many Latin American and several Asian economies. The main element in the drop in total Peruvian agricultural output, however, was the decline in production for export, particularly of cotton. (See Table 3.)

The contrasting performance of manufacturing against that of agriculture is strikingly illustrated by the following estimates. The manufacturing sector was helped not only by a rising level of protection, but also by the increasingly liberal use of tax concessions, particularly on import duties for the import of raw materials and machinery, and on profits taxes through reinvestment allowances. Import duty and profits tax exemptions for industry rose very rapidly in the sixties in relation to total industrial output, as noted below in Chapter IV. The rapid increase in protection for consumer industries, together with the exemptions for component parts, stimulated the creation of assembly industries, notably cars, home appliances, paint, artificial textiles, and pharmaceuticals. All required a high level of protection. A

11

TABLE 3. TRENDS IN AGRICULTURAL AND MANUFACTURING OUTPUT, 1957-1968

	1957/59	1961	1962	1963	1964	1965	1966	1967	1968
Agric. production index (incl. food)	100	124	125	122	130	127	127	125	118
Food production index	100	120	119	118	126	125	128	134	121
Food production per person index	100	110	106	102	106	102	101	103	90
Food imports (U.S. $ million)	n.a.	73	81	86	96	121	130	140	n.a.
Manufacturing production index	100	138	153	164	179	193	211	221	219

SOURCE: U.S. Department of Agriculture; Central Bank, *Cuentas Nacionales*; and manufacturing output estimates based partly on electric power consumption by manufacturing industry, as computed in Banco Continental, *Quarterly Economic Report*.

few of these industries had a better chance than others of lowering their costs over a period of a decade, but some, such as the car assembly plants, had very little chance of becoming economic for a very long time.

The establishment of the car assembly plants in 1964 gradually generated a debate on whether such industries were in the national interest. The discussion was mostly in terms of whether the establishment of the plants, including the initial inflow of foreign capital, saved foreign exchange at all or not. Hardly any attention was paid to the cost of this saving, if indeed there was any saving of foreign exchange;[8] the cost is not only the fiscal revenue lost, and the diversion of investment away from possibly more remunerative activities for the country, but also the substantial loss of flexibility in the import pattern. If Peru had faced a foreign exchange shortage fifteen or twenty years ago,

[8] This point is discussed below in Chapter IV.

temporary restrictions on certain luxury imports could conceivably have had a positive effect at little political cost; however, in the mid and late sixties, the cost was the unemployment of skilled assembly line workers, a much less acceptable result.

THE ROLE OF THE PUBLIC SECTOR

A striking feature of economic life in Peru, at least until the end of the sixties, was the traditionally limited role of the public sector. The roots of the laissez-faire tradition in Peruvian economic and political life probably lie in the relatively high degree of concentration of power and wealth that in the past was an outstanding characteristic of Peru, even in relation to other Latin American countries. Apart from the low proportion of government expenditure and taxation in relation to the national product—the consequence and outward sign of the small degree of intervention of the state—there were still in the sixties many other signs of relative "laissez-faire" in Peru. Until 1964 taxes were collected and government payments made through a privately owned institution; electric power generation and distribution is still largely in the hands of a privately owned company with a large European shareholding;[9] the same was true until 1970 of the ITT-controlled telephone company serving Lima and a Swiss-controlled company serving the provinces; Peru's two major railroads were owned until 1972 by a Canadian-based British company.

Private management of regulated public services undoubtedly compared favorably in most cases with the few state-run commercial enterprises. Peru had and still has relatively efficient urban electric and water supply at little cost to the taxpayer. At the same time, the small size of the public enterprise sector until the end of the sixties meant that the government budget was relatively free of the sub-

[9] By the beginning of 1974, the government had a controlling interest.

sidy payments that plague the finances of some other developing countries.

With the passage of time, it was inevitable that there should be increasing journalistic and parliamentary pressure for the state to assume a leading role in new prestige enterprises. In the thirties the government took over the bankrupt Peruvian steamship company, and in the early forties it started a pilot steel mill on the north coast: both enterprises expanded as a result of massive foreign supplier credits for equipment, often of marginal use. The quality of management in public sector enterprises was, with occasional exceptions, quite low.

Until the early 1960's the budget had been traditionally a passive instrument of development. On the expenditure side, the major outlays were to keep going the administration and a modest level of public education, to maintain the armed forces, and to carry out a modicum of public investment, particularly for road construction and maintenance. Except in some years when construction on a number of large projects happened to coincide, public investment in the fifties averaged a meager 10 to 15 percent of public outlays, or less than 2 percent of the national product. Aside from direct construction, the government attempted to encourage large-scale agriculture, and also manufacturing and medium-sized mining enterprises through credit by state development banks. Although the Agricultural Bank and the Industrial Bank received their greatest impetus in the sixties, they were already important in the fifties, mostly for short-term financing of production. Both institutions had a heavy private sector representation on their boards and a strong commercial orientation in their activity. Both institutions financed themselves largely out of credits from the Central Bank and U.S. commercial banks.

On the revenue side, the government traditionally paid little attention to the use of taxation for development. The major sources of revenue were indirect domestic taxes—

particularly the stamp tax on domestic transactions, a sort of sales tax—import duties, and profits taxes, which were paid by a few large companies. The emphasis on indirect taxation properly reflected the administration's limited ability to collect income taxes, a common occurrence in economies at a similar level of development, which have a large proportion of rural and semi-employed workers. Taxation was not designed as a means of encouraging or discouraging certain types of economic activity. Custom duties were set to provide revenue, and so was the level of the stamp tax; on the other hand, real estate, a magnet for private funds in times of inflation and political instability, was left virtually free of taxation. Whereas customs duties on consumer goods, and exemptions for raw materials and machinery, were beginning to be used significantly in the early sixties to encourage the establishment of manufacturing plants to substitute imports of consumer articles, government policy traditionally avoided taxing imported foodstuffs, in order to keep the price of staples down. As a result, the government generally resorted to large-scale imports of cereals and dairy products, to the detriment of domestic agriculture.[10]

The limited role of government in the economy was paralleled by a shortage of talent in the public sector. It is of course difficult to measure talent, but Peru was—and may still be—distinctly behind other major countries in Latin America in the level of its administrative sophistication and training. To some extent this is a reflection of the modest managerial resources of the country, which have not kept up with the growth of income. The upper income groups have not encouraged their children to work outside the family firm or estate and to gain outside experience: as a result, the youths who could afford a high-level technical education have not taken advantage of the opportunity to the same extent as in the case of some other Latin

[10] This aspect of agricultural policy was continued by the new government that assumed power in 1968.

American countries. Partly because of relatively modest salaries, upper income groups, at least until the early sixties, avoided government service except in ministerial or diplomatic positions. Peru has been fortunate in having had two good university-level schools of engineering and agronomy: however, when the children of the upper income groups went to these colleges, they often ended up using little of their university training in their future activity.

The small number of available men for salaried managerial positions has inevitably led to the frequent use of imported talent. For example, all the major Peruvian-owned commercial banks in the sixties operated with at least one foreigner as head of their management. A high proportion of manufacturing plants had foreigners as their technical directors, and they were not Peruvians born of foreign parents, but outside managers brought especially for the job.

The public sector did not fare as well as the private sector in the use of this imported talent, because foreigners would obviously be quite out of place in the government, in addition to being legally barred from serving in it. More important, the Peruvian upper class has no tradition of public service. Except for the career diplomatic service, which was well organized, the government attracted few highly qualified younger professionals, particularly in the area of financial management. One exception was that of the Central Reserve Bank, a then fairly autonomous institution, in the period 1962-1969. For most of the government, however, a salary scale that placed excessive emphasis on length of service meant that only people of independent means could afford public posts, but precisely these people were unwilling to work in public administration in anything but ministerial posts. The case of Peru in this respect stands in sharp contrast to Chile, Colombia, or Mexico.

The lack of an even rudimentary financial administration in the government is a major factor in understanding Peru's recent economic history: the public sector's ability to cope with the analysis of economic problems did not improve substantially in the fifties and sixties, a period during which population rose 75 percent, the national product grew in real terms by 180 percent, exports more than quadrupled, the national debt multiplied ten times. Nor can it be said that the press and informed opinion substantially increased their capacity to understand economic problems, at a time when most political issues revolved increasingly around economic questions. The serious university-level study of economics was and is still in its infancy, and much that passes as economics is in fact either accounting or the history of political doctrine. As long as the problems remained simple, this ignorance may in fact have been an advantage. However, in the sixties, large public investment commitments, the enormous rise of public expenditure for education and other social services, the weight of foreign indebtedness—to cite only a few complex problems—all required a more informed administration, Congress, press, and business opinion. These did not exist.

Social Imbalance

An analysis of the social situation in Peru depends on impressions rather than facts, because, except for a few scattered studies, there is no coherent body of social statistics. All observers will agree that Peru has a high concentration of wealth, not only within a small opulent class, but also regionally in the metropolitan area of Lima and the port city of Callao. The type of disparities between the center and the periphery, or between the "modern" and "traditional" sectors, are of course common to most developing economies. So are the disparities between the various levels of income recipients. Whether these differences are significantly more marked in Peru cannot be conclusively established, but available estimates show that Peru is certainly not better off. The existence in the Sierra of about 40 percent of the population in conditions not too different from those of four hundred years ago is bound to be re-flected in wide income disparities. The existing estimates by Webb of the size distribution of income in Peru[11] for the sixties show a marked concentration of income; this is paralleled by a very large difference between the average income of the top groups and that of the groups at the bottom. On the other hand, the average income of the latter—if the statistics can be believed—was somewhat higher than that of their counterparts in Colombia or Brazil, in the latter case presumably because of the very low income levels in some areas of the Northeast. In any event, while the data do not permit precise comparisons, there can be little doubt of the substantial concentration of income in Peru. (See Table 4.)

The concentration of income is paralleled by a substan-tial but unmeasured concentration of wealth.[12] In the past, this wealth was largely in land, but already by the early sixties a rapid shift had begun to urban real estate and industry. While the new assets were probably somewhat less concentrated than land ownership, the close-knit form of industrial organization and the low to moderate effective taxation of profits—with virtually no taxation of real estate wealth—means that the concentration of urban wealth was probably not much less than for landed wealth in the past.

The information on the concentration of land ownership in the fifties and sixties is well known. Although less inexact than in the case of income distribution, the data are still subject to all sorts of caveats. For example, figures on con-centration on the coast include land unusable without irri-

[11] Principally in Richard C. Webb, *The Distribution of Income in Peru*, Discussion Paper No. 26, Research Program in Economic De-velopment, Woodrow Wilson School, Princeton University, Septem-ber 1972. Most of the information is for 1961, but there are impor-tant pieces for later years.

[12] Carlos Malpica, in *Los Dueños del Perú*, Fondo de Cultura Popular, Lima, 1970, gives an account of some of the families that used to own important assets, especially land.

18

TABLE 4. Size Distribution of Income Estimates:
Peru and Other Countries
(estimated percentage shares of national income by group shown)

Groups:	Bottom 20%	Next 40%	Top 40%	(of which top 10%)
Peru	3.5	14.7	81.8	49.2
Brazil	4.2	17.8	78.0	49.0
Colombia	2.5	23.5	74.0	48.0
Mexico	4.2	16.7	79.1	49.9
44 countries (average)	5.6	20.4	74.0	44.0
including: Israel	6.8	32.0	61.2	19.0
Japan	4.7	26.4	68.9	23.0

Sources: Albert Fishlow, *Brazilian Size Distribution of Income* in *American Economic Review*, Papers and Proceedings of 84th Annual Meeting, May 1972; Colombia: Miguel Urrutia and Clara Elsa de Sandoval, *La Distribución de Ingresos entre los Perceptores de Renta en Colombia—1964*, in *Revista del Banco de la República*, Bogota, July 1970; Mexico: Ifigenia M. de Navarrete, *La Distribución del Ingreso en México—Tendencias y Perspectivas* in *El Perfil de México en 1980*, Siglo XXI Editores, Mexico D.F., 1970; 44 countries— Irma Adelman and Cynthia Taft Morris, *An Anatomy of Income Distribution Patterns in Developing Nations*, World Bank Economic Staff Working Paper No. 116, 1971; Peru—Webb, *The Distribution of Income in Peru*. Except for Israel and Japan, the 44 countries selected by Adelman and Morris are generally considered "developing" economies.

gation: the picture of concentration may be accurate, but not the inference that income arising from this land would be as concentrated. For this reason, the figures below refer to crop or arable land, and therefore understate concentration to the extent of the ownership of land that could be used in future if it were irrigated. Still, the concentration that emerges as of the early 1960's, especially at the upper end of farm sizes, is high even if compared to the average for South America. This was paralleled in the coastal areas by a high level of concentration of access to water for irrigation. (See Table 5.)

TABLE 5. Estimated Distribution of Cropland Ownership: Peru and Other Countries, 1960

Size of farm	Under 1 ha.	1-5 ha.	5-50 ha.	over 50 ha.
Peru				
% of owners with				
>1 ha.	—	73.8	22.9	3.3
% of total cropland	4.3	26.5	25.3	43.9
Range of average				
farm size (ha.)	0.4	1.8	3-10	72-313
Colombia				
% of owners with				
>1 ha.	—	50.3	40.4	4.1
% of total cropland	1.9	15.4	41.0	39.7
Range of average				
farm size (ha.)	0.3	1.8	3-10	56-103
South America (total)				
% of owners with				
>1 ha.	—	36.4	45.8	17.8
% of total cropland	0.7	7.9	34.3	57.1
Range of average				
farm size (ha.)	0.4	2.8	4-10	68-160

Source: Data and estimates shown in *Report on the 1960 World Census of Agriculture*, Vol. 5, United Nations Food and Agriculture Organization, Rome, 1971.

The regional concentration of income is perhaps a phenomenon of a different nature. There is no statistical doubt about the concentration of activity in the Lima area. When metropolitan Lima at the end of the sixties had about 22 percent of the total population, one half of the GNP originated there, compared to 40 percent in 1960. To cite a few random indicators, Lima had 70 percent of the doctors, 85 percent of the private cars, and 40 percent of the literate population of the country.[13] The population of the Lima area has grown at a much faster rate than the national average of 3 percent. Migration into the main cities, par-

[13] Data for 1969-1970.

ticularly into Lima, has been stimulated, as in most developing countries, by the attraction of bright lights and by the supposed comfort of Lima in comparison with stagnant incomes in the countryside and the drabness of life there. The stagnation of agriculture in the last decade has been a major cause of accelerating migration into the cities, perhaps even more than in Colombia, Mexico, or Chile. Available estimates show that the labor force in agriculture, including peasant farmers, grew at a much slower rate in recent years than did population or employment in other sectors. Altogether, agriculture, manufacturing, and government in the first half of the sixties absorbed only less than 60 percent of the increase in the labor force, thus leaving a large part to be absorbed by the so-called "services," a category that hides very low incomes or underemployment or both. (See Table 6.) The emigration from the countryside, combined with the scarcity of remunerative employment, mean that Lima is today surrounded on three sides by the most conspicuous slums in Latin America. Although the lack of vegetation exaggerates this eyesore, and although many shanty-town dwellers do in fact have steady jobs

TABLE 6. PERUVIAN LABOR FORCE, 1950-1966
(thousands)

	Census			Average Annual % Change	
	1950	1961	1966	1950/61	1961/66
Agriculture and fisheries	1,522	1,704	1,846	1.0	1.7
Manufacturing and Mining	335	435	510	2.4	3.2
Government	104	176	240	4.9	6.4
Other	623	912	1,124	3.5	4.3
Total	2,584	3,227	3,720	2.0	2.9
Population	8,070	10,420	12,103	2.4	3.0

SOURCE: Central Bank, *Cuentas Nacionales.*

21

and literacy and some have electricity and television sets, the slum problem in all its ramifications is gigantic and immediate. Its roots lie not only in the dislocations generally associated with modernization, but especially in the relative impoverishment of the countryside, which results in a large migration to urban areas. This phenomenon has been accentuated in Peru, as in other Latin American countries, by the policies of governments to keep the prices of food staples low and if possible stationary, with the result that peasant agriculture has in most years faced declining terms of trade in relation to domestic manufacturing.

The concentration of wealth in Lima led to periodic efforts on the part of the government to encourage investment outside. The Planning Office regularly, since its inception in 1962, came out in favor of more decentralized investment. A laudable point of view, it had little practical impact on private investment, which inevitably gravitated to the only really large urban center in Peru. It is doubtful if the virtually complete profits tax exemption that was granted new industries in the Sierra and Amazon regions under Belaúnde did much to encourage investment in those areas, except for investment that would otherwise have taken place anyway because of the proximity of natural resources, such as the manufacture of wood products. The attraction of the Lima market and the fact that tax exemptions there have in any case been generous have generally outweighed the attraction of investment in manufacturing outside the area. Another device was the creation of so-called industrial parks, near Arequipa in the south and near Trujillo on the north coast. These parks, within which manufacturing plants were free from all taxes, including turnover taxes of 5 percent normally applied to purchases of materials, had some measure of success in attracting new plants, such as canneries, although at considerable fiscal cost for the investment realized.

One more case of deliberate encouragement of investment outside Lima was the creation in the first half of the sixties of various regional commercial banks. The idea was that through local control these banks would give closer attention to the provincial areas they served than the branches of Lima banks already established in those areas. The seven regional banks were simple commercial banks, making short-term loans, and they are in no sense development institutions. In practice, the purpose of the regional banks was not fulfilled. The banks were able to capture only a small share of deposits, and these funds were lent out largely to the main shareholders of each bank. The proportion of uncollectable loans was high, and most of the banks survived only through continuous Central Bank rediscounts, with one or two of them permanently on the verge of bankruptcy (they were taken over by the state banking system in the new government). It is obvious that deposits equivalent to two or three million dollars were quite insufficient to support a commercial bank, especially one with branches. Although, on the positive side, the development of some entrepreneurial local pride can be mentioned, the regional banks in fact contributed little to the diversification of investment outside Lima.

The basic features summarized above did not change in substance during the period of the Belaúnde administration. Five years is too short a span for that. However, there was undoubtedly some evolution,[14] which income distribution estimates—more than ten years old by now—have not measured. Change was as much the result of the trend of economic modernization as of deliberate government policy, which was especially influential in education and health. It is doubtful, however, if the growth and change were sufficient to provide remunerative employment for the expanding labor force—growing annually by 120,000—especially from 1967 on, when the financial crisis became paramount.

[14] See the end of Chapter III.

23

CHAPTER II

Dramatis Personae

FERNANDO BELAÚNDE TERRY

When Fernando Belaúnde Terry[1] was inaugurated as President of Peru on July 28, 1963, a new era began. A military junta, faithfully keeping its promise to return the country to civilian rule within one year, had allowed the June 1963 elections in which Belaúnde defeated the chieftain of the APRA (Alianza Popular Revolucionaria Americana) by a small majority. Despite the fact that he obtained only a plurality of the vote, Belaúnde was an extremely popular figure, capable of drawing and inspiring a crowd at a moment's notice. He was the first president who had a real and wide knowledge of the interior of the country, having visited the remotest regions of the Andes and the Amazon basin during his two previous electoral campaigns in 1956 and 1962, and throughout his political career.

Belaúnde, born in Lima in 1912, comes from one of Peru's patrician families noted for its public service. His father, Rafael Belaúnde, was prime minister in the Bustamante administration (1945-1948) and his uncle, Victor Andrés Belaúnde, was a major figure in Peruvian diplomacy for many years. Aside from three years as a Congressman (*diputado*) in 1945-1948, Fernando Belaúnde himself has been an architect all his professional life and has always been a man of modest financial means.

Belaúnde's philosophy was dominated by a plea for the

---

[1] A description of Belaúnde's early career can be found in Frederick B. Pike, *The Modern History of Peru*, Praeger, 1969; an illuminating analysis of the ideological development of Belaúnde and Acción Popular is in Francois Bourricaud, *Power and Society in Contemporary Peru*, Praeger, 1970 (French version, 1967).

participation of all Peruvians in the political process, especially those outside Lima. The view emphasized not only participation of all regions in the political process—in the 1963 election, for example, Lima provided 43 percent of the voters even though it contained only about one-quarter of the voting-age population—but also integration of the rest of the country in the economic life of the country, which was dominated by Lima. Belaúnde developed his views between his 1956 and 1962 campaigns for the presidency, a period during which he covered a large part of the interior, often on horseback or even on foot, reaching areas where no national politician, let alone a presidential candidate, had ever set foot. These views were expressed in a series of speeches and books, centered around catchy titles.[2]

Popular participation came to be expressed not only in the revival in 1963 of elected municipal government for the first time in forty years, but also by giving the people a stake in economic development through a work program, Cooperación Popular. The latter idea went back to Belaúnde's interpretation of development under the Incas, who had not had money to build their roads, terraces, and fortresses but had known how to put labor to productive use. Peru had somehow to get around its "déficit de soles y abundancia de brazos." Even though Cooperación Popular had many political and financial difficulties and was to lose, toward the end of the Belaúnde administration, the drive of the first years, its achievements were impressive. This was not only in physical terms but especially in giving lower income groups a feeling that the government—hitherto a distant and vague entity, whose contact with the groups was often only that of sending the army into an area to press young men into military service—was concerned with their efforts. The idea that the government was not just a welfare

---

[2] Among them: *Pueblo por Pueblo*, Lima, 1959; *La Conquista del Perú por los Peruanos*, Ediciones Tawantinsuyo, Lima, 1959. An English translation of the latter was published in Lima in 1965 under the title *Peru's Own Conquest*.

agency, but that it encouraged self-help and participation was a most important idea that is increasingly recognized by planners of economic development.[3]

It is true, as Bourricaud says,[4] that "Belaundism is an impulse rather than a dogma." It was a feeling for priorities, not a detailed program. But the reorientation proposed was undoubtedly right: the interior instead of Lima; political decentralization and local participation instead of appointments from the capital; reorienting new agricultural investment away from the coast to the "*Ceja de Montaña*."[5] The difficulties, of course, arose in the execution: the rapidly industrializing urban sector (basically Lima) had other priorities (such as higher tariffs, urban expressways, higher salaries). Belaúnde never really accepted the problem of conflicting economic claims; he tried instead to satisfy competing claimants. An equally important if not greater obstacle was that of the relations with Congress, especially APRA.

Belaúnde was elected with an opposition Congress. Until the end of his term his party was faced in Congress by the majority opposition alliance of APRA and UNO—Union Nacional Odriista, led by General Odría, military ruler of Peru between 1948 and 1956. This apparently incredible alliance of two groups that until then had feuded bitterly was in part made possible by the increasing conservatism of the APRA leadership and the realization by Odría that he was powerless alone. A major factor in the parliamentary

[3] See, for example, Robert S. McNamara, speech to the Board of Governors of the World Bank, Nairobi, September 1973, pp. 11-12, 17.

[4] François Bourricaud, *Power and Society in Contemporary Peru,* Frederick A. Praeger, New York, 1970; quoted phrase appears on p. 253.

[5] The eastern slopes of the Andes, facing the Amazonic region, a belt of generally unexploited land about 1,000 miles in length and ranging in width from 50 to 100 miles, at elevations of 1,000 to 3,500 feet. Physically, it is probably best suited for cattle and for oil-seed development (such as African palm).

26

stalemate was of course the strength, due to the proportional representation system of election—"la cifra repartidora"—of the Christian Democrats, on the one hand, and UNO, on the other. The Christian Democrats, formally the allies of the government and Acción Popular, in fact accentuated even further the lack of unity in the Acción Popular leadership.

Faced with such an opposition Congress,[6] which was unchangeable since there were no mid-term elections, Belaúnde could easily have made a show of force with the help of the army, which supported him during most of his term in office. Nevertheless, he constantly refused to do so and to take any measures that in any way might even remotely bypass the constitutional rights of Congress. Obtaining approval for fiscal measures, particularly tax measures, became a herculean task that was achieved only in the last months of the Belaúnde administration.

President Belaúnde was above all a builder. He saw the country as a vast terrain on which an architect could exercise his skills. While he saw the need for useful economic infrastructure investments of various kinds—such as roads, irrigation, schools, health facilities, and housing—the financial aspects of this investment interested him little. Somehow economic and financial considerations would bend in face of the priority of developing at all costs. While Belaúnde admired the idea of personal savings, the importance of national savings for development was not apparent to him with the same force. His attitude to financial questions was a deeply ingrained one and evolved only slowly as a result of persistent advice pressed upon him in the latter part of his term of office.

The Managers of Public Finance

The Ministers of Finance of that period are an important part of our story. Most of them—there were seven between

---

[6] The composition of Congress is shown below in Chapter III.

1963 and the coup on October 3, 1968; four of whom held office in the last year of the government—were hemmed in between a spending Cabinet and a Congress, supported by most of the press, which vociferously refused to admit even the smallest tax increase. Congress itself was generally against tax increases, but not always against unfinanced expenditures. With the exception of the last Minister of Finance, none received the united and uncompromising support of the Cabinet for the tax measures that virtually all of them requested from Congress.

One element of continuity in the Finance Ministry was Luis González del Valle. He was a rare example of that supposedly non-existent species, the permanent and competent high-ranking Latin American civil servant. González del Valle managed to survive a succession of ministers by deftly avoiding the limelight. He did not want to be identified with any group. Proud of working in a ramshackle office, rarely seeing outside visitors, he was in fact the center of policy-making in the Finance Ministry, and the only element of continuity. Although he was a one-man operation, he was never afraid of giving blunt advice to his ministers. Together with the Central Bank economic advisers, he formed a team that was cordially loathed by the Lima elite, some of whom thought there were sinister motives in the emphasis given by the economic advisers to the need for more tax revenues.

As the Finance Ministers changed, so did the boards of the Central Bank, although with less regularity. The board and the chairman of the Central Reserve Bank had less operational importance than the Finance Minister, but they were important in preserving the role of the institution as a reasonably independent economic adviser to the government. A key figure was Fernando Schwalb, chairman of the bank from February 1966 to the beginning of 1968. A distinguished lawyer, supporter and friend of Belaúnde from the earliest days, Schwalb came to the Central Bank in 1966 after having served Belaúnde for two years as Prime Minister and Foreign Minister. His background was largely diplomatic and legal, not economic, but through his connection with the government he gave the younger economists of the bank an opportunity to advise the Ministry of Finance on a hitherto unknown scale. These efforts culminated, somewhat belatedly, in the fiscal measures taken at the end of the administration.

The chairmanship of the Central Bank was not generally regarded as a full-time activity, although the holder of the office had considerable discretion in what he did. However, his relations with the government, and especially with the president, were crucial. In the period 1966-1967, there was sometimes a reluctance on the part of the chairman of the bank to confront the president with the reality of the financial problems facing the country. As a result, the professional staff of the bank acquired a visibility it did not seek. At the head of the staff during that period was Javier Otero, who had spent twenty-five years at the bank and had been a driving force in modernizing it and assembling a professional economic staff. He had been helped in that task by Carlos Rodriguez-Pastor, a lawyer then in his early thirties, who succeeded Otero in 1968, and by Richard C. Webb Duarte, who had done his graduate work in economics at Harvard. When Rodriguez-Pastor took over as head of the staff in January 1968, the average age of the three-man management team of the bank, including Webb and the author, was thirty-one.

As a result of a program begun in the early sixties with help from the Ford Foundation, the Central Bank had by 1967-1968 assembled one of the best-qualified teams of economists in any Latin American country at that time. The selection process was a good example of opening careers to talent. Each year about twenty of the best economics students from universities around Peru were selected by the research department of the bank. Those chosen were then put through an intense three-month course taught by full-time professors (usually one from Princeton or Harvard,

29

and one from the Catholic University of Chile). At the end of the course, half a dozen or so were selected to enter the bank, and were usually sent for two years of graduate study abroad at the expense of the bank (usually to Chile, Mexico, or the United States). By 1967-1968, about twenty of them had returned with graduate degrees and were well established in the bank. Almost all came from families of very modest financial means. The Central Bank subsequently provided much of the economic talent available to the public sector.

The cast of characters of the 1960's would not be complete without a description of the institutional context within which they moved. The two main political parties and the newspapers are perhaps the most important. Their main characteristic can perhaps be unsympathetically described as a certain lack of adaptability to the modern world.

APRA

The principal organized political party was APRA.[7] As the name Alianza Popular Revolucionaria Americana suggests, APRA in its inception—in the late twenties—was a revolutionary party, preaching urgent and drastic land reform, the redistribution of wealth, and dignity and help for the Indian masses, all this not only for Peru but on a Latin American scale. For many years, the program of APRA was considered radical and modern. APRA preached economic integration before economists became interested in it. The original APRA generation had known suffering and violence. In 1932 several hundreds of them were executed by the army at Chan Chan, the pre-Columbian fortress on the

---

[7] For a more comprehensive analysis of the principal political parties in Peru at the time, see Carlos Astiz, *Pressure Groups and Power Elites in Peruvian Politics*, Cornell University Press, Ithaca and London, 1969, pp. 88-130. See also Grant Hilliker, *The Politics of Reform in Perú—The Aprista and Other Mass Parties in Latin America*, The Johns Hopkins Press, Baltimore, 1971.

outskirts of the northern city of Trujillo—the traditional APRA stronghold—as retribution for the assassination of a group of army officers by APRA hands. The relations of the army and APRA were strained for the next forty years, and so far no APRA president has been allowed to take office. In 1945 President José Luis Bustamante y Rivero, an independent with APRA support, did take office but he remained in power only until 1948, when he fell in the midst of civil strife between the APRA and the armed forces.

Since the beginning, the leading figure in APRA has been Victor Raúl Haya de la Torre—born in 1895—who has kept a firm monolithic control over the party. The outward unity of its message, together with the only effective grass-roots political organization in Peru, especially in the north, were the main assets of APRA. Against this, its leadership has not evolved with the times and APRA has not managed to communicate a forceful and attractive program to urban voters, who make up the vast majority at election time. During the second Prado administration from 1952-1962, APRA had tried to get closer to power through the so-called *Convivencia*, or "living together," under which APRA collaborated significantly with the executive. In 1962, Haya de la Torre won the largest vote, but there was some question as to whether APRA had the one-third minimum required by the Constitution. In the 1963 election Haya was beaten by Belaúnde.[8]

The frustration of not being able to wield executive power, combined with a dominant voice in Congress—as a result of the coalition with the Union Nacional Odriista (UNO)—explains much of APRA's attitude in the Belaúnde years. The Belaúnde program was quite similar in several respects to that which an APRA government might have supported, but APRA built up a growing opposition to it, citing the government's amateurism and easy spending methods.

[8] See beginning of Chapter III.

Acción Popular

The government party, Acción Popular, stood in sharp contrast to APRA. It was more of a movement than an organized political machine. Centered around its creator, Fernando Belaúnde, who founded the party in 1956, it possessed a crop of youthful and enthusiastic leaders, unafraid to speak out, often out of turn. The organization of Acción Popular did not compare with that of the APRA, and coordination within the party was often sketchy, with Acción Popular congressmen opposing their own ministers; sharp disputes often broke out in the party's conventions. Whereas the government needed well-organized support in Congress, with a strong central coordination capable of keeping mavericks in line and negotiating calmly with the majority opposition, it got the opposite, exacerbating a tense situation. The possibilities for negotiated agreements on the main issues—chiefly land reform, expenditures, and taxes—were made even more difficult by the temper of the Christian Democrats, the small but vociferous group allied to the government party.

The Press

The press is an essential part of the political makeup of Latin American countries. The tremendous surge of literacy in the last two decades in Peru has considerably widened the market for newspapers, which are the favored reading material for the largest part of the public, who have neither the means nor the education to read books. From 1955 to 1965 the population of Peru rose from 8.8 million to 11.7 million and the percentage of people over fifteen able to read and write rose from about 52 percent to 70 percent.[9]

[9] Source: estimates based on data published for 1961 and 1970 (61 and 75 percent, respectively) by the U.S. Agency for International Development. A figure of 47 percent for 1950 was estimated

In Lima alone, literacy rose from an estimated 70 percent to virtually 100 percent, while the population went from slightly over 1 million to over 2.5 million at the end of the sixties. Lima had seven major morning papers—plus the official gazette, required reading for business and professionals—and three evening papers. Perhaps the paper least associated with a particular and predictable point of view was *Expreso*, which grew to have the largest circulation countrywide (though not in Lima). Its principal owner, Manuel Ulloa, generally supported Acción Popular.[10] There were also several magazines. The most widely read and influential was probably *Caretas*, edited by the independent journalist Enrique Zileri.

The influence of the press upon politicians and political opinion was concentrated largely in the hands of the traditional Lima dailies, *La Prensa* and *El Comercio*, and of the families who own them. The Miró Quesada family had directed the destinies of *El Comercio* with a firm grip, imprinting upon it their own view of Peru and the world. The paper was run for many years by Luis Miró Quesada, who was in his late seventies at the time of our account. As with many of the leisured classes brought up at the turn of the century on French culture, his preference was for Europe or the Old World—pictured as intellectual, nonexploitative, willing to experiment in novel systems such as Socialism or Fascism—as against the world of Uncle Sam, who was seen as a rather amiable but oafish economic bully far too close to home. *El Comercio*, behind the staid facade of its conservative-looking front page, was generally in

by the Organization of American States (*Latin America's Development and the Alliance for Progress*, Washington, D.C., 1973). The raw data are those of the Oficina Nacional de Estadística y Censos, as adjusted in the above secondary sources.

[10] *Expreso* was subsequently taken over by the new regime in 1969. The remaining newspapers were taken over by the authorities in July 1974.

favor of nationalism combined with conservatism. It also maintained a tactful support for most governments, reserving the right to change that stance into merciless opposition, as was the case towards the end of the Belaúnde government.

La Prensa cannot be divorced from its owner and publisher, Pedro Beltrán. Active in national life since the 1920's, a delightful host and conversationalist, the owner of one of the most beautiful farms on the south coast and of a Lima town house that was a veritable museum, he has been in Peruvian politics for over fifty years. He was always a foxy politician; some would even have called him devious. His aristocratic and intellectual appearance, and his somewhat professorial tone did not endear him to the voters; he has not been able to fulfill his ambition of rising to the presidency. A graduate of the London School of Economics, "Don Pedro," as he was often called, holds liberal views in the best sense of Cobden and Bright: free trade, the least possible amount of government taxation and intervention, and personal liberty. He has even gone to jail on a couple of occasions in support of liberty of the press. He took the leading part in 1958 in the creation of Peru's flourishing savings and loan system; at the same time, he has steadfastly maintained that government expenditure should be held back stringently. He did not often conceal his opinion that most of Belaúnde's development schemes belonged, in his view, to the realm of the Mad Hatter and Tweedledum and Tweedledee.

La Prensa prescribed Beltrán's medicine for the economy with increasing frequency and intransigence during the Belaúnde years. The message in much of its editorial writing was that the government should follow the recipe put into effect by Beltrán himself when he was Prime Minister and Finance Minister in 1959-1961, a period of general economic buoyancy due to the sharp increase in production for exports.

THE CHURCH AND THE MILITARY

In addition to the politicians and the press, there were several other sectors and groups of importance to development. The most obvious were the military establishment and the clergy. However, their participation in the events described in this book was limited. Perhaps the most important development in the participation of the church in economic debate was the increasing concern of the younger priests with social justice. The trend, which was part of the wider ferment in the church, especially in Europe, came to Peru later than to other Latin American countries such as Chile, where foreign priests were more influential.[11] The Maryknoll missionaries from the United States were especially active in Peru and contributed to the intellectual modernization of the Peruvian church. Father Joseph Michenfelder was especially influential. Among the Peruvian clergy, several names stand out: the activist Bishop Luis Bambarén, and, on a more radical bent, Father Salomón Bolo and the Jesuit Romeo Luna Victoria. Bolo, a picturesque populist leader was an important figure in the early and mid-sixties in leading demonstrations against landlords and organizing invasions of unused lands around Lima. Luna Victoria is perhaps a more intellectual figure; he has lectured and written widely on the "change of structures" needed in Peru; his vocabulary borrows heavily from Marxism, and his analysis of basic economic variables tends to be strongly ideological, but there can be little doubt about the relevance of his thesis, which is shared by most of the younger priests. The church hierarchy neither actively opposed nor supported the younger priests, and was relatively self-effacing during the Belaúnde administration.

[11] Still, a significant proportion of the clergy in Peru has come from abroad as the interest of the local youth in the church has waned. France, Ireland, and Spain have provided many of these expatriate priests; there was also a sizeable contingent from the United States.

35

The role of the military was more complex and more important. Compared to its population, Peru is in the upper ranks of Latin American countries in terms of the size of its armed forces (about 39,000 men in the Army, 8,000 in the Navy, and 7,000 in the Air Force)[12] and of its defense expenditures in relation to GNP (about 3 percent in the late 1960's). However, compared to some countries in Asia and the Middle East, these proportions are quite low, reflecting the fact that a possible threat justifying defense outlays is also less evident. During the Belaúnde administration, defense absorbed about one-fifth of the expenditures of the central government, with the proportion tending to rise in the later years.

The Army has always been the largest of the three services. Although generalizations are difficult, the social origins of its officer class are probably wider than in the case of the Navy or Air Force.[13] In a real sense, the Army has served as an avenue of social advancement: three of the four presidents of military origin in the last forty years were men of economically humble origins. The armed services, and especially the Army, have thus been no strangers to politics. In the Belaúnde administration, their involvement was formally limited to their normal tenure of the three armed services ministries. But, more important, the potential involvement of the armed forces was always there: the Pérez Godoy and Lindley Junta of 1962-1963 had taken over in 1962 and allowed the 1963 elections. The process might thus be repeated again, a threat that existed throughout the Belaúnde years.

Much has been written about the training of the officer

---

[12] In the mid-1960's.

[13] The detailed work of Professors Luigi Einaudi and Carlos Astiz on the Peruvian officer class has dwelt on other variables, which were more easily measurable. See Carlos Astiz and José Z. Garué, "The Peruvian Military. . . ," *Western Political Quarterly*, December 1972; Luigi R. Einaudi and Alfred C. Stepan III, *Latin American Institutional Development: Changing Military Perspectives in Perú and Brazil*, Rand Corporation, Santa Monica, 1971.

class in the Centro de Altos Estudios Militares (CAEM), founded in 1950.[14] CAEM was indeed ahead of its time compared to other Latin American countries, but would not be an unusual institution in the United States or in Europe. Indeed, it has been an accepted practice in the United States—at the three service academies and the National War College—that the officer class should receive wide training in non-military scientific and humanistic subjects. The innovation in Peru was to superimpose this training on an already existing officer class that had not had it. However, the training has to be correctly described as a way of encouraging intellectual curiosity—"crear inquietudes"—rather than actual detailed training.[15] Courses were generally short, with at most two or three weeks devoted to a subject such as economics. Nevertheless, CAEM was important in creating an awareness of national problems among the officer class. In the period 1963-1968, while the politicians argued, the officers debated in the seminar rooms in Chorrillos. However, there was probably a wide variety of opinion among the officer class, and it would be a mistake to infer that the existence of CAEM meant that most officers were uniformly concerned with social issues or that they were formally trained for government as a result of their stay in CAEM. If there was a discernible general attitude among the officer groups in the early and mid-sixties, it was probably that of "anti-communism." The gradual waning of this theme began after the Army successfully helped the police put down the guerrilla revolt in 1964-1965 and came into more direct contact with the poverty and social problems of some of the remotest Andean areas. The guerrilla episode also greatly enhanced the pride of the Army and was undoubtedly important in awakening political consciousness among the officer corps.

[14] See, for example, Einaudi, *Latin American Institutional Development. . .*, Rand Corporation, 1971.

[15] My Central Bank colleagues and I did some occasional teaching at CAEM.

37

CHAPTER III

The Early Belaúnde Years, 1963-1966
I: The Development Effort

MINORITY GOVERNMENT

Few governments in Peruvian history have begun with the degree of vocal popular support the Belaúnde administration enjoyed at the time of its inauguration on July 28, 1963. Partly as a result of the times, and mainly as a result of his own inclinations, Fernando Belaúnde Terry became President of Peru after he had made the need for basic economic and social change his main battle cry in his three campaigns for the presidency. Although the mood of 1963 election was one of popular enthusiasm, Belaúnde obtained only a relative majority in the June 1963 elections: out of about 1,814,568 votes,[1] Belaúnde received 708,662,[2] as against 632,501 for Haya de la Torre and 463,085 for retired general and former strongman President Manuel A. Odría.

Aside from the modernizing and reformist platform of the new government, there were several features of importance about the political situation when the new government came in. When one looks towards the past, the most important was the fact that a civilian government was taking office in 1963 after one year of military rule. The June 1962 elections, at the end of Manuel Prado's second term as

---

[1] Or about 40 percent of the voting age population. Literacy requirements, distance, apathy, and the complicated documentation required to obtain a "Libreta Electoral," which remained in force after 1963, kept the voting population down, although the 1963 turnout was a significant improvement over the 1956 vote of about 33 percent.

[2] Or 39 percent of the total, more than the one-third required by the Constitution.

38

president, threw up an extremely close and disputed result in which, according to the official results, Haya de la Torre had led by a hair's breadth, obtaining 32.97 percent of the vote against 32.13 percent for Belaúnde and 28.45 percent for General Odría. According to these figures, APRA failed to obtain the one-third of the vote required by Article 128 of the Constitution. The figures, however, are even today the subject of controversy. Still, the results were inconclusive and were made questionable by widespread rumors of fraud. Faced with this situation, APRA appeared to agree to gives its votes to Odría when the issue was to be decided in Congress. Odría, who had run last of the major candidates,[3] would thus have been elected president. Faced with this situation, the armed forces—who had been accepted by the major parties as "guarantors" of the election—annulled the election and ousted President Prado only ten days before the scheduled July 28 inauguration.[4]

A year later the Junta, despite some internal army rumblings, kept its promise to hold elections and to return the government to civilian hands. Politically the 1962-1963 episode naturally left scars of resentment in APRA, which had come within inches of achieving its never-fulfilled goal of electing its own chief as president. Also, the 1962-1963 interlude made clear that civilian rule existed at the tolerance of the armed forces, although this was nothing new in Peru. The leaders of Acción Popular were only too well aware of this fact. For example, a few days after the Junta had taken power in July 1962, two Acción Popular leaders, Fernando Schwalb and Celso Pastor, brother-in-law of Fernando Belaúnde, went on a well-publicized visit to the presidential palace to salute the new head of state.

In July 1963 the main political fact facing the incoming Belaúnde administration was that it was a minority govern-

---

[3] He still got 481,000 votes, mostly in the Lima area.

[4] For a history of the 1962 coup, see Arnold Payne, *The Peruvian Coup d'État of 1962: The Overthrow of Manuel Prado*, Institute for the Comparative Study of Political Systems, Washington, D.C., 1968.

ment, since the opposition coalition had a clear majority in Congress. The government coalition of Acción Popular and the small Christian Democratic contingent was in a minority both in the Senate and the Chamber of Deputies, with 20 seats against 18 for the APRA and 7 for the Odriistas in the former, and 50 against 58 for the APRA, 27 for the Odriistas and 5 of various other groups in the Chamber. Very soon, in the elections for the presiding officers of both houses, APRA and UNO (the Union Nacional Odriista) teamed up, reviving the unusual alliance that began in embryo during the political maneuvers following the disputed 1962 election. The "Coalición" was born. For virtually the whole of the next five years, it was to stand in unchanging opposition to the government "Alianza."

The baffling nature of this APRA-Odría coalition stems not only from the past history of both groups, but from the divergence between their political beliefs. In 1948, General Odría had led a bloody coup against the APRA, sending virtually all the leaders to exile. The APRA was outlawed for the whole of Odría's government, and Haya de la Torre himself spent six lonely years in the Colombian Embassy, surrounded by police, trenches, and searchlights. It was only in 1955 that he was granted safe conduct out of the country. The enmity between APRA and the Army, and the personal hatred of most APRA leaders for General Odría, should have been reason enough to preclude a rapprochement within the memory of living men. In addition, of course, there were and still are vast ideological differences, with APRA a reformist party of professionals and trade unionists with excellent grass-roots organization, and UNO predominantly a right-wing grouping of Odría's personal followers, albeit not without popular support, especially in Lima, where the Odría administration's expenditures in housing and schools, at a time of growing incomes and employment, are not forgotten.

The marriage of convenience between the two parties in 1963 did, however, have some more recent roots. There had, of course, been the *Convivencia* between APRA and the Prado administration in 1956-1962. In the case of APRA and UNO, perhaps the main uniting factor was the position of Belaúnde in the 1962 and 1963 campaigns during which, in order to gain the votes of the left, he took positions on land reform and the International Petroleum Company issue that turned out to be considerably more radical than his actions once in office. Another factor making it easier perhaps for APRA and UNO to join up was the age of their leaders compared to the much more youthful and upstart organization put together by Belaúnde. Nevertheless, these historical accidents are not enough to explain the *Coalición*, which had little to hold it except its opposition to the executive. The APRA party, with its credo largely taken from the revolutionary twenties and thirties, has not evolved an economic philosophy to deal with Peru's domestic economic problems; it is not surprising, therefore, that APRA soon found Odriísmo's opposition to heavier taxation a convenient platform, particularly since it held back some of the government's pet projects. APRA persistently voted down any tax increases and by 1966 coined the slogan "No más impuestos" ("No more taxes"), a major influence upon the history of the last two years of the Belaúnde administration.

As the Belaúnde government began on July 28, 1963, therefore, it faced two potential opposition forces: a Congress that was soon to show its negative attitude to the government, especially in economic matters, and an army that, although it was very favorably disposed to Belaúnde personally, had a year earlier been willing to step in when the civilians did not seem to be able to handle the affairs of state to the armed forces' liking.

FINANCIAL STABILIZATION UNDER PEDRO BELTRÁN, 1959-1961

An account of the development effort under Belaúnde must begin with the tenure in 1959-1961 as Finance Minister (and Prime Minister) of Pedro Beltrán. The pattern of export-led growth that prevailed in the 1960's began on a large scale during Beltrán's tenure of office. Moreover, in the following years, his fiscal and monetary measures stood as a shining example to the business community, and as the epitome of regressive stabilization efforts to the left.

Beltrán was eminently successful in solving the 1958-1959 fiscal and balance of payments crisis. The Prado government had let expenditures far outrun revenues, with the result that pressure began to build upon the exchange rate. *La Prensa* led a chorus of press attacks against the Prado government, fueling the depreciation of the freely floating exchange rate. When the rate reached a low of soles 30 to the dollar, compared to soles 19 a few months before, President Prado was virtually forced to call Beltrán to form a new Cabinet in July 1959. Beltrán immediately obtained a loan from the Central Bank—just the kind of paper loan *La Prensa* had been against—sufficiently large in amount so that he would not have to come back again for a second round. He sought and received assurances of support from the U.S. Export-Import Bank for a balance of payments general purpose loan to encrease international reserves. These measures coincided with the impending start of large-scale copper exports by the Toquepala Mine—a major U.S. investment begun under Odría—and with the incipient fishmeal boom. Private sector confidence thus returned rapidly and the Sol started appreciating. Beltrán halted the appreciation and after a few weeks pegged the rate at a level which wisely left an ample margin of undervaluation.

The important part of his policy concerns the budget. Although some cuts were made, overall Central Government expenditure in fact went up, albeit at a somewhat slower rate in comparison with previous years and in relation to Gross National Product. The largest contribution towards balancing the budget came from a phenomenal increase in tax revenues, stemming from the introduction of a tax on interest on loans and of pay-as-you-go on income and profits taxes, the application of profits taxes to oil companies, and mainly from the first profits tax payments of the Southern Peru Copper Corporation out of Toquepala. As a result of the measures, the tax ratio went up sharply while expenditures increased at a slower pace. The policies followed by Beltrán had the desired effect, and they were put into action with obvious political skill and courage, and, most important, with the help of a pliant Congress. The measures taken, however, were not what many in Peru subsequently came to believe they were. The point was not so much to reduce expenditures, as *La Prensa* was to prescribe in 1967-1968, but to hold their growth down sufficiently so that tax measures and revenue increases would lead to a strengthening of public savings. (See Table 7.)

TABLE 7. SUMMARY OF CENTRAL GOVERNMENT REVENUES AND
OUTLAYS, 1957-1961
(millions of soles, current prices)

		1957	1958	1959	1960	1961
A.	Central Government expenditures[a]	5,058	5,474	6,377	7,236	9,270
B.	Central Government current revenues (mainly taxes)	4,803	4,761	6,122	8,151	9,666
C.	GNP in current prices	35,535	39,549	46,260	55,518	62,294
D.	Ratios A as % of C	14.2	13.8	13.8	13.0	14.9
	B as % of C	13.5	12.0	13.2	14.7	15.5

[a] Excluding debt amortization.
SOURCE: Central Bank, *Cuentas Nacionales*.

The export-led growth that began in earnest at the time that Beltrán was Finance Minister set the pattern for the 1960's.[5] There were no real alternatives for Peruvian eco-

[5] His basic policies were continued by Alex Zarak, his successor as Finance Minister in 1961-1962. An outside analyst's view of the eco-

nomic expansion at the time, but there were obvious weaknesses in the type of export growth, since it relied largely on the once-only effect of previous investment in the fishmeal industry and in one copper mining enclave.

THE LEGACY OF THE 1962-1963 JUNTA

The armed forces' Junta that took over just before the end of President Prado's term of office left a creditable legacy to the incoming civilian government. Although GNP growth slowed down in the wake of a temporary stagnation in export earnings, the 1962-1963 government introduced a number of useful institutional reforms and generally kept the wheels of government turning. Several of these reforms, described below, in fact originated with President Prado's able and aggressive Minister of Public Works, Jorge Grieve. Among the innovations of the Junta were the reform of the Lima water and sewerage authority (COSAL) and the creation of a government housing bank, which expanded the functions of an existing agency. Despite its location on the desert coastline, Lima in the 1960's was one of the few Latin American metropolitan centers that enjoyed an efficient water and sewerage system, self-financed through water rates sufficient to cover operating and expansion costs. This was largely the result of COSAL, and of the technical leadership it enjoyed. The housing bank created in 1962 was given very broad powers; although the bank subsequently spent most of its energies supervising and financing the savings and loan system, it was instrumental in its first year in organizing on a significant scale the inflow of foreign private capital and official loans into "popular" (in fact middle-class) housing. Under the Junta also, the Peruvian

---

nomic policies of Beltrán as Finance Minister is that of Rosemary Thorp, *Inflation and Orthodox Economic Policy in Perú*, Bulletin of the Oxford Institute of Economics and Statistics, August 1967, Volume 29, No. 3.

Corporation, a Canadian company that owned Peru's two principal British-built railroads, obtained a World Bank and Export-Import Bank loan to modernize its by then almost historic rolling stock and locomotives. Although these loans were subsequently criticized because of the company's inability to meet debt service without government assistance, they prevented a much more costly operation. The financial problem of the railways was due to the fact that trucks had to meet only part of their road user costs (as a result of low license fees and the relatively small taxes on fuel, especially diesel). As a result, the railway, which had to meet its full maintenance costs, would not have been able to raise its tariffs (the government, in any case, would not authorize it) without losing traffic and thereby worsening its financial problem. This is of course the classic problem faced by most non-subsidized railways. Without the improvement in equipment, the plight of the railways would have been much worse: service would have rapidly deteriorated and the government would probably have been obliged to take over the enterprise, compounding the substantial financial losses that would have by then existed.[6] In addition, the heavy traffic of minerals from Cerro de Pasco and La Oroya (see map on p. 46) would have been diverted to the road, with heavy costs to the government in road maintenance.

The Junta took office at about the time the Alliance for Progress was making its initial and well-publicized steps and

[6] The two Peruvian Corporation railroads, built in the 1880's with the funds of widows and orphans, in the heyday of British railroad investment abroad, are among the curiosities of Latin America. The Central Railway climbs by conventional means from sea-level to over 16,000 feet in less than one hundred miles. The Southern Railway links the Pacific to Cuzco, and also Bolivia across Lake Titicaca by means of some of the oldest lake steamers in the world. The oldest one was brought in pieces by muleback and ran from 1869 to 1970. Lake Titicaca lies at 12,500 feet. The Peruvian Corporation railways were taken over by the government in 1971, after the government had met the external debt service of the railways since 1967.

45

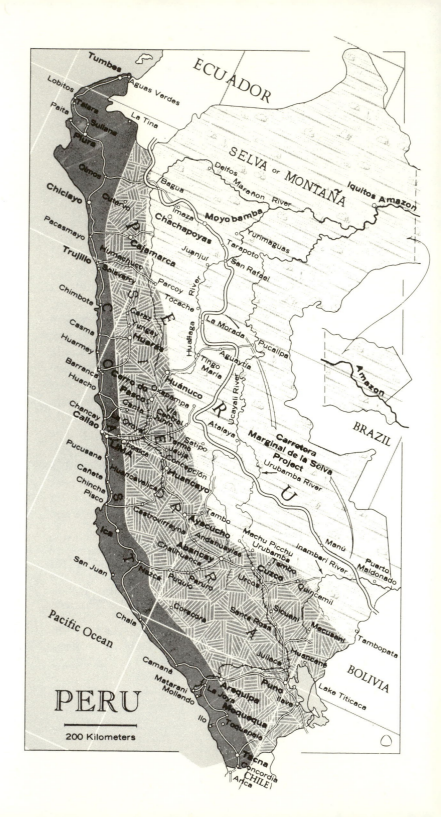

the establishment of economic planning machinery was much in vogue in Latin America. Although the Planning Institute established by the Junta subsequently bogged down—not unlike many of its counterparts in other countries—in blueprints unrelated to the possibilities of financing them, its initial start under the then Colonel Valdivia was promising. An inventory of public sector tasks and financial needs was made, so as to include all public expenditures in the annual government budget. This all-inclusive budget, which went under the title of "program budget"—since expenditures were classified by broad functions and programs rather than by administrative units—undoubtedly made for a more useful presentation of the government accounts. The logical sequel to the program budget—namely, proper expenditure forecasting and control at the level of the various ministries and agencies—was in fact not enforced until the very end of the Belaúnde administration.

The introduction of program budgets happened to coincide in time with a sharp increase in expenditures in 1963. Although the entry of the Belaúnde government for the last five months of the budget period contributed somewhat to the rapid growth of expenditure, the 29 percent increase in current expenditures over 1962 levels was largely built into the budget from the beginning, partly by design and to some degree also because of inadequate planning. The government's fiscal advisers, among them a team from the Organization of American States and the United Nations Economic Commission for Latin America (ECLA),[7] were generally in favor of a significantly faster growth rate of public expenditure, reflecting the government's own point of view. (See Table 8.)

Although revenue growth kept up with expenditure in 1963, this was accomplished through an increase in the

[7] Incidentally, the team included the economist Pedro Vuscovic, who later became Minister of Economy at the beginning of the Allende Administration in Chile.

47

TABLE 8. Summary of Central Government Finances, 1961-1963

	1961	1962	1963
A. Central government expenditures[a]	9,270	10,978	13,195
Of which current expenditures	(8,120)	(9,531)	(12,311)
investment expenditures	(1,150)	(1,447)	(884)
B. Current revenues	9,666	10,924	13,111
C. Surplus or deficit	396	−54	−84
D. A as % of GNP	14.9	15.3	16.8

[a] Net of debt amortization.
Source: Central Bank, *Cuentas Nacionales.*

stamp or turnover tax,[8] a measure that had an immediate revenue effect but was regressive and also had limited potential for further revenue growth in the future. The main expenditure increases were for salaries and for grants to state agencies, particularly to universities. The tax and expenditure policies of the Junta continued to a significant degree under the Belaúnde administration.

Although the 1962-1963 Junta proceeded cautiously in its economic and social measures, there were a few younger elements in the military who would have liked more deliberate action in such areas as land reform and the expropriation of the installations of the International Petroleum Company. The ideas of these middle-level army officers came together at the Centro de Altos Estudios Militares (CAEM), already described in Chapter II.

ECONOMIC GROWTH UNDER BELAÚNDE, 1963-1966

The export-led growth that had begun under Beltrán continued during the first three years of the Belaúnde adminis-

[8] Basically a tax on sales large enough to involve documentation. Between January 1963 and August 1964, the stamp tax was raised from 2.5 to 5 percent.

tration. The increase in average per capita GDP was well above the Latin American average. However, there were important changes in the character of this expansion under Belaúnde. While in the earlier period 1959-1962 there had been a very sharp rise in exportable output, in the years 1963-1966 most of the growth of export earnings came from higher international prices, especially for copper and fishmeal, while exportable output rose only marginally. In a sense, of course, it would have been unrealistic to expect a repetition of the extraordinary coincidence of two or three large new export ventures of 1958-1960; on the other hand, exports were going up on 1963-1966 only because of favorable international prices, which were outside the control of Peru.

Another source of weakness was the stagnation of investment in 1962-1964. This was the result of various factors, including the political uncertainties of 1962-1963, the reaction of the private sector to Belaúnde's platform of advocating a solution to the IPC question and a large land reform, and probably also to a larger than usual accumulation of over-capacity in manufacturing. Private investment in fact fell in the years 1962-1964, and it was only because of the start of a massive program of public works and of the shift of private savings into residential construction—a not unusual tendency in times of uncertainty—that total investment kept up at all. Output of manufactures—largely serving the Lima area and a few other towns—nevertheless continued to rise rapidly, stimulated by the higher import tariff introduced in 1964, but farm output continued its virtual stagnation.[9] Thus, while the average output per person continued to expand at a respectable rate above the 2.5

[9] This aggregate conceals a decline in export agriculture combined with a 4 percent annual growth in food production, which, despite its rapid rate of growth, was too little to meet domestic food demand without a rapid rise in food imports. Most of this food production increase took place on large farms on the coast, especially on land formerly used for cotton, as cotton became less profitable.

annual percentage increase adopted in 1961 in the Charter of Punta del Este, the combination of sagging agriculture and large increases in profits of a few export industries probably led to some deterioration in income distribution. This was offset to some extent by the surge of private sector building and manufacturing and by the government's own programs, but employment and income from these sources were barely sufficient to offset the declining relative importance of agriculture as an employer. (See Table 9.)

TABLE 9. Some Indicators of Aggregate Growth:
Peru and Latin America, 1961-1966
(annual average percentage changes, 1961-1966)

	Peru	Total Latin America
GDP per capita at factor cost	3.2	2.0
Merchandise export earnings, f.o.b.	10.0	5.3
Export prices (including petroleum)	5.0	1.7
Volume of exports (including petroleum)	4.8	3.6
Agricultural output	1.6	3.3
Manufacturing output	9.2	6.2

Sources: Organization of American States, Latin America's Development and the Alliance for Progress, Washington, D.C., 1973; U.S. Department of Agriculture, Indices of Agricultural Production for the Western Hemisphere, Economic Research Service, issue of April 1970: U.S. Agency for International Development, Summary Economic and Social Indicators for 18 Latin American Countries, 1960-71, June 1972; International Monetary Fund, International Financial Statistics.

Perhaps the clearest indication of the government's economic philosophy in those years lies in its motto "El Perú construye" (Peru builds). The phrase, which might better be translated as "Peru hard at work building," conveys not only physical construction but also the idea that the country can actively do something for itself, that development is an imperative task.

The major manifestation of this attitude was a massive

increase in public investment and in current government outlays. In virtually every area of public investment, the Belaúnde administration, especially up to 1966, was characterized by massive increases in expenditures for construction. At the same time, equally large increases occurred in current outlays for social services, particularly for education and health. Although a number of individual investments and programs became failures or at least fell considerably short of their objectives, there can be little doubt about the correctness of the desire of the Belaúnde administration to give the public sector a more active role in investment for infrastructure and social improvement.

The problems were the relative neglect of agriculture—except for large-scale coastal commercial farmers—and the unwillingness to realize until much later in the administration that higher expenditures would have to be accompanied, at least in some degree, by more revenue. The public investment effort of course very much reflected Belaúnde's own priorities. As an architect, he was more interested in physical achievements than in policies that might achieve a result not tangible for several years. The major public works planned or underway were displayed in scale models in the main banquet hall of the presidential palace. Foreign dignitaries would inevitably get a tour of the exhibit with a detailed description by the president of the main projects and of the regions in which they were situated. A large-scale effort in project preparation was made in the early years of the administration.

Belaúnde displayed a healthy skepticism toward economists, and his love of Peru and its people often led him to digress from a financial discussion into a monologue on some new physical achievement of his government: how an Amazonian village had been reached by plane for the first time after the inhabitants had by themselves—under Cooperación Popular—built an airstrip; how the housing agency had just delivered the five thousandth apartment in a new public housing complex; how the first of a new series

51

of ships for the state shipping line had just been launched in Spain.

PUBLIC INVESTMENT

President Belaúnde was probably more interested in *roads* than in any other aspect of physical development. Peru had by 1966-1967 and still has only about 2,750 miles of asphalt roads, mostly on the coast, and about another 4,200 miles of so-called "all-weather" roads. The rugged topography and the scarcity of roads meant that there was no need for sophisticated analysis to realize that the transportation network was very much in need of improvement and extension. The two paved roads are the coastal Panamerican Highway, almost 1,600 miles long and in poor condition at its northern and southern ends, and the Central Highway, which climbs from Lima up to 16,000 feet and over the continental divide to the eastern foothills of the Andes. Except for this road, which reaches a tributary of the Amazon, the rest of the road network had in the past been aimed largely at the coast and had served the interior badly. The Amazonic region was devoid of any roads.

There were good reasons for Belaúnde to shift some public investment toward the Amazonic area. Although the Amazonian flatlands are said to have poor soils, this is not true of the eastern foothills of the Andes. The long-term potential of these lands, particularly for cattle farming and for the production of vegetable fats and oils, together with the obvious appeal of attempting to shift some of the surplus population from the Andes to potentially more prosperous areas east—as was begun in Bolivia in the 1950's—instead of west towards the overcrowded coastal oases, were some of the bases for Belaúnde's idea of the *Carretera Marginal*.[10] Literally the "highway on the edge," it was

[10] Pedro Beltrán, when he was Prime Minister, established the Instituto de Reforma Agraria y Colonización (IRAC). One of its aims

planned to run along the Piedmont region on the edge of the eastern tropical lowlands.

The inspiration for *La Marginal* has both Peruvian and continental origins. With the exception of Bolivia, the Andean countries have developed away from the Amazonic east. The question of whether to channel agricultural development towards the coast or towards the Selva has been particularly acute in the case of Peru, which, unlike Ecuador, has limited coastal lands that can be developed only at high cost through irrigation. At the same time, the Sierra, in relation to the available agricultural land, has a very high population density. Some of the Andean valleys, such as Cajamarca in the north with its small and medium dairy farms, have a long-term agricultural potential, but for the bulk of the Andean population, despite the relatively lower natural growth rate of population (about 2.3 percent annually at the end of the sixties), the choice is to emigrate or starve. In fact, about one-third of the population increase spills over into immigration to the coast. This helps to swell the rate of growth of population on the coast to extremely high levels of close to 5 percent annually.

Although land redistribution can alleviate the economic problem in a few selected areas of the Sierra, no amount of land redistribution will by itself substantially increase the income of the Sierra, although there are of course good social and political reasons for a more even pattern of land distribution in that area. To have economic impact, land redistribution would have to be accompanied with a massive influx of education and technical aid, and investment in transportation, which would bear fruit only after a long period. Even then, the impact on incomes would be doubtful because of the poor resource endowment of much of the Sierra for agriculture. With limited economic prospects for

---

was to encourage migration to the *Montaña* or *Selva* (the Amazonic region).

the gigantic irrigation schemes on the coast that would be needed to provide additional gainful agricultural employment, the move to the east is a logical one, although its effects are likely to be visible only after fifteen or twenty years.

The *Carretera Marginal* project was officially launched with much fanfare and a preliminary economic and engineering report prepared by a U.S. consulting firm and made public in April 1965. The study was organized by Belaúnde with the support of the Ministries of Public Works of Colombia, Ecuador, and Bolivia, and the Interamerican Development Bank.

By launching his project with the support of three other countries, Belaúnde attracted the attention of the Andean countries to the Amazon basin. Although the potential of the lowland Amazon jungle is a matter of dispute and conjecture, there is no such doubt about the Piedmont area, where good management has already in some areas produced encouraging results in cattle, and in some vegetable oils. As Brazil pushes west with road-building that will reach the border of Peru before the mid-seventies,[11] the Andean countries, with the exception of Bolivia, have made no effort to study the possible resources of the Amazon basin. Only in the case of a few oilfields has this general neglect been put aside.

Of the 1,200 or so miles that the *Carretera Marginal* is to cover in Peru, about half are already built to minimum standards. Some of the work was, in fact, an extension of penetration roads begun before the Belaúnde administration. The *Carretera Marginal* was generally derided by the opposition in Congress and by Peru's business class. *La Prensa* used it frequently as a symbol of grandiose and spendthrift government policies. The opposition to *La Marginal* was partly politically motivated; it also reflected the

[11] A jeep truck in fact reached the Brazilian border in Madre de Dios in mid-1969.

inability of many of Peru's leading citizens to take a broad view of the country's development problems. A criticism often made was that the road was a drain on the budget: in fact, most of the 750 miles that were passable in 1968 were built with 80 percent of the financing from a 40-year low-interest AID loan and a long-term U.S. Export-Import Bank loan. The cost to the Peruvian taxpayer from 1963 to 1967 was about 300 million soles per year, or an average of less than 2 percent of the Central Government budget. Perhaps the main valid criticism against *La Marginal* was that the Ministry of Public Works devoted so much of its attention to it that it tended to neglect other important road construction projects, such as the old Central Highway, which links up with *La Marginal.* As in many other developing countries, road maintenance was in general inadequate.

Road construction was also important in Lima. A fifty-mile turnpike to the south was built almost overnight, putting Lima's beaches within easy reach of an increasingly numerous fleet of cars and buses. Lima's politically ambitious mayor, Luis Bedoya, head of a splinter group of the Christian Democrats, launched the construction, with partial debt financing from the Bank of America, of an expressway to the more prosperous and motorized suburbs. The rest was largely covered by a betterment levy on properties improved by access to the highway (the so-called *derechos de mejoras*). Nevertheless, although the road was an aid to the relief of congestion in a city with 150,000 motor vehicles, a few critics felt that the funds might have been better spent on socially more useful investments, such as a greater effort to provide water, sewerage, light, and paved streets to the worst of Lima's slums.[12] Moreover, no effort was made to make the beneficiaries of this investment (mainly private

[12] The slums, known as *barriadas*, were re-christened *pueblos jóvenes* (or young communities) by the new government. Some of the important work of modernization in the slums has been done by foreigners, including missionaries.

cars) pay for it through higher license fees or gasoline taxes (the price of gasoline remained until mid-1968 at about 20 U.S. cents for a U.S. gallon of middle-octane quality). Despite some defects of execution, the Belaúnde strategy in pressing for construction of new roads to the east was a major break with the past, and represented a high-priority initiative. While the work is unfinished, a good beginning was made and eventually a new orientation to Peru's population and agriculture will ensue if complementary investments in basic facilities are made.

The government's program of *port* construction suffered delays, but during the Belaúnde administration, the berthing capacity of public ports—as opposed to the ports owned and managed by the sugar estates, and the various publicly owned lighterage ports—rose by 50 percent. The government continued the works already begun under the Prado administration for the port of Callao, and undertook new expansion both on the Pacific coast and on various small Amazonic river ports.

The aims in the other major sectors were perhaps less spectacular than the *Carretera Marginal*, but they were in general well conceived and made an attempt to do something about Peru's social problems.

In *housing, health, and water and sewerage*, increases in investment were extremely rapid, especially up to 1966. The emphasis was not exclusively in the large urban areas, but down to the middle-sized provincial centers. Some projects turned out to cost much more than planned and others misjudged the market. Such was the case of one large unit housing project in Lima, the cost of which turned out to be so much higher than originally planned, that the apartments had to be sold to professional and middle-to-upper income families instead of to the workers for whom they were intended. Nevertheless, the achievement of four years was substantial: virtual doubling of public housing facilities, the expansion of the public sewerage system from a coverage of 50 percent of the urban population to 65 percent, a 50 percent increase in hospital facilities.

One area where investment increased more slowly was *school construction*. The government concentrated, at least in its first years, on getting the existing classrooms filled. The quality of both public and private education left, and still leaves, much to be desired, and the machinery of educational planning remained archaic, but the achievements in public education were nevertheless impressive. Not only did enrollment increase very sharply, but the number of graduates also. Primary school enrollment rose from 56 percent of the population aged 5 to 14 in 1962 to 74 percent in 1968, compared to a Latin American average of 50 percent in 1962 and 58 percent in 1968. During the same period, the number of primary school graduates rose by 100 percent (although the number of graduates was still a low proportion of total entrants). Secondary school enrollment increased from 240,000 to 560,000, with a proportionate increase in the number of teachers.[13]

The record in investment for *irrigation* was creditable. The government continued the San Lorenzo irrigation scheme begun in the fifties near Piura: although the project has suffered considerably because of exceedingly optimistic forecasts of water availability—as a result, over a third of the canals and other facilities have been slowly covered over by sand—San Lorenzo is the first major irrigation scheme in Peru designed from the beginning for units other than latifundia, although average farm size (about 300 hectares) is still very large. A similar scheme was begun in 1965 at Tinajones near Chiclayo, also in the north, to settle 60,000 hectares of land that had until then not received enough water. The first part of the Tinajones scheme

[13] Data from U.S. Agency for International Development, *Summary Economic and Social Indicators, 18 Latin American Countries, 1960-1971*, Washington, D.C., June 1972. See other data later in this chapter.

57

began to be settled after 1968; with it, the area under permanent irrigation on the coast rose from about 450,000 hectares in 1963 to 580,000 hectares in 1969.[14]

The progress in irrigation and in opening up new lands in the selva was unfortunately not accompanied by policies designed to give the farmer better prices. The traditional practice of holding down prices of basic foods, particularly meat, milk, and rice, through duty-free imports, was continued, thus denying the farmer the price advantage necessary to bring the new lands near the selva rapidly into production and to offset high transport costs to the main coastal urban markets. It was only later, in the last months of the administration in 1968, that an attempt was made to change this policy.

Slow at first, the upsurge of public investment accelerated sharply in 1965 and 1966. Although the role of public investment was still small in comparison with private investment, its growth in relative terms far outstripped that of private investment. With the President personally interested in the details of virtually every item of public works, and the bulk of foreign medium and long-term loans and supplier credits available only for equipment and public works, it was not surprising that public investment received most of the attention from the government and from lenders abroad. (See Table 10.)

Parallel with expenditures on public works, the two major state-owned development banks pushed forward with an unprecedented increase in their lending for commercial agriculture, manufacturing, and fishmeal. The growth of both banks was part of a deliberate policy of granting them exceptionally favorable reserve requirements, and was also made possible by a large-scale inflow of short-term loans from U.S. banks in order to finance production for export, in the form of renewable loans secured by acceptances on existing stocks of fishmeal, sugar and cotton. By the end of

[14] 1 hectare = 2.471 acres.

TABLE 10. PUBLIC INVESTMENT, 1960-1967
million soles, current prices)

	1960	1961	1962	1963	1964	1965	1966	Est. 1967
Central and local govts.	659	1,228	1,545	993	1,775	3,047	4,250	5,101
State enterprises	583	1,640	1,254	2,100	2,805	3,131	3,732	2,866
Total	1,242	2,868	2,799	3,093	4,580	6,178	7,982	7,967
By sectors:								
Roads	{327	{484	{645	{261	{1,071	{1,330	2,255	2,736
Ports and airports							323	413
Irrigation	27	75	107	164	129	342	480	608
Housing	20	35	49	550	842	1,214	521	321
Health and water				264	701	565	672	692
Industry	{868	{2,274	{1,998	{1,854	500	460	827	324
Energy					568	536	566	666
Other					769	1,731	2,338	2,207
Total as % of GNP	2.2	4.6	3.9	3.9	4.8	5.5	6.0	5.2
Private fixed investment as % of GNP	16.0	17.8	19.0	17.9	14.3	14.3	13.7	14.1

SOURCE: Central Bank, *Cuentas Nacionales*; and partial sector data.

1966, the two banks owed about U.S. $48 million abroad in these types of loans compared to U.S. $5 million four years earlier. In the period 1964-1965 the lending of the two banks expanded by over 150 percent, even faster than commercial bank credit, which increased by 67 percent.[15] Including the smaller Mining Bank, credit outstanding from the three state development banks accounted for 21 percent of banking system credit at the end of 1966.

[15] During the same three-year period, the various price indices rose by an average of about 40 percent.

Cooperación Popular

One of the first actions of the Belaúnde administration in August 1963 was to establish the program of "Cooperación Popular." The idea of popular participation in public works—perhaps better described as community self-help—was rooted in life in the Inca Empire. The institutions of community effort survived the Spanish colonial period and continue to this day in one form or another in the 3,000 or so "Comunidades" that exist mostly in the Sierra. The total population in the "Comunidades" is perhaps 2.5 million. One of the main themes of Belaúnde's speeches and writings before becoming president was the example of Inca times in succeeding to put to work an abundance of men ("abundancia de brazos") without the use of money but through community spirit and action.

The idea of popular community self-help does not appear novel to those accustomed to English and North American tradition, but it was a new thought in the Hispanic atmosphere of Lima. Belaúnde was particularly interested in helping "Los Pueblos Olvidados" (The Forgotten Villages), most of which were in Andean regions almost completely by-passed by the public works programs of earlier governments. The presidential message of 1964 summarized some of the aims of Cooperación Popular:

"The government that took office on July 28, 1963, faces the social reality of underdevelopment economically, in education, and socially, in most of the rural areas of the Andes, Selva and the coast. . . . In the past, in Lima and the Interior, the so-called Public Works were carried out, often unfinished, and in the great majority of cases imposed by the Central Government or its local spokesmen, without taking into account the sincere goodwill of the local inhabitants or beneficiaries to contribute themselves to those works. . . . It was thus necessary to change the centralist approach and to confront problems and seek their solution from the point of view of the community. Fortunately, this approach to development had been a feature in Peru for more than a thousand years through community self-help or Acción Popular."[16]

The physical achievements of Cooperación Popular were not likely to live up to the ambitions of its founders. To have reached such a goal would have required a wholesale transformation of government. Yet the idea itself was probably more important in its time than the physical results. Until the idea of Cooperación Popular was launched, "helping the poor" was something left to the government or to a few enthusiasts. The type of approach used by Belaúnde avoided any hint of paternalism of the type that appears in most anti-poverty programs.

The physical effort enlisted a wide variety of participants. For example, university participation brought about 3,000 university students annually during their summer holidays to help with teaching in villages; reforestation was begun; local health services were started; and a wide variety of public works (especially roads, schools, and public water supply) were carried out. At its peak, in 1964-1965, the annual rate of expenditure was a modest 270 million soles annually or U.S. $10 million at the prevailing exchange rate. About one-third of the expenditure represented direct government outlays for equipment and administrative salaries, and most of the rest was the imputed cost of volunteer labor, valued at U.S. $1 per day.[17] In all, probably close to 200,000 Peruvians, or about 4 percent of the labor force, worked at one time or another in Cooperación Popular programs. Cooperación Popular programs were sometimes undertaken together with those of the Fondo Nacional de Desarrollo Económico, an agency established by Belaúnde in 1963 primarily in order to finance provincial public works.[18]

[16] El Perú Construye, 1964 Annual Presidential Message, Lima, July 28, 1964, p. 136.

[17] El Perú Construye, 1965 Annual Presidential Message, Lima, July 28, 1965, pages xxxix-xli and 380-395.

[18] The annual volume of capital outlays of the Fondo was about 500 million soles in the mid-sixties.

The Cooperación Popular program aroused strong opposition from the APRA-UNO majority in Congress. It was felt that the program was primarily political and that the administrative ranks of the agency were swollen with the Acción Popular faithful. Much of this was inevitable, since the idea of the program was at the core of the Acción Popular platform. The staff was led with enthusiasm by Eduardo Orrego, an architect who had been a pupil of Belaúnde. Orrego's strong political motivation eventually forced his departure, and a less activist leadership was installed. Another factor in this change may have been that the president probably got worried about the influence upon the agency of university students, such as Ricardo Letts and Luis Pássara, who had become quite radicalized after their stay in the field. APRA resented the political success of the program, which identified Acción Popular with "The People." Cooperación Popular works usually bore an inscription that stated: "El Pueblo lo Hizo" ("Built by the People"). APRA-UNO severely cut the appropriations for Cooperación Popular (they were less than 1 percent of the budget) and forced the government to reduce the status of the program from an inter-ministerial one to a simple department of the Ministry of Development and Public Works. In the last years of the Belaúnde administration, when government attention tended to focus on financial problems, Cooperación Popular did not receive the attention it should have.

LAND REFORM AND RURAL UNREST

With the well-known skewed distribution of farm land already described above in Chapter II, it was not surprising that Belaúnde should have made land redistribution a major part of his political platform. Ten months after taking office, on May 21, 1964, he signed an Agrarian Reform Law (Law 15037). Despite this early start, however, the achievements were relatively modest. This was due to problems in the law itself and in its application. The land issue itself was an important part of the social and political history of the early years of the administration, but perhaps the greatest significance of the Land Reform Law and machinery was that it provided the legal and administrative background and experience for the much greater effort begun by the armed forces' government in 1969.[19]

The land question in Peru is complex. It is not simply the problem of the uneven distribution of the ownership of agricultural land, but also of the economic potential of the land in question, which varies greatly by regions and within those regions themselves. Except for fertile river valleys, virtually the whole of the coast is a desert, entirely useless for agriculture without the construction of enormously expensive irrigation schemes.[20] The distribution of irrigated land, which is particularly uneven, is thus a central issue on the coast. In the Sierra, only less than 5 percent of the total land area is arable; of the remainder only a small part is suitable for very extensive grazing, and the rest is made up of escarpments, scrub, high peaks, and glaciers. In the Sierra, with its deeply rooted rural population of about 4 million vying for about 800,000 hectares of cultivated land—much of it of poor quality and sloping terrain, and an additional undetermined amount of grazing land—overpopulation is clearly a major economic problem. The skewed distribution of the available land and of agricultural services exacerbates the problem considerably. Not

[19] A comprehensive summary of the history and main issues of land reform in Peru up to 1970 is that of Thomas F. Carroll, *Land Reform in Peru* (54 pages and bibliography, unpublished paper presented to the U.S. Agency for International Development for its spring 1970 review). Other comprehensive reviews are those by John Strasma, to which references are made in the bibliography. I am particularly indebted to Professor Strasma for comments on this section.

[20] Since most of the coastal river water is already used, new schemes have to rely on the diversion of waters that would have flowed to the east of the Andes (as in the Majes project near Arequipa) or into a different area (as in the Chira-Piura diversion scheme in the north near the border with Ecuador).

surprisingly, the surplus population has gravitated to Lima and other cities on the coast, rather than to the Amazonic Piedmont region, which has been relatively inaccessible, with scant public services, and hot and humid weather. A long-term solution to the "agrarian problem" of Peru must therefore emphasize the creation of employment opportunities in other sectors, such as manufacturing, services (including government), and, to the limited extent possible, fisheries and mining. The development of Peru's scarce agricultural potential[21] is a very expensive task and requires a variety of measures, including the well-known (but seldom achieved) combination of education, extension, fertilizer, credit, transport and marketing, plus, of course, a less uneven distribution of the ownership of land or at least of the access to it.

In the 1960's, the issue of land reform was almost exclusively that of land distribution. The redistribution of land was the principal political problem in the countryside, especially in the Sierra. Peasant organizations began to be formed in the Sierra in the 1950's. Much of this activity was concentrated in the valley of La Convención near Cuzco, in which a few families owned most of the cultivated land. The estate workers squatted on hillside plots above the valley. They soon discovered that coffee would grow on the slopes, and many were soon earning more from sales of coffee than from estate work. When the landowners realized

[21] There is controversy about the size of Peru's potential farm land. The Inter-American Committee on Agricultural Development (CIDA, following its Spanish initials), sponsored by the Organization of American States, in 1966 concluded a comprehensive study on land tenure and agricultural potential (*Peru—Tenencia de la Tierra y Desarrollo Socioeconómico del Sector Agrícola*, Washington, D.C.) which is the principal source of information on the question. The main point of disagreement concerns the Sierra, for which some feel that a major low-cost potential exists (for example Jacques Kozub, *Agricultural Development Priorities in Peru*, Washington, D.C., 1968, unpublished). There is no disagreement about the very high cost of developing coastal and Amazonic lands, although the agricultural potential of the latter is quite uncertain.

that the hillsides were valuable and tried to take possession of the land and the coffee trees, conflict was bound to break out. The peasant movement in La Convención was already advanced when in 1960 a young agronomist from Cuzco, Hugo Blanco, entered the scene. The movement, at least the group that followed Blanco, became much more aggressive and undertook a number of invasions of hacienda land. In July 1962 the government recognized some of these land claims, but the unrest continued and culminated on Christmas Day 1962 in a bloody battle between police and Hugo Blanco's group. He was captured and imprisoned early in 1963, while the military junta was in power.

The unrest spread to the Central Sierra and on July 28, 1963, the day of President Belaúnde's inauguration, 3,500 *comuneros* (members of an Indian community) invaded a large hacienda in the central Sierra department of Junín. This and other land invasion disputes were settled by the government. However, a few intellectuals, perhaps the main one of whom was Gonzalo de la Puente Uceda from the APRA offshoot called APRA Rebelde and others from the MIR (Movimiento de Izquierda Revolucionaria), succeeded in stimulating the restlessness and placed themselves at its forefront. They were evidently inspiring themselves by the feats of Fidel Castro in the Sierra Maestra five years earlier and had received training and encouragement from Cuba. However, the central and southern Sierra of Peru (the various small bands operated mostly in the area between Huancavelica and Cuzco) was very different from the Sierra Maestra: it was largely barren, cold, and far from any significant cities. Most important, there was no dictatorship in Lima, as there had been in Havana, but on the contrary a popular and elected government. The guerrilla movement never really caught on. However, the guerrillas inflicted serious damage on the police, who were in charge of pursuing them. In mid-1965 police contingents were ambushed at Púcuta and Mesa Pelada in the Central Sierra, and one of them was completely wiped out. President

Belaúnde became seriously concerned that the unrest would spread, and he reluctantly asked the army to step in. The army sent its crack "Ranger" troops—which appear to have received some covert U.S. government training and support—and in a few months the guerrilla-like tactics of the Rangers had wiped out the rebels. De la Puente Uceda and various other leaders were killed and the armed bands decimated. The efficiency of the army, together with the lack of popular support for the rebels, led to the final outcome.

An important consequence of the role of the army was to awaken the activism of younger officers, many of whom for the first time saw at close quarters the poverty of the Sierra. The prestige of the army was also greatly enhanced. Another consequence of the episode was a wave of anti-communism in the APRA-UNO coalition, some of whose leading parliamentarians began McCarthy-like investigations of government departments. No "communists" were found, except for one. Nevertheless, the executive was under constant harassment, and several ministers were censured by the majority in Congress, which had to resort to often flimsy excuses to bring down the ministers. When his first cabinet resigned under congressional pressure, Belaúnde decided to call Acción Popular parliamentarians to the ministerial posts, in the hope that APRA-UNO would become more responsive.[22] Prime Minister Schwalb resigned and in 1966 became president of the Central Bank. He remained friendly with Belaúnde, but his absence from the Cabinet deprived the president of a close source of political and economic advice at the time he needed it the most.

The guerrillas had been only indirectly linked to the agrarian issue. In the course of 1965, as the army pursued

[22] According to Schwalb, the APRA leadership, through Luis Alberto Sánchez, told him that the attacks in Congress had nothing to do with him personally; the leadership hoped he would stay on. Nevertheless, the pressure of APRA-UNO in Congress was intense, leading to the resignation of the Cabinet. Luis Alberto Sánchez, born 1900, is a leading author and intellectual, and for many years one of the senior members of the leadership of APRA.

the guerrillas, the land reform law was already being implemented, but with several problems. The law approved by Congress was milder than that proposed by the president with the support of Edgardo Seoane, first vice-president of the Republic and head of the presidential level land reform office (ONRA, Oficina Nacional de la Reforma Agraria). Congress excluded from expropriation the "agro-industrial complexes" (coastal sugar plantations) and efficiently farmed estates. APRA had close links to the sugar producers, all of whom were on the north coast, the bastion of APRA strength; another motive for the omission of the estates was the then widely accepted point of view that sub-dividing the estates, which were highly productive, would lead to a large decline in output.[23] The omission of the estates invalidated much of the political impact of the law, since they were the most visible remnants of the then already rapidly declining power of the large landholders.

The President decided not to fight the issue of the coastal estates, since he felt he had already gone as far as he could. Besides, in order to introduce land reform legislation, he had to get approval for a reform of article 29 of the Constitution, a major undertaking, in order to permit deferred instead of cash payment for expropriated land. Under the new law, land redistribution was supposed to begin with public lands, followed by unused and improperly managed lands. Payment for expropriated land was to be part cash (between soles 50,000 and soles 200,000, depending on the quality of exploitation of the farm, or about U.S. $2,000 to U.S. $8,000 at the then prevailing exchange rate) and the rest in long-term low interest bonds.[24] The recipients of the bonds were able to use them for the payment of taxes and also to acquire shares in a trust fund—which was in fact

[23] In fact, under the land reform carried out from 1969 onward, the sugar estates have been kept as units managed by cooperatives with military and civilian advisors.

[24] For a comparison of the features of the 1964 law with those of the 1969 Decree-Law, see Thomas F. Carroll, *Land Reform in Perú*, U.S. Agency for International Development, unpublished, 1970.

never established—of the Industrial Bank for the establishment of new industries. The landholders were thus supposed to become industrialists; this feature of the law had hardly any influence in speeding the industrialization that was in any case already taking place. Furthermore, the majority of the large landholders already had industrial interests.

For President Belaúnde the issue of land reform was not only the land reform law and its application; he attributed just as much importance to the drive toward the Selva, and particularly the building in that region of basic services and "infrastructure," of which the *Carretera Marginal* was the most obvious example. Land redistribution, he felt, was needed to correct an injustice, but it could not be relied on by itself to solve Peru's agrarian problem. To a large degree, he was right. On the other hand, his views served perhaps—in the mind of government officials concerned with land reform—to rationalize a rather slow approach to the task of actually redistributing land.

By the time the law was passed, Edgardo Seoane was on his way to Mexico in golden exile as Peru's ambassador. He felt strongly that the new law was not strong enough and was particularly incensed at the fact that under the new law ONRA was no longer to be at the level of the presidency. He thus began his gradual estrangement from Belaúnde, which was to culminate in 1968, when Seoane formed his own Acción Popular splinter party and supported the coup against Belaúnde.

ONRA soon faced financial problems. It was supposed to receive 3 percent of the Central Government budget, a sum it was probably not equipped to spend in its first year or two; even so, after the budget emerged from Congress and from the budget-cutting at the Finance Ministry, it received only about 1 percent of budgeted expenditures.

A major drawback of the effect of the announcement of the comprehensive law, while it was being slowly enforced, was its negative effect on agricultural investment. Private investment in agriculture fell steadily during the 1960's; as noted in Chapter II, the growth of farm output during the decade was extremely slow. There were other causes, of course, such as the increasingly unfavorable terms of trade for agriculture, a decline temporarily interrupted after the 1968 devaluation. However, there is little doubt of the prolonged effect upon investment in commercial agriculture of impending land expropriation, which in fact began to materialize on a significant scale only in 1969, once the new government began putting its own land redistribution into effect. Up to 1968, the bark of land redistribution was certainly greater than its bite.

Nevertheless, a significant beginning was made under the Belaúnde administration. About 700,000 hectares were actually expropriated and an additional 1.4 million hectares of idle land reverted to the state. By 1968, about 300,000 hectares of this area of 2.1 million hectares had been redistributed to 11,000 families; 3,000 of these families received the Algolán estate in the Central Sierra, which was expropriated in 1965. Before he left office, Belaúnde had completed the steps, except for the signed decree, for the expropriation of the Cerro de Pasco Corporation 200,000-hectare sheep livestock farm in the Central Sierra. In addition, about 55,000 squatter families received provisional rights over the land they occupied. A supervised credit program was established within the Agricultural Bank: the bulk of the credit went to about 12,000 family farms on the Coast. The average size of farm was in the 6-to-10 hectare range (well above the *minifundio* range), but with about 40 percent of the credit going to larger farmers in the San Lorenzo irrigation project in the north near the Ecuadoran border. San Lorenzo had been started in 1957 under President Prado with the help of a World Bank loan.[25]

Seen in a national context, these figures are modest.[26] A

25 For an account of the vicissitudes of this project, see Albert Hirschman, *Development Projects Observed*, Brookings Institution, Washington, D.C., 1967.

26 To put these various figures in perspective, in the mid-1960's Peru had about 22 million hectares of farmland, of which one-tenth

more telling yardstick, perhaps, is whether there was increasing progress during the four-year period of land reform under President Belaúnde. Much of the effort was in the first two years and tended to fall behind in the scale of governmental priorities as the financial problems of 1967-1968 moved to the center of the stage. The decision was not exclusively that of the executive: a major factor was the attitude of the majority in Congress who were critical of ONRA. In view of the urgent need for Congressional approval of fiscal measures, the president was understandably reluctant to open a second front against the Congress in which he had no majority.

The land reform episode in Peru from 1964 to 1968 inevitably raises the question of whether a major land redistribution program is possible in a parliamentary system in which the executive does not have an overwhelming majority, reflecting a broad national consensus on the issue. The evidence of other countries tends to parallel that of Peru and shows that a major land reform—if undertaken at the stage of development of most of the developing countries, in which agricultural land is still the major capital asset—requires a degree of national agreement that is very rarely found.

MIDDLE-CLASS PROSPERITY

What did the government achieve in its first three years for the well-being of Peruvians? The normal process of modernization undoubtedly accelerated expansion of the urban "middle class." The fact that this "middle class" probably represented the top 5 percent of income groups[27] does

---

were cultivated. The number of rural farm families in Peru numbered about 1.1 million; the number of permanent squatter families qualifying for occupancy under Title XV of the land reform law was about 160,000. See Thomas F. Carroll, *Land Reform in Peru*, pages 9 and 24, and *El Perú Construye*, Annual Presidential Message, July 1964, pages 132-133, and July 1965, pages 469-472.

[27] The same is true to a lesser extent of most industrialized coun-

not diminish the fact that there was a widening of incomes and opportunities. A large proportion of white-collar workers and of workers in industrial establishments would be included in the top 5 to 10 percent of income groups. One indication of the relative satisfaction of this special group was the small number of major strikes; this was partly the result of the willingness of most of Belaúnde's Labor Ministers to step into disputes and press for large wage settlements.

A three- or four-year period is not long enough to detect a major improvement in income distribution, short of drastic measures. In terms of national aggregates, however, the period of the Belaúnde administration probably coincided with a sharp increase in the relative share of income going to the fully employed urban groups (basically industrial, government, and some service workers) and with the relative impoverishment of the largest income group, the small farmer and the landless rural laborer. Output and employment of this group probably rose at no more than 1-2 percent annually,[28] well behind the growth of large-scale commercial agriculture and of urban incomes. The public works of the government and the participatory programs of Cooperación Popular probably had some effect in keeping up incomes of rural inhabitants.

The national accounts show that wages and salaries, and also business profits, increased their share of the nation's income, while the share of traditional sources of income—namely farming, rent from real estate, and interest earnings—fell. There was a sharp rise in white-collar income,

---

tries. There are many "middle class" youths in the United States who go to a college that costs their parents $5,000 or more per year. I have taken here a wider definition of the "middle class" than in Webb, *The Distribution of Income in Peru*, p. 6, where he takes the top 1 percent of income recipients, or about 40,000 persons in 1961. The minimum qualifying income of this latter group in 1961 was the equivalent of about U.S. $3,000 per capita.

[28] Author's estimate, based on the annual increase in agricultural output by small farms.

influenced by large government salary expenditures for civil servants in general and for school teachers in particular. The tax-free profits of enterprises also rose sharply, reflecting the liberal tax concessions granted to manufacturing industry and also the high level of profits in mining, as a result of rising copper prices in 1966. The national account data suggest that significant changes in sectoral income distribution took place in the short span of the early years of the Belaúnde government: the strengthening of the city against the countryside, of industry, construction, and services against rent, and of the urban working- and middle-class against the two most traditional elements in the population: those living off rent, whose significance diminished sharply, and the mass of the Sierra population. (See Table 11.)

TABLE 11. SHARES OF NATIONAL INCOME, 1962-1966 (percentages of national income)

	1962	1966
Wages and salaries	46	48
Of which: Blue-collar workers	(24)	(23)
White-collar workers	(22)	(25)
Other incomes, excluding interest	29	27
Of which farmers	(14)	(11)
Profits of enterprises	16	18
Of which tax-free profits	(12)	(15)
Rent and interest income	9	7
Total	100%	100%

SOURCE: Central Bank, *Cuentas Nacionales.*

Paradoxically, for a President one of whose major interests was developing the interior, economic growth during 1963-1968 was largely an urban phenomenon. On the other hand, this pattern of development is not surprising and is similar to that of most developing countries in the post-war period. During the 1950's there was probably a redistribution of income not only towards the cities, but, within the cities, towards the white-collar "lower-middle" income masses, while blue-collar workers approximately held on to their share. The numbers in the consumer boom of the mid-sixties make it clear that this was no binge of the so-called oligarchy, but a deepening change in urban areas. Nor did the change begin with the new administration in 1963, although the large-scale increase in the government wage-bill thereafter accelerated the process.[29]

The rapid creation of additional employment stimulated in urban areas by the construction boom, together with a sharp expansion in public school enrollment, created a widespread impression for the lower half of income groups that opportunities were expanding and that they were not boxed in the existing regressive pattern of income distribution. The massive effort in public education after 1963 was striking and contributed to this impression.[30]

[29] Among some indicators of this "middle-class" material prosperity, the following available ones can be cited (years 1960, 1963, and 1967): passenger cars: 65,000, 111,000, 195,000; TV sets: 75,000, 150,000, 285,000; radio receivers: 1.1 million, 2 million, 3.1 million; other indicators are the number of insured under social security schemes (from 670,000 in 1960 to 1,035,000 in 1967, an increase from 21 percent to 27 percent of the employed population) and the number of shareholders of mutual savings and loan associations (from 11,000 in 1962 to 220,000 in 1968).

[30] In addition to the figures shown earlier in this chapter, the following data from UNESCO compare the progress in school enrollment with those of other Latin American countries:

Estimated gross enrollment ratios as a percentage of the relevant age group[a]	Primary		Secondary	
	1960	1965	1960	1965
Peru	50	63	18	31
Mexico	54	59	12	21
Brazil	45	46	18	26
Colombia	45	43	16	23
Chile	69	69	34	41

[a] For purposes of international comparability, UNESCO uses the 5-14 age group for primary schooling, and the 15-19 age group for secondary schooling.

The economic program of the first years of the Belaúnde administration was reflected mostly in visible and physical achievements—roads, housing, health facilities, education. Although the deliberate attempt at reorienting development policy away from the traditional coast and sierra regions toward the Amazonic eastern part of the country was not reflected in economic aggregates during the 1963-1968 period, it was a very important signal for future development. As far as the distribution of income is concerned, the trend was mixed, and an analysis of the problem over time is hampered by the lack of information. At least it can be said that a powerful basis for potential change was established through the massive widening of education.

CHAPTER IV

The Early Belaúnde Years, 1963-1966
II: The Financial Problem

THE SETTING FOR GOVERNMENT FINANCIAL POLICY

The financial policies of the early Belaúnde years were concealed by the glow of achievement in public investment and modernization, and the continued growth, albeit in fits and starts, of export earnings. While there were government policies for public investment, there was little direction on how to finance the development effort. In a sense, with the enthusiasm of a youthful government with a fresh outlook, this was understandable. At the same time, however, it reflected in part the primitive condition of financial policy-making in the public sector.

The public finances of a country such as Peru, with its rapid growth of foreign exchange earnings, ought to have been manageable to administer. Nevertheless, by 1963, Peru had not yet developed the talent or the institutions necessary to give the kind of minimal economic advice likely to be useful or to be listened to. The four agencies then principally responsible for economic policy—the Finance Ministry, the Development and Public Works Ministry, the Planning Office, and the Central Reserve Bank—were not brought together in coherent coordination. In any case, the talent available to them was scarce, partly because of low pay, and also because of the tradition of the economic elite of not participating in government at the civil service level. The Finance Ministry had not developed an effective system of expenditure control, nor did it until much later; what existed was in the form of a posteriori statistics by the Office of the Comptroller General. The Ministry had no economic staff, with the exception of Luis González del Valle, who in fact performed many of the operational duties of the minister. Expenditure and tax administration fluctuated with the coming and going of each minister. During the Belaúnde administration there were altogether seven holders of the portfolio in slightly more than five years.[1] The Central Reserve Bank, by reason of its relative independence and the growing strength of its economic staff, could have been expected to play an important role in economic policy, but this did not begin to happen until 1965, after Alfredo Ferreyros replaced Enrique Bellido as chairman of the board. The Ministry of Development and Public Works had generally concentrated on public works, and the 1963-1966 period was no exception: industrial, energy, and mining policy tended to receive less attention than public works.

In an atmosphere where economic analysis was either not forthcoming or, if available, rarely welcome, financial policy was bound to depend heavily on the pressures of the politicians and various interest groups—the manufacturing lobby foremost among them—and on the personality of the Finance Minister. Although the 1962-1963 Junta had begun to loosen the purse strings significantly, the incoming Belaúnde administration inherited, from the days of Pedro Beltrán, a manageable budget. As noted in Chapter II, the gap left by the Junta was not large. The incoming Belaúnde administration could naturally be expected to increase expenditures considerably, but it had done little thinking on how it would finance the increase.

[1] Javier Salazar Villanueva (July 1963 to October 1964), Carlos Morales Machiavello (October 1964 to September 1965), Sandro Mariátegui (September 1965 to September 1967), and then in one year, Tulio De Andrea, Raúl Ferrero, General Francisco Morales Bermúdez, and Manuel Ulloa. In this last period, Pablo Carriquiry served at various times as interim minister while he held the Development and Public Works portfolio.

An important feature influencing fiscal policy in the early years of the Belaúnde administration was the view by some in the government that inflation was a good thing, as an inevitable concomitant to development. Because fiscal stability had become associated with Pedro Beltrán, it was felt that those who supported a moderately non-inflationary budget must be political supporters of Beltrán and therefore "oligarchs." A sporadic discussion developed between the Central Bank and the Planning Office, marked by rigid positions on both sides. The Planning Office, which had received substantial technical assistance from the U.N. Economic Commission for Latin America (ECLA) tended to accept the ECLA view that the main problems of development stemmed from the inadequate structure of supply. The management of total demand through fiscal and monetary means was looked upon as of secondary importance. The early 1960's were the heyday of the conflict between the so-called "ECLA" and "IMF" views, and the conflict between Planning Office and the Central Bank tended to mirror the international institutional difference. While, in retrospect, much of the discussion was consumed in semantics, the prevalence of one point of view or the other certainly made a practical difference in fiscal policy. Finance Minister Morales Machiavello, an architect by profession, was particularly impressed by his Planning Office advisers, for whom financial stability was not a top priority. Although the emergence of the budget deficit as a major destabilizing force in the economy was not due to any one man, the relative ease with which the idea of inflation was accepted at the Finance Ministry in the period 1963-1965 was a major factor in the creation of the fiscal and financial problems that came into full view in the following years.

The design and execution of fiscal policy was made difficult by the lack of timely and accurate statistics. The only periodic information was the monthly balance sheet of Central Government payments and cash receipts prepared

77

by the Office of the Controller General. While the information was timely, it was designed to serve the purposes of the Controller, not those of fiscal planning.

Another important point in the analysis of past fiscal policy is the relationship between the Central Government and the rest of the public sector. During the 1960's, Peru had a growing public sector, as the number of decentralized agencies and their activity expanded. Among the agencies were the non-profit service organizations such as the two Social Security organizations (for workers and for white-collar employees), various research institutes, especially the public universities (which had increased to the somewhat unbelievable number of twenty-two by the end of the decade). In addition, there were state enterprises (about twenty of them by 1969) of which the main ones were the state development banks, and enterprises dealing with the merchant fleet, steel, the Mantaro hydro-electric project, guano and fertilizers, petroleum, and various others. With the exception of social security, petroleum, and to a lesser degree the state banks, most of the others were highly dependent on Central Government aid, either in the form of current operating subsidies (especially to the universities) or of so-called capital contributions, a part of which was in fact used to meet interest payments on external debts of various enterprises.

Financial control over the decentralized part of the government was generally sporadic and mostly inadequate. There were therefore very few accurate and timely statistics on the operations of the public sector as a whole, and historic records are spotty since there was no standardized accounting for the various agencies and enterprises. In rough figures, during the 1960's current revenues of the decentralized public sector averaged about one-third of the total for the public sector, while expenditures were 45 percent of the total. A part of the current revenues were in fact taxes assigned by law to various agencies (such as certain import duty revenues that were segregated for specific agencies) and collected by the Central Government. In the end, therefore, the operations of the public sector were reflected to a large degree in those of the Central Government.

The table below summarizes the trend of Central Government current revenues and expenditures, as reflected in the national accounts. The definition of Central Government is a broad one, and includes on the revenue side taxes collected on behalf of independent agencies and on the expenditure side the transfer to those agencies, including the two Social Security organizations. The table shows at a glance the evolution of the fiscal problem. After a successful effort to raise taxes in 1963 in order to keep up with a sharp rise in expenditures, no further significant increase in revenues in relation to GNP took place, while outlays rose quickly, especially in 1964 and 1965. The financing of the deficit contributed substantially to a very rapid expansion of domestic credit—financed in large measure by central bank credit or by short and medium-term foreign borrowing by the state banks. The share of net lending to the Central Government in the total domestic credit expansion was very large in the five years from 1963 to 1967, and it constituted a disproportionately large influence on the growth of money supply. (See Table 12.)

Although the role of the budget in the economy appeared small when measured against GNP, its impact on the monetized sector was much larger. In Peru, as in many developing countries that have a relatively low level of public revenues and expenditures in relation to national income, the unsettling influences of a budget deficit can be much greater than a proportionately similar deficit in an advanced economy. The major explanation for this is of course the absence of an adequate capital market, which in the industrialized countries serves as a channel for private savings to the public sector. Another possible factor is that, when measured against the money supply instead of the GNP, the role of the government budget is often much greater in the poor countries than in the advanced economies.

79

TABLE 12. CENTRAL GOVERNMENT EXPENDITURES AND CURRENT
REVENUES IN RELATION TO GNP, 1961-1967

	1961	1962	1963	1964	1965	1966	1967
Current revenues (percent of GNP)	15.5	15.2	16.7	16.7	17.4	17.3	16.9
Expenditures net of debt amortization (percent of GNP)	14.9	15.3	16.7	18.6	20.3	20.6	21.2
Surplus or deficit (percent of GNP)	0.6	−0.1	—	−1.9	−2.9	−3.3	−4.2
Memorandum: change in net credit to Central Government as percentage of change in							
(a) domestic credit	−16.6	−28.5	39.7	52.9	18.4	66.1	40.6
(b) money supply (M1)	−17.2	−137.9	78.5	84.8	49.3	142.3	73.4

SOURCE: Central Bank, *Cuentas Nacionales*. Estimates of money and credit 1964
1967 derived from *Cuentas Monetarias* (unpublished); 1961-1963: Internationa
Monetary Fund, *International Financial Statistics*, 1972 Supplement.

TAX POLICY AND DEVELOPMENT

In view of the government's desire to expand the role of
the public sector and to engage in social reform, it would
have been natural to expect an active and progressive tax
policy. Instead of such a policy, which would have sought
to strengthen and increase direct taxation on incomes and
property, the initial tax measures of the government reduced taxation of enterprises by widening exemptions on
profits taxes and import duties to be paid by industry. At
the same time, the level of import duties and of the turnover tax were raised. The strategy was to provide a stimulus
to private investment, which had been lagging, while at
the same time to raise revenue through taxes that were easy
to collect. Initially, the measures led to a significant increase
in revenue, but eventually the loopholes that had been
opened became. a major claim upon potential tax revenues.

Moreover, the tax system came to rely even more than before upon regressive forms of taxation.

The granting of substantial tax concessions, especially to manufacturing industry, was the first step towards the creation of a substantial budget deficit. The Executive widened the application of one of the two existing industrial promotion laws (Law 9140 of June 1940) by giving virtually tax-free status to new manufacturing investment in the amazonic ("Selva") area. In itself the new decree was logical enough, since the Selva had some resources, such as lumber, which had a development potential. However, the amount of investment attracted by such tax concessions was minimal. At the same time, the fact that the same decree turned Iquitos into a free port stimulated, over the next few years, large-scale, duty-free imports of unnecessary luxury consumer goods, such as higher grade textiles, jewelry, appliances, and cigarettes—which were then taken openly by travelers or surreptitiously by firms to the Lima area. Statistics showed that wool consumption per capita in Iquitos, a steamy tropical town, was by far the highest in Peru.

Law 9140 also provided the legal umbrella for the creation of a few industrial parks. The idea of industrial parks is one that planners have been enamoured of in many developing countries. While industrial parks are no doubt an incentive to the establishment of new plants in some countries—in Singapore, for example, where overcrowding has driven land prices up to exorbitant levels, and water and electricity supplies are normally inadequate—these conditions did not exist in the principal urban areas of Peru. No available statistics exist on either the output from industrial parks—which was very small—or the costs in terms of taxes lost—high in relation to the output—but the net benefit of the parks to the economy was marginal.

The revenue lost as a result of the Selva and industrial park exemptions schemes was nevertheless small in comparison to the loss from the establishment of the car-assembly plants, which was made possible by Decree 80 of November

81

1964. The decree allowed contracts to be signed between the state and a limited number of automobile assembly plants, enabling the latter to import, in addition to machinery, all the necessary parts at low duty rates for assembling cars locally. Sixteen plants signed agreements between 1964 and 1967; after production on a significant scale began at the end of 1965, the revenue loss to the government became very large.

There are understandable manpower reasons to encourage the development of industries that require and train labor to a relatively high level of skills, particularly if they also require large inputs from other such industries.[2] However, car manufacturing and assembly was unlikely to be such a case and, moreover, direct employment in the auto assembly plants at its peak in 1966-1967 was only 2,500, with another 2,500 in related industries. Most of these related industries, with the exception of tire production, were very high-cost assembly operations themselves, depending largely on imported parts. Due to the tiny volume of the Peruvian auto market and the diversity of factories operating from 1965 onward, costs in the industry were inevitably very high. The label "industry" is a generous one: except for the four largest, most of the plants were glorified tool sheds, where techniques were not much more sophisticated than the home assembly of a bicycle.

The very high costs were largely met out of the government treasury in the form of revenue losses. Locally assembled cars were priced just below the imported price after import duties which ranged from 60 to 100 percent of the c.i.f. value of most imported cars. Locally made cars, therefore, captured the bulk of the market, and in 1966 and 1967 their output was 10,600 and 15,100 units respectively, excluding large trucks. The import duties lost by the govern-

2 Shipbuilding is a case in point, in which Peru has made an encouraging beginning. On the other hand, the car industry is unlikely to be economic for a very long time, even with the smaller number of plants approved by the government in 1971-1972.

ment in those two years can be estimated as follows (see Table 13).

TABLE 13. Estimate of Duties Exempted on Locally Assembled Cars and Small Trucks, 1966 and 1967

A. 1. Numbers of locally assembled cars and small trucks (two years)	25,000 units	
2. Value of parts imports for local assembly (c.i.f.)	U.S. $	55,000,000
3. Duty paid (approx. 15 percent at S/. 26.82 per U.S. $)	S/.	220,000,000
B. 1. Value of imports if complete cars had been imported (c.i.f.)	U.S. $	65,000,000
2. Duty to have been paid (average of 85 percent)	S/.	1,465,000,000
C. 1. Duty revenue lost in two years (B.2 less A.3)	S/.	1,245,000,000
Equivalent in U.S. $	U.S. $	46,450,000
2. Total import duties collected on all merchandise 1966-1967, equivalent to	U.S. $	430,250,000

Source. Author's estimate based on published data on vehicle output and on import tariff.

The illustrative calculation above is admittedly rough and incomplete, since it does not take into account the relatively modest local profits and sales taxes paid in the process of assembly. However, even if the margin of error is large, the estimates still show the large fiscal loss that was incurred in order to establish an industry with a limited market and a doubtful future. The fault was compounded by allowing too many plants, although even one plant would still have been out of place for a market of about 15 thousand cars annually. It is true that the revenue loss was substantial only in 1966 and 1967, when car sales boomed as a result of the cheapening of imports in relation to domestic money incomes. There was of course supposed to be a foreign exchange saving, mainly because of lower freight costs for boxed parts compared to a finished car. However, this saving was probably zero once remittances of profits and royalties abroad were taken into account. A real saving of foreign exchange could have occurred if there had been higher duty rates on the more expensive cars.

If the cars assembled locally had been imported, additional government revenue and spending of S/. 600 million a year would have done more for local purchasing power than the local purchases and salary payments of the plants: even if the government had had no means of disposing of the money and had given it away to the 5,000 skilled and semi-skilled workers who worked in the plants and dependent industries, the annual income per man would have come to almost U.S. $5,000 annually, or three to four times the average industrial wage!

Were there redeeming features in the creation of this "infant"? The main ones usually mentioned are the training that car assemblies provided to the labor force and the establishment of various subsidiary industries that arose as a result of the car industry. These points are no doubt valid, but they are probably quite insufficient to offset the wastage of resources of the assembly plants. Moreover, these same benefits could probably have been achieved by investing in other areas, such as shipbuilding. The yard managed by the Navy expanded rapidly in the late 1960's, and became an employer as large as the car assembly plants had been.

The import duty exemptions for the Selva, the industrial parks and the car plants, were special cases and affected revenues significantly only in the middle years of the Belaúnde administration. Of greater importance was the continuance of the general system already in force for granting exemptions to manufacturing industry. These exemptions were to a large extent encouraged by the tariff system itself, which had and still has unrealistically high duties on inputs needed by most manufacturing plants. It was only natural, after the tariff increases of 1963-1964, which substantially benefitted consumer goods' industries heavily dependent on imports of parts and raw materials, that those industries should exert strong pressure to obtain exemptions of imports of parts and raw materials. Otherwise, these assembly industries could not have competed against imports of the finished goods, even at the high new import duty rates. The process was to some extent unavoidable but the granting of exemptions, which is an administrative decision, probably proceeded too fast and too easily, encouraging the establishment of "import duty mills," surviving exclusively because of tax privileges and making a limited, sometimes negative, contribution to the economy.

The tariff increases of December 1963 and August 1964, the principal taxation measure taken by the Belaúnde administration until 1967, were a success from a revenue point of view, since they more than made up for the revenue lost through exemptions, and enabled public revenues to continue upward when other forms of taxation, especially income and profits taxes, were weakened by lax tax administration, over-generous deductions and exemptions,[3] and widespread evasion. By 1966, however, the increasing importance of import duty exemptions began to erode the import tariff base, and in 1967 customs revenue fell as a percentage of imports, despite a substantial second tariff increase in June of that year. (See Table 14, page 86.)

Despite the erosion of the import duty base, government revenues in the first years of the Belaúnde administration came to rely increasingly on traditional indirect sources of taxation, especially import duties. It is true that import duties taxed the most rapidly growing and easily identifiable taxable quantity, namely imports. But the system also fos-

[3] The value of profits tax exemptions granted to the manufacturing sector, the principal beneficiary, has not been quantified.

85

tered, through high protection and costly special tax privileges, extremely inefficient manufacturing industries heavily dependent on duty-exempt imports. Furthermore, the

TABLE 14. IMPORT TAXATION, 1962-1967

	1962	1963	1964	1965	1966	1967
1. Import duties collected (S/. million)	2,058	2,345	3,619	5,053	5,702	6,34⁵
2. Value of c.i.f. imports (U.S. $ million)	542.9	578.5	587.1	718.6	816.7	822.⁵
3. Value of c.i.f. imports (S/. million)	14,561	15,515	15,746	19,273	21,904	25,48⁵
4. Duties collected as a percentage of imports	14.1	15.1	22.9	26.2	26.0	24.⁵
5. Nominal value of import duty exemptions[a]	n.a.	n.a.	n.a.	1,363	2,491	3,74

[a] It would be unrealistic to consider these amounts as equivalent to import reve nue losses, since imports would undoubtedly have been lower had the full dut been charged. Nevertheless, the upward trend of exemptions is clear.
SOURCE: Central Bank, *Cuentas Nacionales*; and customs authority data.

tax structure, rather than becoming more progressive to parallel the trend of expenditures, became in fact more regressive. Income and profits taxes declined in importance, and the performance of the personal income tax was particularly poor. Generous family deductions[1] meant that most families with an income of less than U.S. $5,000 equivalent (with three or four children, this would equal an income

[1] Until 1967 the equivalent (at the average current exchange rate for the year) of U.S. $1,200 for the spouse, and U.S. $750 for each child, with the deduction for all children up by 50 percent if there were 3 or 4 children, and up by 100 percent if there were 5 or more. Thus a family with an income equivalent of U.S. $20,000 and with 5 children, would pay taxes only on U.S. $11,300, from which the usual deductions for professional expenses, interest paid, etc., could be made.

per head three to four times the national average) were legally outside the range of the income tax. This in effect ruled out personal income tax for any but the top income groups, and the number of taxpayers among this latter group was extremely low, even for a developing country. As an illustration, the total number of individuals paying income tax in 1967 was less than 5 percent of the white collar labor force. (See Table 15.)

TABLE 15. TRENDS IN PROFITS AND INCOME TAXES, 1963-1968

	1963	1965	1966	1967	1968
Number of tax returns (incl. firms)	n.a.	69,288	79,956	81,623	92,987
Number of taxpayers (incl. firms)	n.a.	34,818	38,465	38,802	n.a.
Direct taxes as percent of Central Government current revenues	32.8	24.5	23.7	26.2	34.8

SOURCE: Tax office data published in Central Bank, *Reseña Económica y Financiera.*

The decline in the proportion of direct taxation, together with the increasing importance of exemptions from import duties and profit taxes, meant that the rate of growth of government revenues kept up with that of the domestic product only because of the extraordinary rapid growth of imports and the increase in import duty rates. Central Government revenues stagnated at about 16-17 percent of the gross national product in the period 1963 to 1967, while expenditures were increasing much faster.[5]

[5] For an account of the generally regressive results of tax policies during the early years of the Belaúnde administration, see Richard C. Webb, *Tax Policy and the Incidence of Taxation in Peru*, Research Program in Economic Development, Discussion Paper No. 27, Woodrow Wilson School, Princeton University, September 1972.

GOVERNMENT EXPENDITURES

The trend, both in quantity and quality, of government expenditures in the first years of the Belaúnde administration is more complex to analyze than that of revenues. Certain facts stand out, however. Expenditures grew substantially faster than either revenues or the domestic product. Current outlays rose the fastest, largely because of the increases in teachers' salaries and the growth of subsidies (especially pensions and transfers to universities); military expenditures rose modestly until 1966 and then rose rapidly in 1967, and investment expenditures rose at an annual rate of 20 percent in real terms between 1963 and 1966. In the same period, Central Government spending (as defined in the national accounts) doubled in absolute numbers, and rose from an equivalent of 16.7 percent to 20.6 percent of GNP. Two-fifths of the increase was for education, and well over a quarter for public investment.

Public education had been only slowly improved in previous administrations, which had begun sporadic programs of school building. The quality of teaching had continued to be poor; public schoolteachers were badly paid and most of them did not have the necessary qualifications. The government, probably rightly, believed that building more classrooms would be of little use unless there was a dramatic improvement in the quality and quantity of teaching. Teaching had to be made more attractive. Francisco Miró Quesada, one of the younger and more intellectual members of the family that owned the *El Comercio* daily, was Belaúnde's first Minister of Education until October 1964. He coined the phrase "la dignificación del magisterio" ("giving the teachers dignity") to express these needs. In November 1963 he submitted a bill to Congress proposing moderate salary increases for public school teachers, and a charter providing for increased benefits. Not surprisingly, the proposal quickly became a political football since the teachers and their families could form a large voting bloc and were thus a potentially large single political force. In 1964, the 60,000 public schoolteachers and their immediate relatives probably signified a voting bloc of about 150,000 to 200,000 or 6 to 8 percent of the total number of voters. The APRA, and especially Luis Alberto Sánchez, quickly outbid the government's proposal and after an escalation of salary proposed by Congress, Law 15215, the "escalafón magisterial" (teachers' pay and promotion schedule), was passed by Congress and signed into law by the president in late 1964. Few politicians realized at the time what its costs would be, although it should have been obvious that the four annual across-the-board raises of 25 percent provided in the bill for 1965 to 1968 would by themselves lead to a mushrooming appropriation for education. The law not only established higher salaries, but also included a number of social benefits, most of them well-intentioned but with onerous financial costs. Among some of the new provisions: all graduates of teacher training colleges were to be automatically hired as teachers, maternity benefits were increased, and special allowances were established for teaching posts outside urban areas.[6]

The "escalafón magisterial" was the single most important influence on the rapid rise in government expenditures during the Belaúnde administration. On the one hand, the result of the "escalafón" was indeed the intended one of a rapid real improvement in the income and status of public schoolteachers. In fact, there was a redistribution of income towards the teachers: the share of public schoolteachers in national personal disposable income rose rapidly, from an estimated 3.4 percent in 1963 to 5.6 percent in 1966. Although teachers' salaries were still low, they had become more attractive, and more than made up, in terms of the social satisfaction of the teachers, the ground lost in real earnings through inflation in the previous few years. On the

[6] Just about every teacher qualified for some sort of bonus: being at high altitude, or far from the capital, or in a high cost area, etc. Nevertheless, teachers' salaries were still relatively low.

TABLE 16. COMPOSITION OF CENTRAL GOVERNMENT EXPENDITURES, 1961-1967
(millions of soles in current prices)

	1961	1962	1963	1964	1965	1966	1967
Consumption expenditures	5,535	6,325	7,199	9,624	11,796	13,905	16,565
Wages and salaries	(4,549)	(5,270)	(6,212)	(8,139)	(10,087)	(12,130)	(14,417)
Other	(986)	(1,055)	(987)	(1,485)	(1,709)	(1,775)	(2,148)
Transfers and subsidies	2,405	3,044	4,909	6,191	7,726	9,281	10,579
Interest	180	162	203	217	573	623	893
a. Total current expenditures	8,120	9,531	12,311	16,032	20,095	23,809	28,037
b. Direct capital expenditures	1,150	1,447	884	1,640	2,819	3,754	4,619
c. Total (net of debt amortization)	9,270	10,978	13,195	17,672	22,914	27,563	32,656
Memorandum item:							
Outlays by Armed Forces	—n.a. on comparable basis—				3,286	3,575	5,268
Ratios to GNP							
Current expenditures	12.9%	13.3%	15.6%	16.9%	17.8%	17.8%	18.2%
Capital expenditures	1.8%	2.0%	1.1%	1.7%	2.5%	2.8%	3.0%

SOURCE: Central Bank, *Cuentas Nacionales*. The definitions used in *Cuentas Nacionales* are different from those used in the budget; a major difference is that the latter allows for a "liquidation period" in the following calendar year, but it is computed under the year in which the expenditures were provided for in the budget.

other hand, from a fiscal standpoint, the cost of the measure was much more than the financial authorities had expected and, taking into account the expenditures in other sectors, much more than could be financed without a major tax increase. It accounted for about 40 percent of the increase in Central Government expenditures in 1965 and 1966, the two years during which the salary increases in the law were granted. The complementary provisions of the new teachers' statute had been superimposed on an antiquated administrative system that lent itself, because of poor controls, to an even faster rise of expenditures. It was not until 1967 that a census of teachers was successfully carried out, and only in 1968 were the hiring of teachers and the public school payroll placed under central control.

Although the increase in teachers' share of income was a result of their growing political power because of their rapidly increasing number, it is tempting to reflect whether a similar result could not have been achieved at less fiscal cost.

The benefits and salary increases granted the teachers would not have been of the size approved in the "escalafón" if either the Executive or Congress, or preferably both, had been willing to take a less popular stand, an attitude that would have been feasible if a simple study of the consequences of the salary increase for the teachers had been publicly available. The staffs of the two agencies—the Central Reserve Bank and the Planning Institute—which might have provided the necessary analysis did not have the necessary public stature and support. The general ignorance of elementary financial arithmetic in political circles meant that not even the press, except for a few scattered questions, raised the issue. In the end, if the Executive had wished to exert a moderating influence, it could have used the many weapons at its disposal. Among these means were the enormous personal prestige of the president and the desire of some of the major newspapers, particularly *El Comercio*, to please the Executive, especially at the expense of the

APRA-dominated Congress. But the Executive had not thought through the financial consequences of the measure. The forced redistribution of income towards the teachers was a socially worthy cause. It paralleled, and probably was a factor in making possible, the continuance of the visible improvement in public education that had begun a decade before but sharply accelerated in the Belaúnde period. But the financial size of the measure benefitting the teachers was too large. (See Table 17.)

Another growing item in education was grants to public universities. Beginning under President Prado, in an attempt to decentralize university education and to satisfy regional

TABLE 17. Trends in Public School Teachers'
SALARIES, 1963-1966

	1963	1964	1965	1966
1. Number of public schoolteachers (thousands)	52.9	60.5	67.8	79.4
2. Total salaries paid (million soles, current prices)	2,092	2,182	3,898	5,551
3. Average annual salary per teacher (current soles)	39,500	36,000	57,400	69,900
4. Total national personal disposable income (million soles, current prices)	61,766	72,779	85,248	98,380
5. Share of teachers' income in national personal disposable income[a]	3.4%	3.0%	4.6%	5.6%
6. Share of total central government salaries in national personal disposable income[a]	10.1%	11.1%	11.8%	12.3%

[a] Income taxes paid by public school teachers and civil servants were very small and have not been deducted to arrive at the ratio shown.

SOURCE: Central Bank, *Cuentas Nacionales*, and various official statistics.

demands, public universities were created at an increasing rate, and by the mid-sixties there were twenty universities, most of them in the public sector, with very few departments and faculties of acceptable quality, the Agricultural University being for most of the sixties a notable exception. The public universities depended very heavily on central government grants, which rose from S/. 257 million in 1963 to close to S/. 1 billion in 1967. The achievement in university education, despite the rapid increase in enrollment, is open to doubt, since there was an excessive concentration of enrollment in the humanities and law: over 70 percent of the students were enrolled in those subjects, whereas only a quarter were in scientific studies, and most of these had little applied content. The experience of other countries, with a surplus of dissatisfied professionals in liberal arts subjects unable to find employment equal to their relative educational level, is likely to be repeated in Peru as graduates from the universities increase in number at a faster rate than professional employment opportunities.

While the expansion of government spending on education was deliberate, because it resulted from Congressional and Executive decisions, a sizable part of the increase in other government current expenditures took place quietly, under the shadow of established routine. A large item was the pension budget, which grew from 1963 to 1966 at the same speed as total government outlays. The case of pensions was a clear instance of overgenerous retirement provisions—retirement at 85 percent of full pay after twenty-five years of public service, regardless of age except for a few categories—in relation to the ability of the country to pay. No centralized accounting of government pension liabilities existed, with the result that the pension budget was invariably underestimated, since it was one of the items for which no obvious measuring yardsticks existed and about which both the Executive and Congress tried to make discreet downward recalculations to leave room for more easily identifiable expenditures. But despite these cuts in the estimates, real outlays for pensions galloped ahead at about 20 percent per year throughout the 1960's.

Expenditures for the armed forces increased at a slower rate than the rest of the Central Government budget in the initial years of the administration, and they decreased from about 20 percent of the total in the early sixties to 15 percent in 1965-1966. In 1967, this trend changed and the armed forces received a large increase in appropriations in the middle of the year. As the 1969 elections approached, it was only natural that the APRA-UNO coalition should try to be friendly with the armed forces. A special factor was the role of UNO Senator Julio de la Piedra, one of the more powerful, forthright, and colorful members of the upper chamber. The supporters of defense expenditures in 1967 were helped by the fact that the three service ministries observed the most orderly budgetary practices in the Central Government. It is true that the financial management of the armed forces was helped by import duty revenues directly assigned to them and by the fact that military budgets did not suffer the kind of budgetary cuts made by Congress in other government departments; however, it remains true that the three armed forces ministries did manage to run their financial affairs much better than the rest of the Central Government.

Of all the categories of expenditures, the one that received the greatest public and press attention was that of public investment. This was not a surprising phenomenon, since the chief priority of President Belaúnde was transformation through massive construction programs. However, the Central Government portion of public investment accounted for only a quarter of the rise in Central Government expenditure between 1963 and 1966, a significantly lower share than the rise in spending on education and on other current outlays. The fiscal impact of public investment was nevertheless very important since it could have been much less of a burden on current revenue if long-term foreign loans had been available to finance a significant portion of this investment. Mostly because of the on-and-off attitude of U.S. AID towards Peru due to the IPC question (see Chapter V below) and also because of the lack of expertise in the planning office in dealing with the project preparation requirements of the international financial agencies, the proportion of public investment financed by long-term foreign loans from those agencies and from bilateral public sources turned out to be quite small—less than one-fifth. The lack of such funds led Peru to seek loans from foreign commercial banks, at terms often incompatible with the long-term benefits of the programs financed in that manner.

FINANCING THE DEFICIT

Much of the increase in expenditure between 1963 and 1966 was to a large extent for causes that were in general "good" ones—namely, education and most of public investment—but the fact that this increase in outlays far outran the available resources should have led to a more critical examination of priorities. Both Congress and the Executive were ill-prepared and unwilling to do this. The increase in schoolteachers' salaries was the outstanding example. Furthermore, the critical examination was postponed because both Congress and the government found ways to avoid the issue until 1966 through short-term borrowing abroad and the draw-down of funds accumulated by public institutions, particularly social security funds. Both sources of funds were inflationary means of financing expenditures, but the fact that they were legal saved the conscience of an Executive and a Congress largely unfamiliar with economic arithmetic. (See Table 18.)

There were many points during the four years 1963-1966 at which the rate of increase of expenditures could have been slowed down. A few key ones have already been mentioned. But throughout the period political and personal attitudes towards the fiscal and financial decline ensured its continuation: the refusal of the Executive at its highest

TABLE 18. FINANCING THE DEFICIT OF THE CENTRAL GOVERNMENT, 1962-1967
(millions of soles, current prices)

Calendar Year	1962	1963	1964	1965	1966	1967
1. Current revenues	10,924	13,111	15,843	19,669	23,231	25,967
2. Total expenditures	10,978	13,195	17,672	22,914	27,563	32,656
a. Current	9,531	12,311	16,032	20,095	23,809	28,037
b. Capital (excluding debt amortization)	1,447	884	1,640	2,819	3,754	4,619
3. Current savings (1. less 2a.)	1,393	800	—189	—426	—578	—2,070
4. Deficit (1. less 2.)	—54	—84	—1,829	—3,245	—4,332	—6,689
5. Financing						
a. Long-term external development loans	300	207	400	550	955	1,059
b. Other foreign loans	—	268	209	410	1,295	1,861
c. Borrowing from the Central Bank	263	546	1,225	97	2,055	966
d. Borrowing from the Banco de la Nación	—	—	246	800	1,157	499
e. Increase in the floating debt and other	—	—	—	1,236	39	2,600
f. Less: debt amortization	—450	—607	—907	—1,021	—1,452	—1,324
g. Discrepancy	—59	—330	656	1,173	283	1,028

Sources and note: The revenue and expenditure figures are from Central Bank *Cuentas Nacionales*, and include as revenues taxes collected on behalf of the res of the public sector and as expenditures the transfer of these revenues to the res of the public sector. Since the national accounts are on a calendar year basis, the coverage is different from that in the fiscal accounts, which include a "liquidation period" that takes place in the year following that for which the figures are shown The financing items are taken from external debt and banking system statistics The difficulty of obtaining reliable estimates is highlighted by the large items for discrepancies.

level to become aware of the situation and to call forcefully for a lesser expansion of expenditure and more tax revenue, the refusal of Congress to do likewise, and the desire of its majority to place the blame on the Executive. These shortcomings were very much rooted in personalities and in the historical circumstances described in Chapters I and II; they were very much the product of an economy and society expanding at a very rapid pace while the managerial and technical talent available to the public sector was far behind.

The budget deficit shown here, based on a wide national accounts concept of revenues and expenditures of the Central Government, is broadly comparable in its impact to the overall deficit of the public sector. The financing of the deficit was largely through inflationary means, since other sources of financing of a non-inflationary nature were limited. The main non-inflationary sources of financing were long-term foreign loans for development programs and the tapping of domestic private savings through government domestic borrowing. Neither of these sources made an important contribution to bridge the fiscal gap in Peru during the Belaúnde administration. Foreign long-term loans covered a much smaller proportion of total outlays than in other countries, such as Chile and Colombia, which were large recipients of U.S. AID loans. As for tapping private savings, the government had little success: as in the case of many developing countries, it did little to cultivate regular and orderly borrowing from the public and from institutions, and, on the contrary, sought private savings at the time that the well-publicized fiscal woes removed the confidence of the small group of potential investors. This was the case in 1966 and 1967, when the government introduced a relatively attractive 10 percent Treasury bond redeemable at sight, with tax free interest,[7] yet it was only able to place

[7] The 10 percent interest amounted to real yield of about 13 percent for corporations and high-tax bracket individuals; this was attrac-

97

about S/. 300 million. This was the equivalent of less than 6 percent of total savings and time deposits in the banking and savings and loan systems, which paid lower rates of interest. Most of the issue was eventually placed with government pension funds.

The gap was largely financed by the Central Bank printing press,[8] by drawing down government agency savings accumulated in official banks and by increasing amounts of short-term debt abroad. The threat of criticism by *La Prensa*, Pedro Beltrán's paper, tended to exercise a restraining influence on borrowing from the bank of issue. In 1963 and 1964, the continued export boom and the growth of Central Bank foreign reserves made inflationary financing of the Treasury more acceptable to the press and to the board of the Central Bank, which was made up largely of respected businessmen and commercial bankers—the latter never too averse to the prospect of the growth of deposits brought about by Central Bank credit expansion. In 1965, however, rapidly increasing Treasury needs coincided with the arrival of Alfredo Ferreyros, a tough new Central Bank chairman, and with increased public awareness of the financing problems of the Central Government, brought on by rapidly rising domestic prices. The government, therefore, had to turn to new sources of financing.

One tempting source was the large fund of accumulated deposits of various public sector agencies, particularly the social security agencies, in the Banco de la Nación. Formerly the Caja de Depósitos y Consignaciones, modeled in some respects after its French namesake, this ancient organization had been controlled until 1963 by the private commercial banks and acted, for a fee, as the government's revenue

---

tive, even considering an 8 percent rate of inflation, because the government stood to buy back the bonds at any time, and did.

[8] In popular parlance, "la maquinita" or the "little machine" that is supposed to be hidden in the vaults of the Central Bank and to spew forth an unending stream of new bank notes for use by the government. In fact, all the bank notes were imported.

collector and treasury. In that year, the Caja was nationalized by the Belaúnde administration. The nationalization
of the Caja and its transformation into the Banco de la
Nación, which was supposed to act as the banker for the
public sector, coincided with a rapid increase in the incorporation of workers in the social security system, which
began accumulating deposits at the new bank. It was at
about the same time that the Central Government was
entering its fiscal woes. Although public finance logic, supported by economic opinion from the foreign lending agencies, argued that the surplus of one part of the public sector
should be used to cover the deficit of another, it was equally
clear that most of these funds had been idle in the Banco
for some time. Their release in one lump was bound to be
inflationary.

Although the government began borrowing in significant
amounts from the Banco in 1964, by 1965 the needs were
much greater and the disbursement of existing public sector
funds deposited in the Banco—as inflationary a means of
finance as Central Bank credit—was not enough. The process of transferring government funds deposited in the commercial banks to the Banco de la Nación was therefore
accelerated. Although this withdrew loanable funds from
the commercial banks, the move was in fact also inflationary
because the commercial banks kept reserves (an average of
about 30 percent) whereas the Banco in practice had no
reserves: therefore, on the assumption that the banks were
fully loaned up (an assumption that was in fact realistic
for most of the period 1963-1967), for every 10 soles withdrawn from the commercial banks, only 7 would as a first
step be withdrawn from the credit stream, whereas the
Caja would put back 10 soles into the system through credit
to the government. In the following stages of the banking
system multiplier, some of these funds would come back
to the commercial banks and then be subject to reserve
requirements.

An even more important source of finance in 1965 was a

99

U.S. $40 million loan obtained from a group of U.S. banks. The relative ease with which the loan was obtained fostered the illusion that this type of financing could replace more difficult fiscal decisions. The loan, originally for a term of three years, sharpened the trend towards an increasingly shorter maturity of the public debt. The financing of budgetary operations with short-term borrowing abroad at commercial rates of interest was possible because of Peru's good credit standing in the international financial community.[9] Despite the growing budgetary difficulties and the signs of persistent inflation, most of the U.S. banks familiar with Peru felt that the situation was easily salvageable, and some of the banks thought, with some reason, that the three-year bridge loan would enhance their relations with Peru at little risk. The international reserves of the Central Reserve Bank, at an all-time high of U.S. $175 million (including the proceeds of the U.S. $40 million loan) at the end of 1965, seemed to confirm this prospect.

In 1966, the financing problem became more acute. The government was forced unblushingly to borrow on a large scale from the Central Bank, and discussion of the fiscal issue in the press became more intense. Short-term foreign borrowing was entered into on a larger scale, with the refinancing of the previous year's U.S. $40 million—which yielded U.S. $20 million in new funds after the repayment of U.S. $20 million on the original loan—and the use of a general borrowing authority introduced by Congress in the budget for 1966. Article 114—to cite it since it subsequently became famous—of the budget law for 1966 allowed the public sector to enter into contracts for public works and other investments with foreign suppliers without competi-

[9] In 1966 the international standing of the government was such that a number of major international investment banks approached the government about the possibility of an international long-term public bond issue, a form of financing that until then had been accessible to only very few developing countries in the post-war period (among them Mexico, Venezuela, and the somewhat special case of Israel).

tive bidding, provided that the supplier extended an additional 20 percent of the value of the contract as a cash loan to the government or the agency concerned. This provision led to a number of suppliers' credits being railroaded through bureaucratic channels at great speed so that the cash portion of the projects could be used for urgent public payments. A case in point were contracts late in 1966 for the purchase of 12 new cargo ships in Europe at a total cost of U.S. $50 million plus a cash loan of U.S. $10 million.

By the end of 1966, the budget deficit was running at an actual rate of about 3.5 percent of GNP. For many countries such an amount would certainly not appear to be unmanageable. However, since at least two-thirds of the gap was financed through various means that were either inflationary or likely to balloon short-term external debt obligations, the deficit made the difference between a "normal" rate of inflation of 5 or 6 percent then characteristic of many developing countries and the 13 percent annual average price rise experienced in the period 1964-1966. In addition to these elements, the rapid expansion of credit to the private sector, particularly in 1965, contributed to fuel the flames, with an assist from the Central Bank that increased its lending to commercial banks by almost S/. 1,800 million or 60 percent during the year. Despite a drastic increase in reserve requirements in mid-1965, the Central Bank was unable to sterilize a sufficient proportion of the growth of the short-term loanable resources of the banking system. Through various legal loopholes, such as deposits in the state development banks (which were counted as legal reserves), the commercial banks in 1965 managed to conserve some of the growth in their deposits for use in credit operations, although from mid-1965 on they were supposed to freeze the whole of the increase in their deposits.[10] Despite the measure, commercial bank credit grew by 29 percent that year. (See Table 19.)

[10] Through a "marginal" reserve requirement of 100 percent on any deposit growth after the middle of 1965.

TABLE 19. Price Increases, 1955-1968
(percentage changes, annual averages)

	1955-60	1960	1961	1962	1963	1964	1965	1966	1967	196
1. GNP deflator	9.2	10.0	3.6	5.3	5.8	13.0	13.3	12.2	9.7	
2. Cost of living index			4.5	6.5	6.3	10.4	17.0	8.9	9.8	22.

Note: Data for some years have been left blank because of their doubtful reliabilit
Source: Central Bank, *Cuentas Nacionales* and *Boletín Estadístico*.

As the impact of the substantial tariff increases of 1963-1964 receded, imports became again extremely responsive to internal economic trends. Domestic inflation led to an accelerating demand for imports, which became cheaper than domestically produced goods as the exchange rate was held stable. By 1966, the pressure of inflation was becoming more evident. Complaints about a credit squeeze, a familiar cry in an inflationary environment, began to be persistently heard, even though in that year total domestic credit rose by 25 percent, loans and credit to the private sector by 15 percent, compared to an increase of 8 percent in domestic prices. Inventories rose sharply: although the statistics are sketchy, the sample used for the national accounts shows that inventories doubled in 1966. Partly in order to feed this accumulation of inventories, imports grew sharply, by 23 percent in 1966. The inflationary environment made possible relatively large wage settlements with a minimum of strikes; although wage increases were certainly not the prime mover in the inflationary cycle, they kept up with it. (See Table 20.)

The Judgment of the Experts

Although by 1966 an informed economic analyst would have easily detected the signs of serious economic and financial problems in Peru, the situation appeared by no means

TABLE 20. SIMPLIFIED MONETARY SURVEY, 1963-1967
(millions of soles in current prices, at end of year shown)

	1963	1964	1965	1966	1967[b]
A. Origin of Total Credit	14,147	17,213	22,278	27,833	31,553
Central Reserve Bank	4,384	5,718	6,635	8,202	10,459
Banco de la Nación[a]	−77	−67	975	1,068	1,788
Development Banks[a]	926	1,630	1,650	3,878	4,264
Commercial Banks[a]	9,159	10,135	13,041	14,568	15,315
Float	−245	−203	−23	117	−273
B. Destination of					
Total Credit	14,147	17,213	22,278	27,883	31,553
Central Government	2,431	4,054	4,986	8,660	10,147
Rest of Public Sector	−358	−1,131	−657	−980	−1,119
Private Sector	14,172	16,548	20,785	23,917	25,211
Official Capital & Other	−2,098	−2,258	−2,836	−3,764	−2,686
C. Money Supply					
Money (M1)	9,245	11,159	13,050	15,631	17,656
Money and Quasi-money (M2)	16,543	19,844	24,479	28,321	30,467
M2 as % of GNP	21.0	20.9	21.7	21.1	19.8
Change in credit to Central Govt. as % of change in M1	78.5	84.8	49.3	142.3	73.4
M2	39.2	49.2	20.1	95.6	69.3

[a] Net of credit from Central Reserve Bank.
[b] Foreign exchange accounts computed at exchange rate of Soles 26.82 per U.S. $ which prevailed until August of that year.
SOURCE: derived from Banco Central de Reserva, Cuentas Monetarias (unpublished).

hopeless to the general observer. Aided by the rapid growth of exports due to the good fortune of rising international prices, the Belaúnde administration had shown that it could successfully cope with a social situation more unbalanced than that of many other Latin American countries, and that it could give new directions for the development of the country. The Peruvian Army had successfully eliminated the guerrilla bands that had, with much publicity, roamed

103

a few areas of the central sierra in 1964 and 1965: the Executive and Congress had not hesitated to support the action of the Army, and the cost of the operation had been small. On the economic front, Peru still had one of the highest aggregate growth rates among developing countries, and seemed to accomplish this, mirabile dictu, while maintaining a stable exchange rate and an exchange system free of any restrictions.[11] Even Peru's fiscal difficulties had their positive side, since they appeared to stem from an over-enthusiastic expenditure policy rather than from any fundamental deterioration of sources of revenue, such as was occurring at the time in some oil-producing countries. Also, the fiscal problem certainly seemed, by its nature and magnitude, easier to resolve than, for instance, the cost-push inflationary pressures in Argentina or Chile.

This hopeful appraisal of the Peruvian economy prevailed in July 1966, when delegates from aid organizations of the main European countries, together with those of the United States Treasury and Agency for International Development, and the International Monetary Fund, convened in Paris under the auspices of the World Bank to decide on a coordinated aid package for Peru. Until then the World Bank had organized only a few of these "consultative groups"[12] meetings for Chile, Colombia, Nigeria, and Turkey. The idea for such meetings went back to the early days of the Kennedy administration, when growing pressures on the U.S. balance of payments, together with the large U.S. commitment for foreign aid, led to the view in the U.S. government that Western Europe and Japan ought to bear a higher proportion of the burden of foreign aid. Countries selected

[11] See, for example, International Monetary Fund, *Seventeenth Annual Report on Exchange Restrictions*, 1966.

[12] The World Bank distinguishes between a "consultative group" and a "consortium." The latter is convened in order to obtain definite pledges of assistance from official external assistance agencies, whereas in the former only a general understanding about the attitudes of these agencies is sought, although some of the lenders do use the occasion to make definite pledges.

for consultative groups were supposed to be particularly promising in their financial and administrative capacity to absorb significant quantities of foreign aid, especially of the kind provided by European suppliers with the export credit guarantees of their governments. The delegates at the Paris meeting received as their menu a rather weighty World Bank report, which analyzed the Peruvian Plan (actually a public investment program) for the period 1966-1970. Although the report concluded that a rather large savings effort would be needed to finance the bulk of the public sector program, it was not very specific about the chief economic problems Peru was beginning to face at the end of 1965, when a 21-person team from the World Bank had visited Peru. The report did not elaborate—perhaps it could not—whether and how the building of roads, houses, hospitals, and ports was related to the growth rate of the national product projected in the plan.

After some discussion, some toasting and speech-making, some polite and a few not so polite questions asked of the Peruvian delegates, and a few general undertakings about future foreign aid and suppliers' credits, the delegates returned home happily.

CHAPTER V

Interlude: The IPC Issue and the Question of U.S. Aid

INTRODUCTION

Before we move on to the main events of 1967-1968, it may be useful to pause and look back at an issue that plagued Peruvian political life before, during, and after the Belaúnde administration. The question of relations between Peru and the International Petroleum Company (IPC) became of crucial importance during the Belaúnde years in at least two ways: first, when it became in 1963 a factor that directly affected the granting of U.S. development assistance for the duration of the Belaúnde government, and, second, when it provided an important part of the background to the coup that overthrew Belaúnde on October 3, 1968. Much has been written about the IPC issue.[1] At the risk of becom-

---

[1] The literature on the history of IPC in Peru suffers in many cases from partiality. IPC has had published under its auspices in the early sixties a number of books on the issue. There have been numerous reviews of the history and of particular aspects of it in the *Revista de Jurisprudencia Peruana*. An interesting account by the then chief editorial writer of *El Comercio* is Augusto Zimmermann, *La Historia Secreta del Petróleo*, Lima, 1968. The principal government participants in the August 1968 negotiations with IPC have not published their own account of events. A large number of university theses, both in Peru and in the United States, have been written on the subject, but most of them suffer from a lack of knowledge of the inner workings of government. Among some of the foreign sources worth citing are the following. A comprehensive survey is the *Letter from Peru*, which appeared in *The New Yorker* magazine of May 17, 1969. The author, Richard N. Goodwin, was Deputy Assistant Secretary of State for Interamerican Affairs at the beginning of the Kennedy administration and later a White House adviser and participant in the

ing repetitious, it is necessary for an understanding of the case to go back to its origins in the nineteenth century. Perhaps, before a sketch of the history of IPC in Peru, it is worth looking into why an issue of this kind can come to loom so large in the political life of a country. Admittedly, IPC was in the late sixties the second largest direct taxpayer in Peru,[2] it accounted for three-quarters of the crude oil produced in the country, and was a large employer, especially in the northernmost coastal city of Talara. However, IPC did not play as large a role in the economic fortunes of Peru as, say, the banana companies in some Central American countries or the oil companies in Venezuela, countries that have relied on such enterprises for the largest part of their export earnings (95 percent of merchandise exports in Venezuela in recent years) for two or three decades. There is, of course, a growing number of countries where major foreign-owned export enterprises have been nationalized in recent years (for example, Chile, Guyana, Algeria, Peru itself, and, in 1974-1975, several oil countries including Venezuela) but in none of these cases did the issue simmer for as long or were the respective positions of governments

---

decisions on U.S. development aid to Peru in 1963. An illuminating account of the attitude of the U.S. government towards the IPC case during the Belaúnde administration is that of Juan de Onís and Jerome Levinson, *The Alliance That Lost Its Way*, 1970, pages 146-156. A legal interpretation of the case is that of Dale B. Furnish, "Peruvian Domestic Law Aspects of the Brea y Pariñas Controversy," *Kentucky Law Journal*, Vol. 59, 1971. The *Hearings before the Subcommittee on Western Hemisphere Affairs of the Committee on Foreign Relations*, U.S. Senate, April 14, 15, and 16, 1969, contain the lengthy testimony of Richard N. Goodwin and of IPC executives. A recent review by a U.S. author is that of Jessica Pernitz Einhorn, *Expropriation Politics*, Lexington Books, Lexington, Mass., 1974. Background on the history of IPC in Peru from 1914 to the 1920's appears in Jorge Basadre, *Historia de la República del Perú*, Vols. 12 and 13. I am indebted to David Falk for a particularly comprehensive account (unpublished) of the history of the case, which he was kind enough to let me see.

[2] The largest was the Southern Peru Copper Corporation.

and companies in the final outcome as far apart as in the case of IPC.

In Peru a few special factors probably contributed to drag out the IPC dispute over the years and thus give it growing political importance. The first and most important, although the least easy to identify, was the lack of a unified national point of view on the issue among the Peruvian leadership in the fifties and sixties. There was little uniformity of views as to whether IPC was economically important, whether a break with it would have had a really substantial effect on relations with the United States, and whether it was a political and economic plus to nationalize the oilfield (which was the original subject of the controversy). While both Congress and the Executive were willing to take steps towards diminishing the status or power of IPC, neither—at least until the settlement of the Belaúnde administration with IPC in August 1968 and the subsequent physical take-over by the armed forces two months later—was willing to take a major step on its own responsibility either in the direction of getting IPC out or of keeping it in. In this climate of lack of clear direction, two opposing influences flourished over the years: that of the U.S. Embassy, and that of *El Comercio*, the large Lima daily.

The position of the U.S. Embassy changed over the years and was not always the same as that of the company. Moreover, it was on occasions different in emphasis from that of the Department of State in Washington, only minutes away by phone or telex but still far away when it came to the fine shadings of discussions with the various Peruvian governments. Despite these qualifications, the message that came from the U.S. Embassy in the fifties and sixties was—stated in its simplest form—that to "harm" or "do something to" IPC would be very bad for relations with the United States. It was argued that this was so because action against IPC would constitute a precedent for relations between U.S. petroleum companies and other petroleum-producing countries. The question of a precedent was of course a large

108

exaggeration since U.S. companies in other developing countries that produce petroleum did not have the status that IPC claimed to have in Peru, namely that of full owner rather than concessionaire of the oil deposits. Moreover, Peru was a minor oil producer and a marginal exporter: it is doubtful if any type of action there would have constituted much of a precedent in major oil-producing countries.[3]

In the almost provincial atmosphere of power groups in Lima, the apparent message of the U.S. government appeared disproportionately large. So did the very different message of *El Comercio*, which had increasingly attacked IPC since before the Second World War. Of course, Peru shared in this period in the growing nationalism of developing countries. But it is doubtful if the IPC question would ever have become as much of a political issue without the steady drumbeat of *El Comercio*. Don Luis Miró Quesada, the patriarch of the family that owned *El Comercio*, is said to have stated that his feelings against IPC were aroused when, sometime in the late twenties, he landed at the port of Talara, the center of IPC operations. A sign saying "Talara—Puerto Norteamericano" greeted him at the pier, and there were clear signs of segregation between foreign and local personnel. He is said to have then begun turning his attention to the IPC issue.[4] The concern of *El Comercio* with IPC varied in intensity over the years, but it increased markedly at the end of the 1950's and from then on never really abated. The political preeminence of the issue ten years later was very largely the result, on the one hand, of *El Comercio*, and, on the other, of the equally intense if less overt pressure of the U.S. government.[5]

[3] The doubtful value of the "precedent" argument was ironically shown up in 1971-1974, when the major oil companies had to accept from the governments of the Organization of Petroleum-Exporting Countries (OPEC) financial demands that the companies would never before have imagined.

[4] The episode is reported by Richard N. Goodwin, *The New Yorker*, May 17, 1969.

[5] See, for example, Richard N. Goodwin's statement at *Hearings*

109

A third force was the Army. More than other groups in Peru the Army gradually evolved a position on IPC; while it was not a detailed platform, the position by 1967 or so was that IPC must go in one way or another. It is true that the War Minister, with the apparent support of the principal generals, approved the Belaúnde settlement with IPC in August 1968, but that agreement was, after all, fairly consistent with the line the Army had been advocating, namely that IPC ought to return the La Brea y Pariñas field to Peru. One possible reason for the Army's views was the exposure that many officers had during their service to the IPC installations in Talara, 140 km from Peru's main northern base in Tumbes. Since the northern base was the most important one after the war of 1940 with Ecuador, most officers passed through it at one time or another. The contrast between the prosperous IPC installations—surrounded, like many factories, by fences topped by barbed wire—and the aged barracks of the military was only too apparent. Enclaves often generate ill-feeling, but in the case of the Talara installations the feeling in the military was heightened by the appearance of intrusion into their special domain.

ORIGINS AND HISTORY TO 1963

The beginnings of the IPC dispute go back to the confused history of the War of Independence.[6] The new Peru-

---

before the Subcommittee on Western Hemisphere Affairs, U.S. Senate, April 14-16, 1969, pp. 84-97.

[6] A number of the disputes of Latin American countries with foreign lenders go back to the Wars of Independence. For example, the so-called "sterling debt" of Guatemala originated in a controversial British loan of the 1820's: after various disputes, renegotiations, and various claims by creditors, a settlement was reached in 1966. The final payment on Haiti's external debt arising from its War of Independence in 1803 was made in 1947, after a history of inflated claims by former foreign landowners, defaults, refinancing loans the proceeds of which were only partly received by Haiti, etc.

vian state emerged with heavy debts from the war. In order to help to pay off these debts, Simón Bolivar in March 1825 authorized the state to sell its properties, including mines, with preference to purchasers who had helped finance the independence effort. One of the properties to be sold was a pitch mine at a place on the northern Peruvian coast called La Brea.[7] When there were no bidders, the mine was given to one José Antonio de Quintana, in exchange for loans he had made to the state totalling 4,964 pesos. In September 1826, the deed of transfer of the property was signed. However, under Spanish colonial law, mineral resources beneath the surface were the property of the Crown. Exploitation of these resources could be undertaken either by state monopolies or by concessionaires for a payment of a surface tax.[8] La Brea had been a state monopoly: if pre-revolutionary law had been followed, no actual sale by the state could have taken place. The Constitution of 1823 by and large adopted the Spanish legal system, except that it prohibited state monopolies. While La Brea could thus not continue as a state monopoly, it was not clear whether the state could in fact sell the mine, instead of granting a concession on it. In any event, the deed of transfer of the property in 1826 set forth that the state, through its representatives, renounced all rights to the mine, allowing the new owner to dispose of it as he wished.

In the simplest sense, therefore, the origins of the IPC dispute go back to the sale of 1826. The new Peruvian state, pressed by its financial poverty after independence, did something that was not strictly legal: the fact that state monopolies were no longer supposed to exist did not mean that the state could legally renounce all its sub-soil rights. On the other hand, a law of March 1825 had allowed the state to sell off its properties, including mines, in order to

[7] "Brea" means pitch. The "Pariñas" part of the property was acquired in 1830 by a subsequent purchaser, José de Lama.

[8] Concessions lapsed in case the resources were not exploited or the tax was not paid.

pay for the debts of the War of Independence, and the recipient of La Brea believed that he was the *owner* of the mine. These contradictions carried through in one way or another for the next 130 years or so, with attempts on both sides to prove or disprove ownership.

Nothing of significance for the future happened during the next forty years, except that the property was sold and bought a few times. In 1868 petroleum was discovered in Peru, and in 1873 a law was passed establishing a system for the exploitation of oil and coal. A procedure for granting concessions was established; concessions were to be divided in even-shaped lots (*pertenencias*) of 40,000 square meters each, and the *pertenencias* that were not worked for a year would be considered abandoned and could not be reclaimed by the concessionaire. Moreover, in order to validate their claims, holders of rights to oil and coal mines had to present them to the Lima Mining Tribunal. A law of 1877 established a tax of S/. 15[9] per *pertenencia*, which had to be paid annually in order to maintain the right to the concession.

The then holder of La Brea y Pariñas, Genaro Helguero, neither paid the tax nor presented his claim, on the grounds that he was a fee simple owner and that the new laws applied to concessionaires. No fines were levied against Helguero for non-payment of the tax and in 1887, after a petition by Helguero, the government declared that he was indeed the owner of the mine at La Brea y Pariñas; however, the government also declared that Helguero should pay the surface tax. This apparently contradictory opinion did not deter an Englishman, Herbert Tweddle, from buying the mine in 1888. In the meantime the area of the mine had been measured by the local court and divided into ten irregular *pertenencias*, taxable at the then going rate of S/. 30 each.

The area then changed hands among various English

[9] In those days, approximately equivalent to U.S. $12.

112

owners, who in 1890 granted a 99-year lease to the London and Pacific Petroleum Company, which immediately began developing petroleum production in earnest. The size of the output and the minute tax revenues it generated eventually brought protests in Congress that the original measurement into ten *pertenencias* was patently wrong.[10] In 1911, the government ordered that the area be measured. After various protests by the English owners, the Peruvian Corps of Mining Engineers measured the area at 41,614 evenly shaped *pertenencias* of 40,000 square meters each (or a total of about 416,000 acres), a far cry from the 10 original *pertenencias*. The tax payment now due was S/. 1,284,420[11] annually, instead of S/. 300. Clearly, the original measurement had been either very incompetent or less than scrupulously honest. Another major event in 1914 was the entry into the scene of the International Petroleum Company, a U.S. company,[12] which subleased La Brea y Pariñas from London and Pacific. Thus, when the government in 1915 refused to reconsider the new measurement and taxation of the area, not only the British but also the United States government protested on the grounds that La Brea y Pariñas was a property, not a concession, and therefore not subject to the mining legislation of Peru. Nevertheless, in order to continue operating, London and Pacific paid the surface tax now due into an escrow account.

In the gunboat diplomacy atmosphere of those days, the Peruvian government and Congress somehow had to pay attention to the diplomatic protest of two "big brothers." After much controversy, at the end of 1918 a law was

[10] In the meantime, when the system for recording real property transactions was established in Peru in 1899, the mine at La Brea was registered as the property of its English owners.

[11] The total annual Peruvian budget in those years was about S/. 28 million.

[12] Subsequently, IPC became a company registered in Canada, but by then over 99 percent of it had been acquired by Standard Oil of New Jersey.

passed, the only article of which stated that the Executive was authorized to enter into an agreement with the British government "for submission of the pending controversy between the state and the company operating the La Brea y Pariñas oilfields to a definitive award by international arbitration."[13] Almost three years later, in August 1921, the two governments entered into an agreement for arbitration. Article 10 of the agreement stated among other things, that if the two governments reached a settlement of the controversy on their own before the Arbitration Tribunal rendered its award, that settlement would be incorporated by the tribunal in its decision. Such a settlement was in fact reached in March 1922. Following that, the tribunal, made up of three representatives (Dr. Fritz Ostertag, President of the Swiss Federal Court, who presided, a Peruvian, and a British representative) met in Paris and made known its decision in April 1922.

The award (or *Laudo*), including the two agreements that immediately preceded it—namely, the agreement to submit to arbitration and the actual settlement—has been a subject of controversy in Peru ever since that date. The award of the tribunal is indeed a strange document. There is no attempt to explain why La Brea y Pariñas was "owned" by those who had leased it to London and Pacific. The document[14] merely states that "the heirs of the late William Keswick and the London and Pacific Petroleum Company Limited, who are the owners and lessees respectively of La Brea y Pariñas, and their respective heirs . . . shall pay for a fixed and inalterable period of fifty years . . . by way of tax based on surface, tax on production, royalties and all other contributions and taxes, the following": a tax of S/. 30 per *pertenencia* they chose to exploit, and S/. 1 for each of the *pertenencias* they chose not to exploit. Elsewhere, the decision stated the only other tax to be paid as a result of the exploitation and refining of La Brea y Pariñas products

13 Law 3016 of December 26, 1918.
14 *International Legal Materials*, 1968, p. 1203.

was an export tax. The other major elements of the decision were payment of back taxes totalling U.S. $1 million and the rescission by the Peruvian government of its various decisions making La Brea y Pariñas subject to the general mining legislation of Peru. There was no provision in the award for any future procedure to modify arrangements if both parties wished to do so.

The tribunal, far from answering specifically the basic question posed by the two governments (whether La Brea y Pariñas was or was not subject to the general mining laws of Peru), seems to have papered over the cracks. With a British and a Peruvian member, it was almost inevitable that the tribunal should in fact merely enunciate the agreement already arrived at in March 1922 by the two governments. In subsequent discussion of the award, one important point that stands out is the contention that the tribunal went far beyond its terms of reference in providing a detailed fiscal arrangement for La Brea y Pariñas, without answering clearly the central question of the status of the area. A related argument is that the Executive, in working out the fifty-year fiscal arrangement with the British government, went beyond the intention of the law approved by Congress. As against this, it is argued that Peru accepted the award, which has the status of an international treaty. It was registered by Peru with the League of Nations. The award, it is argued, represented an international obligation of Peru.

It thus appears that the award met all the necessary formalities of international law. The question is whether the content of the award was consistent with Law 3016 of 1918, which authorized international arbitration. The answer is that the award went beyond the enabling legislation but that its legal form was correct and that it could be rescinded only through an agreement of the parties to it. It is a little as if two minors enter into an agreement before a notary public to buy and sell a property: the transaction would be null and void even though the document itself met all the legal formalities. In order to invalidate the transaction, it would not be enough for one of the parties unilaterally to rescind his part of the bargain; rather, a procedure would have to be followed before a competent judge in order to declare the initial transaction null and void.[15]

Leaving aside the legal problems, which were still being analyzed until recently,[16] the award was undoubtedly irritating to progressive elements of Peruvian opinion. It is very doubtful if a government other than that of civilian dictator Augusto B. Leguía, well known even in the lax financial atmosphere of the 1920's for its excessive deference to foreign investors and lenders, would have accepted the settlement. There have of course been many subsequent allegations of corruption in the settlement: although these have not been proved, the record of some members of the Leguía administration did little to dispel such allegations.

In February 1924, after the arbitration decision and subsequent actions by the Peruvian government, IPC, using an existing option, purchased La Brea y Pariñas from the then owners, whose status as owners appeared to have been confirmed beyond doubt. As a result of the formal entry of IPC as an "owner," one of the parties to the award—the British government—ceased to retain any material stake in it. The Peruvian government now had to deal with a private enterprise that naturally enough had no interest in reopening a question about its very existence. Less than ten years later, under the administration of Luis M. Sánchez Cerro, Congress passed a law[17] that authorized the Executive "to file through international legal channels a petition for the revision of the international award . . . ; and the declaration of

[15] I am indebted to Fernando Schwalb for this simile.

[16] Particularly by some external official lending agencies, which had to determine whether Peru could be expected to pay compensation for La Brea y Pariñas and various former IPC facilities before Peru could meet certain internal requirements for obtaining loans from those agencies.

[17] Law 7511 of April 1932.

116

its nullity. This authorization also includes the petition for revision and nullity of the agreement of settlement of March 2, 1922." It is doubtful if such an initiative would have got very far, since the British government could not very well revise an agreement the beneficiary of which was now a private U.S. company, which was not even a party to the agreement. The Peruvian Foreign Minister of the time, Luis Miró Quesada, was warned that the ten-year prescription period would end soon, after which the award would no longer be subject to appeal to the International Court at The Hague. In any case, in the turmoil of the Sánchez Cerro government, the authorization was not used, although the government did inform the International Court at The Hague that it intended to contest the award. The government itself ended shortly afterwards, on April 30, 1933, with the assassination of Sánchez Cerro.

Nothing of great significance happened until 1959. In the 1930's, when the finances of the government were very shaky, IPC on a few occasions advanced tax payments to the government. In 1951, IPC agreed to submit to the normal income tax regime of Peru for its La Brea y Pariñas operations. In 1957, at the initiative of IPC's local general manager, Jack Ashworth, an Englishman with a degree of forward vision not shared by his successors, IPC petitioned the government of Manuel Prado for the transfer of La Brea y Pariñas to the concession system of the 1952 Petroleum Law. The petition, however, was rejected—partly because IPC wanted to continue paying taxes at the lower special rates applicable to it—and Ashworth, who had not had the full backing of the IPC management in Coral Gables, Florida, resigned. With his departure the company took on a harder line and began to rely on the U.S. Embassy to get across its point of view. Throughout most of this period, of course, Peru had the business-oriented conservative governments of Marshal Oscar Benavides, 1933-1939; Manuel Prado, 1939-1945; General Manuel A. Odría, 1948-1956; and the second Manuel Prado government, 1956-1962. Even the

117

APRA-dominated and mildly nationalist government of Luis Bustamante y Rivero, 1945-1948, did not raise the issue of La Brea y Pariñas. The state of suspense in the relations between IPC and Peru ended in 1959. In that year, Prime Minister and Finance Minister Pedro Beltrán, as a consequence of the large devaluation of the sol and as means of increasing IPC profits tax payments, allowed an increase in the price of gasoline. In order to sweeten the pill, the decree that set the price increase also allowed the government to negotiate a regular concession for La Brea y Pariñas under the 1952 Petroleum Law. A key feature of the proposed concession was the obligation of IPC to reinvest 50 percent of its net profits and depreciation in its petroleum operation in Peru. The proposal to work out an arrangement was condemned both in and out of Congress. Within Congress, a vocal group led by Alfonso Benavides Correa, Germán Tito Gutierrez, and Alfonso Montesinos[18] roundly condemned the increase in gasoline prices and the proposed arrangement with IPC. Although the vote of censure of the Beltrán Cabinet failed— the government normally had a very substantial majority in Congress—the arrangement with IPC never got to the stage of signature. A number of bills for the nationalization of La Brea y Pariñas were introduced during the debate; even though none were approved, they served to show the public a new alternative.

One of the features that is often alleged to have turned some of the elements of the military government of 1962-1963 in favor of Belaúnde was his stand on the IPC issue. Belaúnde was considered by many of the business and conservative elements in Lima in the 1962 and 1963 presidential campaign as a dangerous extremist, close to the communists. In fact, his promise on the day of his inauguration was simply that he would propose to Congress within ninety days a definitive solution ("arreglo definitivo") of the IPC

[18] All of whom played important civilian roles in the first years of the government after October 1968.

question.[19] He did not advocate nationalization. But there was to be no "solution."

It was not for lack of trying, however. The president named an independent, Mariano Velasco, to head the negotiations. Velasco, a businessman with mining interests, was a solid negotiator, but he was unable to budge IPC from its requirement for "full control" of operations at La Brea y Pariñas. The proposals discussed with IPC were in several ways similar to those eventually accepted by IPC in August 1968: IPC to stay as operator of its refinery and distribution facilities with the La Brea y Pariñas oil deposits transferred to the state. There were two basic differences in the 1963 proposals compared to the provisions of the agreement of 1968: first, whereas in 1963 the government was prepared to leave IPC for a period of 25 years as operating manager of La Brea y Pariñas, in 1968 IPC agreed to hand over immediately the fields and their management to the government; and, second, in 1968 there was the issue of alleged back taxes, due to "unjust enrichment," an issue that had not arisen by the time of the 1963 discussions. By 1968 any good will towards IPC had largely evaporated, and the government insisted on a harder bargain. Had IPC been willing to accept the 1963 proposals, it would undoubtedly have worked out an arrangement much more satisfactory to itself than anything acceptable to the government in later years. It is unlikely that a 1963 agreement would have lasted for more than a few years, but even so the basic problem would already have been defused. However, this was not to be, with IPC holding out in 1963 and in the next few years, for "full control" of La Brea y Pariñas, so that government ownership of the sub-soil would have amounted to little more than a formality.

[19] Some commentators (e.g., Richard N. Goodwin, *The New Yorker*, May 17, 1969, p. 58, see quotation below) state that Belaúnde had promised to "resolve" the IPC issue within ninety days. Strictly speaking, he had promised to submit to Congress within ninety days a solution to the problem.

No agreement was reached with IPC after the 90-day period. However, Belaúnde sent to Congress a draft law that restored to the state the ownership of the sub-soil claimed by IPC. Instead of passing the proposed measure, Congress within a few days, in November 1963, passed two substitute laws by a large majority. The first revoked the law of 1918 that had authorized the Executive to submit the issue to arbitration, and the second one declared the agreement and award of 1922 to be null and void. Both laws (Laws 14695 and 14696) were signed by President Belaúnde.

Thus, from the point of view of Peru, the IPC issue was back to the status quo ex ante of forty-five years earlier. The immediate response of the U.S. government to the new laws was to refuse to recognize the unilateral action. In the meantime, however, in February 1964, the APRA-UNO majority in Congress—where IPC had a few friends— passed another law (Law 14863) directing the president to find a solution to the La Brea y Pariñas problem and to submit it to Congress for approval. The Executive was thus put in a position of negotiating from a position of weakness, since the other side knew that any agreement would have to be discussed in Congress, where the government party was in a minority. Further, the Executive itself harbored different opinions on the subject, ranging from the views of Celso Pastor, Belaúnde's brother-in-law, who was ambassador in Washington, to the much more radical position of several of the Acción Popular leaders. On the other side, IPC had the trump card of U.S. development assistance.

Despite its weak negotiating position, the government was not inactive in the next three-and-a-half years: there were various beginnings of negotiation, especially early in 1964, when Belaúnde appointed Tulio De Andrea and Pablo Carriquiry to appraise the value of IPC installations. Widening the terms of their mandate, De Andrea and Carriquiry revived the negotiations on La Brea y Pariñas. The points of agreement were again that Peruvian ownership would be

120

recognized, with IPC administering the property under a 25-year service contract. However, the negotiation collapsed once again over the meaning of IPC "full control" of La Brea y Pariñas operations.

U.S. FINANCIAL ASSISTANCE AND THE IPC ISSUE

Clearly, a key factor that stiffened the attitude of IPC was the apparent linking on the part of the State Department in Washington of substantial U.S. Agency for International Development (AID) assistance to Peru with a "settlement" with IPC. In a formal sense, of course, there was nothing to settle: at stake was a renegotiation of the status of the company in Peru, which remained substantially the same in legal terms until the two laws of November 1963, and in practical terms until August 1968, as it had been since February 1924. A satisfactory account of the attitude of the U.S. government on the IPC issue will have to await the revelation of U.S. government primary sources.[20] What was clear to most moderately well-informed observers in Peru was that throughout the Belaúnde administration the U.S. government conditioned in varying degrees the availability and volume of AID funds[21] to the IPC issue, even though no part of IPC operations was physically expropriated during the period. The policy was an ambivalent one: first, it varied in intensity with the changes of the various Assistant Secretaries of State for Interamerican Affairs (there were five during the period of the Belaúnde administration: Edwin M. Martin, Thomas Mann, Jack H. Vaughn, Lincoln Gordon, and Covey T. Oliver);[22] second,

---

[20] For background, see Jessica Pernitz Einhorn, *Expropriation Politics*, Lexington Books, Lexington, Mass., 1974.

[21] Export-Import Bank financing was not directly at issue.

[22] Undoubtedly, the hardest position was taken by Mann, but in general the fundamental policy remained the same throughout, with some change attempted under Vaughn and Gordon, until the agreement with IPC of August 1968.

121

the policy was never explicitly stated, with reliance being placed on the "message getting across" because of the scarcity of AID assistance to Peru; third, it was not based on any explicit law on the U.S. side, since the main possible legal justification, the so-called Hickenlooper Amendment to the Foreign Assistance Act of 1961, applied only in the case of actual expropriation without prompt and adequate compensation;[23] and, fourth, and perhaps most important, the State Department appeared unwilling to do anything of substance on its own to diminish the problem. This "hands off" and "go slow" attitude left the Peruvian government to argue it out with IPC, a private company, giving the latter one strong bargaining advantage, since IPC knew that U.S. AID would move in on a large scale only if the Peruvian government and IPC reached an agreement. This negotiating situation was quite different from that prevailing forty-five years earlier between London and Pacific and the Peruvian government, when the discussion in the end took place directly between two governments.

The results of this policy were simple: Peru got little U.S. AID assistance during the Belaúnde government, and the IPC issue was driven even more to the forefront of the domestic political scene in Peru. The first problem was, together with the fiscal situation and the overvalued exchange rate, one of several factors that pushed Peru towards large suppliers' credits for capital-intensive projects and towards medium-term borrowing from U.S. banks to finance the fiscal and balance of payments gap. The resulting pattern and size of external indebtedness led to the large debt repayment problem that began in 1967. The pressure on the aid front made reasoned and quiet negotiation with IPC even more difficult than would otherwise have been the case.

It is of course difficult to assess the extent to which the

[23] The amendment had been applied only once, in 1963 in the case of Sri Lanka (then Ceylon).

reduced amount of U.S. AID assistance made a substantial difference in Peru's development plans. Set against the other obstacles in Peru at that time—principally domestic political ones, namely, the stand-pat APRA-UNO coalition and the fragmentation of Acción Popular leadership, and also the weak economic planning machinery—the small size of external concessional assistance was clearly not the major obstacle. However, in terms of opportunities lost, especially in agriculture and education, the damage was substantial. It is true that Peruvian government agencies were slow in coming through with suitable projects. On the other hand, the negative signals about U.S. assistance were a deterrent to mounting a determined project preparation effort in areas where alternative funds from other sources were unlikely to be available. This was indeed particularly true of education and agriculture. Nor did the local AID mission help to make up for inadequate domestic efforts. The direct project preparation work of the AID mission in Peru was small, despite its relatively large professional staff. With the resources spent on this manpower and concentrating it in key areas, it would certainly have been possible to make an effort at helping Peru in project preparation. In addition, there were various special missions on contract to AID, including an agricultural team from the University of North Carolina.

A striking feature of the negative U.S. assistance policies in Peru was that they began immediately after Belaúnde came to power. Aid was to be used as a bargaining tool in the IPC issue. According to Goodwin:[24]

"Dreamer or not, Belaúnde was just the sort of national leader that the United States was hoping for in Latin America, and a logical recipient of generous American assistance.

"Therefore, immediately after Belaúnde's inauguration, Teodoro Moscoso, President Kennedy's Coördinator for the

[24] Richard N. Goodwin, The New Yorker, May 17, 1969, p. 58.

123

Alliance for Progress, flew to Peru with offers of immediate and substantial United States aid. There was only one problem. On taking office, Belaúnde had promised to resolve the La Brea y Pariñas question within ninety days. Moscoso realized that even the most reasonable settlement would create political difficulties for Belaúnde, so he decided to withhold action until the ninety days were up. Thus, the announcement of aid could be used by the Peruvian Government to help blunt any opposition. No effort was made to pressure Belaúnde, and the aid was to flow whatever the outcome might be."

If this statement correctly reflects the U.S. government position, it is not clear how a policy to "withhold action" (i.e., aid) is consistent with the statement that "no effort was made to pressure Belaúnde."

The table below summarizes U.S. AID assistance to Peru in U.S. fiscal years 1964-1968 (July 1963 to June 1968, almost exactly the period of the Belaúnde administration), compared to other Latin American countries. The difference in levels of assistance is striking. The imbalance was to some extent offset by long-term loan commitments from the Inter-American Development Bank (U.S. $102 million over the period shown in the table, including U.S. $19 million on soft repayment terms from the U.S.-financed Social Progress Trust Fund) and from the World Bank (U.S. $109 million). However, this assistance could not come near in volume or in the concessionality of the terms to that which AID, at the time the predominant lender for development in most of Latin America, could have provided. (See Table 21.)

A review of the IPC issue during the first four years of the Belaúnde administration brings out the difficult position in which he found himself, negotiating with a private company while being pressured by a foreign government that itself was not publicly involved in the negotiations. At the same time, there is little doubt that the moment for aggressive initiative on the part of Peru was at the begin-

124

TABLE 21. COMMITMENTS OF U.S. AID CAPITAL ASSISTANCE AND
GRANTS, AND COMMITMENTS OF THE WORLD BANK AND
THE INTER-AMERICAN DEVELOPMENT BANK TO
SELECTED LATIN AMERICAN COUNTRIES,
JULY 1963 TO JUNE 1968

	U.S. AID		World Bank and IADB	
	Total ($ millions)	Per Capita[a] ($)	Total ($ millions)	Per Capita[a] ($)
Brazil	1,067	12.54	687	8.07
Chile	346	40.09	221	25.61
Colombia	353	18.98	282	15.16
Peru	90	7.49	211	17.57
Dominican Republic	244	67.03	39	10.71
Nicaragua	73	43.19	53	31.36
Panama	88	69.29	21	16.53

[a] Based on 1966 population.
SOURCE: U.S. Agency for International Development (A.I.D.), *U.S. Overseas Loans and Grants*, May 24, 1972.

ning of the administration. As time went by, the issues
inflated in political importance, and some form of solution
became progressively more difficult. In retrospect—an admittedly unfair vantage point—it was unfortunate that more
decisive action was not taken by Peru in 1963. Such a step
would undoubtedly have required using the threat of take-
over or nationalization, admittedly a much more common
and accepted form of action in the early 1970's than it was
ten years earlier.

CHAPTER VI

Crisis, January-September 1967: Devaluation

On April 15, 1967, President Belaúnde disembarked at the Lima-Callao airport from the gleaming Aerolineas Peruanas jet that had brought him and his delegation back from the Hemispheric Presidents' Conference at Punta del Este. The welcome was tumultuous, with fifty to a hundred thousand people crowding the beautiful new airport, and dancing in the streets of downtown Lima. For weeks afterwards, the recording of the president's speech at Punta del Este sold at record pace and was played over and over in Lima's noisy music stores. In April 1967, President Belaúnde was indeed at the pinnacle of his popularity.

The Punta del Este speech had been a brilliant oratorical performance. The content was an apologia for the public investment policies of the government, and explained why South America should look to the Amazon basin in its future development.[1] The speech proposed a new scheme for dollar-linked hemispheric bonds[2] and appealed, naturally

[1] President Belaúnde was interested in new schemes for hemispheric development. He mentioned, among others, an idea he had talked about with the Hudson Institute (of Herman Kahn fame) that involved the construction of a dam across the Amazon so as to turn part of it into a vast inland lake that could be used as an easy means of prospecting for oil.

[2] Belaúnde had originally had the idea of marketing agrarian reform bonds, suitably discounted, in order to attract foreign capital, but he came to see that this was not possible. Instead, he worked on a scheme to create a market for dollar-denominated government bonds within Latin America, with central banks acting as agents. With good management, it might have been a profitable way to invest a portion of Latin American reserves, possibly attracting a reflow of capital. The proposal was informally discussed with other Latin American cen-

enough, for a reawakening of U.S. aid to Latin America, of which Peru had received little in the previous three years. Avoiding any notes of bitterness, the speech was delivered, as was Belaúnde's habit, without notes and was an inspiring piece of oratory. Less intellectual than the speech of President Frei, the other great speaker at the event, Belaúnde's performance came from the heart and for a moment uplifted the assembled delegations, who had spent the week discussing a series of resolutions that most of the participants would have some difficulty in remembering today.

THE BALANCE OF PAYMENTS, 1959-1967

By the time President Belaúnde returned from Punta del Este, fears had arisen among a few economic policy-makers and businessmen that Peru's record of unbroken exchange stability since 1959 might not survive long. At the beginning of 1967, the Peruvian balance of payments stood between the apparently dynamic performance of the previous eight years and an uncertain future. The nature of the two main causes of the dynamic performance of the previous three years—the growth of exports and of loan inflows to the government—were also the two principal danger signals for the future of the balance of payments.

The phenomenal growth in the volume of exports that had occurred from 1958 to 1962 was unique since it had been caused by the one-time combined effect of the opening of the large-scale Toquepala copper mine in 1959 and by the uncontrolled growth of the fishmeal industry. From about 1962 on, however, increases in export output were marginal, and in the next four years the volume of exports

---

tral banks, but did not stimulate interest among the countries with relatively high reserves. The Inter-American Development Bank has for several years placed two-year issues of its bonds among the central banks of its member countries, as has also the World Bank among its members.

127

grew by an average of only 1.5 percent per year. (See Table 22.) The political uncertainties caused by the election of 1962 and the subsequent coup, and later the adverse reaction of business to the incoming Belaúnde administration's 1963 electoral platform, led to a general stagnation of investment in 1962, 1963, and 1964. The export sector probably suffered more than the domestic economy, since the owners of the large sugar and cotton farms felt that they would eventually be the target of land reform.

TABLE 22. MERCHANDISE EXPORT INDICES, 1958-1968 (1963 = 100)

	1958	1959	1960	1961	1962	1963
Export volume	56	62	82	96	102	100
Of which: copper	33	30	102	120	104	100
fishmeal	11	29	55	74	111	100
Export prices	81	97	98	94	96	100
Of which: copper	70	96	105	98	100	100
fishmeal	91	105	75	91	98	100
	1964	1965	1966	1967	1968	
Export volume	109	103	109	111	121	
Of which: copper	108	106	119	95	125	
fishmeal	137	125	135	153	200	
Export prices	114	114	130	146	195	
Of which: copper	107	126	197	219	304	
fishmeal	99	148	151	130	192	

SOURCE: derived from International Monetary Fund, *International Financial Statistics*.

Special circumstances also affected various products. Between 1964 and 1966, fishmeal output stagnated as a result of a series of crises in the industry. In 1965, the schools of *anchovetas* were too far from the coast as a result of an outward shift of the cold Humboldt current, making fishing difficult and costly.[3] In most years, a large number of the smaller fishmeal plants faced serious financing problems since the very high ratios of debt upon which they had been built could be sustained only by a rapidly growing and easily available fish catch. As for mining, where enormous copper resources awaited development, the two major foreign-owned companies were unwilling, despite continuously rising international prices, to expand their investments. They did not want to begin discussions on new projects with the government until Congress approved a special statute assuring the companies of tax benefits and other guarantees not contemplated in the mining code. The companies believed that they needed this special statute because the Internal Revenue of Peru had opened a case in 1965 against Southern Peru Copper—with a great deal of publicity in Congress and in *El Comercio*—casting doubt on the tax provisions of the contract of 1954 between Southern Peru and the government, a contract that incidentally had been approved by a previous Congress. The tax case was finally settled by the Tax Court in 1967 in favor of Southern Peru.

The special difficulties that affected the principal export products were reinforced for other export products by the rapid increase in domestic costs in the face of a fixed exchange rate. Since the rate of S/. 26.82, which had been in effect since 1959,[4] had been intentionally set by then Finance Minister Pedro Beltrán with what was generally considered to be a wide margin of undervaluation, there was substantial room for domestic costs to increase before the bulk of exporters began feeling the pinch. The sugar and cotton producers were probably the first to be affected: cotton prices were stagnant from 1963 to 1966 and sugar

[3] The same thing happened on a much more drastic scale in 1972-1973, placing the future of the fishmeal industry in doubt. As of 1974, the *anchovetas* are back, but at a lower level of potential production.

[4] In fact the rate was revalued from S/. 27.70 per U.S. dollar at the end of 1959 to a rate of S/. 26.82 established in January 1961.

129

prices declined in the same period, although increases in the controlled domestic price made up part of the loss. Falling profits and the prospect of land redistribution limited production to the most efficient irrigated areas, and the cultivation of marginal areas declined substantially, or else they were turned over to corn and rice.

A simplistic purchasing power comparison, such as that in the table, shows that the exchange rate became increasingly overvalued in the first half of the 1960's. The largest reduction in the international purchasing power of the Sol took place in 1965, which—not coincidentally—was also the year of the sharpest increase in imports and of a decline in export volume. (See Table 23.) The rapid increase in the value of exports concealed the deteriorating trend to most

TABLE 23. INDICES OF TRENDS IN THE EXCHANGE RATE, 1959-1966
(averages for years shown)

		1959	1960	1961	1962	1963	1964	1965	1966
A.	Exchange Rate: Soles per U.S. dollar	28.00	27.00	26.82	26.82	26.82	26.82	26.82	26.82
B.	Index of exchange rate	104	101	100	100	100	100	100	100
C.	Terms of trade (i ÷ ii)	99	98	94	96	100	113	110	121
	i. Export prices	97	98	94	96	100	114	114	130
	ii. Import prices	98	100	100	100	100	101	104	107
D.	Domestic prices[a]	76	83	88	94	100	111	129	141
E.	Apparent international purchasing power index of the Sol ([C ÷ D] ÷ B)	125	117	107	102	100	102	85	86

[a] In view of the lack of other adequate series, consumer prices are shown here, despite evident limitations as a proxy for domestic prices.

SOURCE: derived from Central Bank, *Boletín Estadístico*, and International Monetary Fund, *International Financial Statistics*, Supplement 1972.

observers. Since the growth of exports was due almost entirely to price increases for copper, profits of the mining companies rose faster than the increase in costs in the period 1965-1967, particularly in 1966, so that their profit remittances abroad increased substantially, leaving a proportionately smaller growth of net export proceeds available for foreign exchange payments. Looked at in this way—net of profit of remittances arising from exports—foreign exchange inflows from export earnings were in fact virtually stagnant after 1964, despite the increases in export prices, a far cry from the rapid export growth seen by most observers in and out of Peru for the period of the mid-sixties. Clearly, as the exchange rate became more overvalued, the incentive to remit projects abroad increased. (See Table 24.)

TABLE 24. NET MERCHANDISE EXPORTS, 1962-1967
(in millions of U.S. dollars, current prices)

	1962	1963	1964	1965	1966	1967
1. Merchandise exports (f.o.b.)	556	555	685	685	789	755
2. Remittances abroad of profits arising from exports[a]	−60	−65	−63	−74	−102	−132
3. Net merchandise exports (1 less 2)	496	490	622	611	687	623

[a] Although no exact classification of remittances exists for the years shown, about 90 percent of them were remittances of companies in the export business. The adjustment has been made to the table.
SOURCE: derived from Central Reserve Bank, *Cuentas Nacionales*.

The effect of an overvalued exchange rate, combined with the excessive domestic credit expansion of 1965 at a time when there began to be some awareness that the rate was overvalued and that "it could not last forever," contributed to the dramatic rise of imports in 1965 and also in 1966. Part of the increase was accounted for and financed by increasing amounts of foreign medium-term supplier credits to the public sector and by the small amounts of long-term loans from the Washington agencies. But the bulk of the increase in imports was by the private sector and might be called "autonomous," or "non-financed," having been brought about by rising domestic income and output, and by the gradually increasing attractiveness price-wise of imported goods. The trend of these "autonomous" imports is clear: capital goods imports fell from 1962 to 1964 as investment stagnated and then recovered rapidly to a record level in 1966 as a number of new private investments came in, especially for the installation of the car assembly plants. Food imports rose rapidly since the domestic increase of the output of food was not enough, and higher incomes led to higher bread, meat, and dairy products consumption; the traditional policy of not giving protection to domestic production of meat, dairy products, and fats and oils, together with the increasing price advantage of imports as domestic prices rose led inevitably to rapid growth of food imports. The remaining imports—or "other" in the table below, made up of raw materials and consumer goods—are the bellwether of price and income trends in the internal economy, and they increased by almost fifty percent between 1964 and 1966, and by another third in the crisis year of 1967 alone. As is shown in the table, the growth of these imports was held back in 1964, largely as a result of the import tariff increase, which affected this type of imports in particular.

A digression on the causes of import growth may be useful. Any estimate is hazardous that attempts to quantify what part of this growth up to 1966 was the result of income growth, and more specifically of industrialization, and what part was the result of domestic inflation, which made imports relatively cheaper in relation to the rapidly increasing money costs in Peru. Early in 1967, the Central Bank prepared a memorandum that attempted to quantify the reasons for the growth of imports in the period since 1960.

132

The main conclusions were reproduced in a published letter from the Central Bank to the Minister of Finance in July 1967.[5] According to this estimate, slightly over half the increase in imports was due to the growth of real incomes, and most of the rest to excess domestic demand stimulated largely by the budget deficit of the public sector. The key assumption was that the income elasticity of demand for imports was only slightly larger than 1 (in other words, a 1 percent increase in income would increase the demand for imports by slightly more than 1 percent). In fact, the income elasticity of demand for imports might well have been higher, closer to 1.5 or even more, a proportion that would not have been surprising in an economy with a "middle-class" consumption boom.[6] The policy relevance

[5] Central Bank, *Boletín Estadístico*, July 1967. This was one of a series of letters in 1967-1968, several of which were published, from the Central Bank to the government, calling attention to the need for fiscal measures. The practice of the Central Bank's sending public admonitions to the Minister of Finance was an old one. The frequency of these letters increased in 1967-1968 as a result of the fiscal and financial crisis.

[6] In an estimate of the income elasticity of demand for imports, the relevant measure of imports is that of "autonomous" imports, excluding public sector imports directly financed by medium- and long-term foreign loans, since the demand for these imports is not directly a function of domestic income (although under certain circumstances this exclusion might be debatable). At any rate, autonomous imports, so defined, rose by 61 percent between 1962 and 1966, real GDP by 23 percent, and the relative price attractiveness of imports—allowing for the 1963-1964 tariff increase—by approximately 30 percent. On these bases, and assuming, in line with experience in economies at a similar stage of development, an elasticity of demand of imports to income of 1.5, and of imports to their relative domestic price of 0.5, 34 percentage points out of the 61 percent increase were the result of general income growth, and 15 points the result of domestic inflation. The remainder was due to special factors, such as the shortfall in domestic food output. These calculations are not only rough but based on averages: for example, it is likely that the rapid growth of an urban consuming class meant that the marginal income elasticity of demand for certain consumer durable imports was much greater

133

of a higher elasticity estimate was quite important: the higher elasticity estimate would have meant that most of the growth of imports was the unavoidable concomitant of income growth and that Peru would have to undergo periodic devaluations as long as the high propensity to import continued. The conclusion of using the lower elasticity estimate was that the fiscal deficit had as much to do with the rapid increase in imports as did income growth, and that a solution to the fiscal problems would go a long way toward diminishing the balance of payments problem. The second of these approaches was the one taken by the Central Bank in 1967-1968. While there was no doubt that the bank was correct about the need for fiscal measures, the economists of the bank—myself included—may have exaggerated the impact that fiscal measures would have on the balance of payments (although, as it turned out in June 1968, after the tax measures were approved, there was a favorable impact of fiscal measures upon business confidence).

The chief available means to finance the balance of payments gap were foreign private investment and foreign borrowing other than that to finance imports. Without sharp fluctuations, direct foreign investment stayed in general at very low levels, largely because of the absence of substantial investment in mining. Foreign short-term loans to the private sector were important in the form of short-term credits for export production, which increased rapidly until 1965, giving the economy in effect a growing advance on future export receipts. But the gap could not have been covered without the substantial borrowing undertaken by the public sector from foreign commercial banks in 1965 and 1966 to cover general government local expenditures. The main such loans were U.S. $40 million obtained in 1965; another U.S. $40 million in 1966—which provided U.S. $20

---

than 1.5, and the price elasticity of demand for those imports less than 0.5.

134

million in new money; a private bond issue in the United States, also in 1966, of U.S. $12.5 million, and a cash loan of U.S. $10 million towards the end of 1966 as part of the order of twelve cargo ships from Finland and Spain. These loans, all of them obtained at commercial terms of five years or less, enabled the government to maintain the level of Central Bank foreign exchange reserves. In 1966, however, despite a 12 percent increase in net exports due to increased prices for copper, and a record volume of foreign loans to the public sector, the foreign reserves of the Central Bank fell by U.S. $24 million.

What are the main conclusions that can be drawn about balance of payments and exchange developments in the years 1963-1967?

First, the deterioration in the balance of payments accelerated suddenly in 1965 and 1966. However, even without domestic inflation, certain latent weaknesses were imbedded in the balance of payments before 1965, and did not come to the fore because of rising export prices and of the slow growth of imports, which had been held back by the stagnation of investment in the period 1962 to 1964. Secondly, the tremendous growth of imports in 1965 and 1966 could not have been sustained without the large increase in borrowing, mostly from commercial sources, undertaken by the public sector. This borrowing created a significant debt repayment burden for the future, especially the years 1968 to 1971, but had not until 1966 and 1967 had more than a limited impact on external debt service. Finally, the increase in the period 1962-1966 in net export earnings, due to the lack of expansion in export volume and the increasing remittances of higher profits arising from rising export prices, was insufficient to finance the rapid rise in payments for imports and services. Taxation of export profits partially offset the tendency, but certainly not with the same effectiveness as if there had been a sliding scale export tax, varying according to price.[7] (See Tables 24, 25, and 26.)

[7] According to the mining code, such a tax could not be imposed

135

TABLE 25. MERCHANDISE IMPORTS, 1962-1967
(in millions of U.S. dollars, current prices)

	1962	1963	1964	1965	1966	1967
1. Total merchandise imports, f.o.b.	478	518	518	660	811	823
2. Capital goods imports directly financed by loans to public sector[a]	41	62	71	80	109	92
3. Autonomous or non-financed f.o.b. imports (1 less 2)	437	456	447	580	702	731
a. Basic foods	67	71	80	101	108	115
b. Capital goods other than in 2[b]	168	157	137	174	252	177
c. Fuels	15	15	17	19	22	22
d. Other[c]	187	213	213	286	320	417

[a] Disbursements of loans directly related to the payment of imports. These imports are entirely capital goods, and include imports of capital goods by the official sector and by the private sector with official financing or financing with a Peruvian government guarantee. There are no data on private sector imports with private long-term financing not guaranteed by the state.

[b] All capital goods, except those directly financed by loans to the public sector. Excludes cars.

[c] Raw materials, and consumer goods, including consumer durables.

SOURCES: Central Bank, Cuentas Nacionales, and unpublished data on the composition of the external debt.

The development of the balance of payments since 1959 had thus been quite uneven. In the three years 1959-1961, Peru reaped the benefits of an 80 percent rise in the export volume due to the opening of one mine—Toquepala—and the sudden growth of one industry—fishmeal. In the subsequent three years, the stagnation of domestic investment held back the inevitable explosion of imports brought about by higher incomes. When domestic investment mushroomed in 1965 and 1966, all the forces making for the rapid growth of imports appeared together: the investment boom, a large

on mineral exports. The new tax regime for large mines introduced in April 1970 has as one of its objectives the progressive taxation of profits in proportion to the return on capital.

TABLE 26. SUMMARY OF FOREIGN EXCHANGE FLOWS, 1962-1966
(in million of U.S. dollars, current prices)

	1962	1963	1964	1965	1966
Net f.o.b. exports (after remittances)	496	490	622	611	687
Non-financed f.o.b. imports (net of loans to finance imports)	−437	−456	−447	−580	−702
Balance of trade payments[a]	59	34	175	31	−15
Services	−48	−46	−81	−81	−78
Private capital (net)[b]	41	−8	−34	45	−8
Foreign loans to official sector[c]	10	15	18	78	128
Amortization of external public debt	−31	−30	−30	−22	−67[d]
Other, including unidentified capital movements	−25	54	−23	−36	16
Total and change in Central Bank foreign reserves (minus equals decline)	6	19	25	15	−24
Total Central Bank foreign reserves at year end	116	135	161	175	151

[a] The difference between export earnings after remittances arising from exports, on the one hand, and non-financed imports, on the other, not the conventional definition of the trade balance. See previous two tables.

[b] After deducting profit remittances of the export sector from exports.

[c] Excluding loans to directly finance imports, which are already deducted from imports, thus leaving loans freely disbursable in foreign exchange.

[d] Includes the prepayment of U.S. $20 million due in later years.

SOURCES: derived from Central Bank, *Cuentas Nacionales*, and previous two tables in this chapter.

fiscal deficit, the increasing weakness of domestic food production, and, of course, the product of all these, rising domestic costs.

THE CRISIS BEGINS

The descent into devaluation on August 31, 1967, was precipitous. Until the beginning of 1967, devaluation was a remote possibility talked about among a few cognoscenti, and occasionally mentioned in the press. On television, de-

137

valuation was more frequently mentioned, especially by Eudocio Ravines, the old-time communist turned conservative demagogue. A protégé of Pedro Beltrán, Ravines held a regular evening program, where he articulately and with increasing frequency, especially in 1967, inveighed against government financial policies and called for a large devaluation. There was little doubt among his listeners that the ideas expounded by Ravines were in fact those of Beltrán. To the large majority of the Lima bourgeoisie, however, who had become accustomed in the span of a few years to the life of appliances and automobiles and even to the lower-level civil servants, schoolteachers, and the urban working class, enjoying the prospect of a real upward mobility and reaping the benefits of reasonably full employment, the word devaluation was synonymous with catastrophe. Nevertheless, as the year 1967 unfolded, it appeared as if every gesture of the politicians, both in Congress and in the Executive, was designed to bring devaluation about sooner rather than later.

On the evening of January 17, 1967, the management of the Central Bank completed a lengthy memorandum that it immediately took to President Belaúnde. Copies were also sent to the leaders of both sides of Congress. The memorandum had been prompted by the evident and very large deficit that was contained in the budget just approved by Congress, and also by the 1967 balance of payments projection just completed by the bank. The document accompanying the projection concluded that 1966 results showed the signs of future trouble; despite a large increase in export receipts and extraordinarily large inflows of foreign loans to the public sector, the Central Bank had suffered a significant reserve loss. For 1967, the projection foresaw—if everything else went well—a reserve loss of at least 30 percent or about U.S. $50 million, largely as a result of the drop foreseen in export prices, particularly of fishmeal.[8]

[8] The f.o.b. fishmeal export price had reached U.S. $150 per metric ton in the course of 1966, or 50 percent above the average of the

138

Further, the prospects would be worse unless something was done about the budget deficit. It was clear to the bank that the budget passed at the eleventh hour on December 31, 1966, by Congress was quite unrealistic since it accentuated the practice of recent years of grossly overstating revenues and underestimating expenditures. Combined with lower export receipts, the large unfinanced budget deficit would lead to a reserve loss of over U.S. $100 million. Hence the memorandum.

The bank had already in 1966 alerted the government on several occasions in memoranda about the general financial deterioration. By January 1967 the magnitude of the problem was much clearer and the bank decided to spell out the problem and possible solutions in black and white to the president. According to the memorandum, after eight years of exchange stability coupled with rapid industrialization and a fairly constant inflation, devaluation would be an almost inevitable consequence of the characteristics of the economic development of recent years. The memorandum conceded that a depreciated exchange rate would not lead to a significant expansion in the volume of exports—an assumption that later turned out to be too conservative—since cost pressures had so far significantly affected only sugar and cotton exports. Although the main problem—the excessive demand for imports, foreign travel, and foreign exchange to deposit abroad—could be mitigated by a higher import tariff and other taxes, the opinion in the memorandum was that while an increase in the domestic price of imports was indeed urgent, it should be moderate since it would increase the already excessively high levels of protection; an import tariff by itself would

---

previous five years. This was considered a high price. The memorandum considered that an average of U.S. $100 per ton might be expected in 1967. Several years later, in 1973, the price was about U.S. $500 per ton, partly because of the shortage of fishmeal but also, and more important, because of the sharp rise in world grain prices, including soybean meal.

not counteract other pressures for foreign exchange purchase. The reintroduction of the certificate exchange system—essentially the compulsory sale to the Central Bank of all export proceeds and the establishment of a dual market with official support only to the official or certificate market—that had been suspended in 1960, was also commented upon: the introduction of a dual market at the rate of S/. 26.82 would immediately sound the alarm and set off a rapid depreciation of the free market, which would after a short time make the official market unsustainable, a premonition that turned out to be all too true later in the year.

The main conclusions of the memorandum were that, whatever the exchange system, devaluation would have to come but that the inflationary results of devaluation would be much worse, and probably annul the favorable balance of payments effects, unless the government obtained first from Congress the tax and expenditure measures needed to close the yawning gap in the 1967 budget. These fiscal measures were viewed as a matter of national urgency.

The discussion of the memorandum was to be repeated many times in the course of the next months, as the Central Bank tried increasingly to convince the Executive to make decisions on the fiscal issue. The President and Minister of Finance Mariátegui possibly thought the *técnicos* of the bank exaggerated. After a couple of days of comings and goings, the discussion was largely shelved.

At least one practical result came out of the incident, however. From that point onward, the Central Bank senior staff met every week with the President, on Thursday before lunch, to inform him of developments. The meetings must have been wearisome for the President. Despite the informality of the Central Bank group, their insistence on the urgent need for fiscal measures and the fact that there was a continuing erosion of foreign reserves cannot have been pleasant for the President.

A problem that exists in the relationship between *técnico* and politicians is the degree to which they trust each other.

The politician tends not to believe gloomy predictions by the *técnico*, who therefore feels that he will not be listened to unless he exaggerates. This type of problem occurred between President Belaúnde and his Minister of Finance (and other members of his Cabinet) on the one hand, and the advisers on the other. It was only natural for the Executive to be more inclined to listen to rosier predictions that emanated from agencies other than the Central Bank and, on occasion, from some of the staff of the bank.[9]

At the end of 1966 two events had taken place that deeply influenced economic events in the first months of 1967. Early in December, the fishmeal industry solved a strike of several weeks by fishermen by accepting a 30 percent raise in their wages decreed by the government. The reluctance of the industry to accept such a large increase, equivalent to a net increase in costs of about 10 percent, was outweighed by the relatively high level of export prices at the time. The other event was the eleventh-hour approval at the end of December by Congress of a Central Government budget that obviously contained a very large deficit. Minister Mariátegui's budget request included S/. 1.5 billion for additional revenue from higher income tax rates, and the introduction of a real estate tax and of a tax on the share capital of enterprises. Not only did Congress not approve the tax request, it also eliminated the pay-as-you-go income tax payment system established a year earlier. It then simply inflated the revenue estimate, approving budgeted current revenues of S/. 23,391 million or 29 percent over the S/. 18,000 million current revenue performance of 1966. The expenditure estimate was S/. 24,640 million, including debt amortization, against a comparable total of S/. 25,400 million in 1966.[10] To make the budget look less unrealistic, Congress simultaneously approved for 1967 a freezing of all public

[9] Including one officer who, without the knowledge of the others, was in the employ of the Army intelligence service.

[10] These figures are not strictly comparable to the national account data used in Chapter IV.

sector salaries, including those of schoolteachers, except in the case of promotions to new functions. Nevertheless, the 1967 budget was patently unbalanced.

Why was such a situation allowed to arise? In a formal sense, the Minister should not have accepted the unbalanced budget. But the real responsibility was much wider, and belonged to both the Executive and Congress. President Belaúnde was evidently disinclined to enter into a controversy with a Congress publicly adamant on the subject of taxes. He may have been right on political grounds: even if he had had a majority in Congress, the unorganized Acción Popular and Christian Democratic Alianza, with its lack of a disciplined leadership, would almost certainly not have provided the necessary support. In 1958, President Prado, even with a majority in Congress, was unable to get the necessary fiscal measures through, and had to wait until the appointment of Pedro Beltrán in July 1959 to get essentially the same measures approved. In 1966, the APRA-UNO coalition had an overwhelming majority in Congress and claimed that the Congress was the "first power in the State" ("primer poder del Estado"): if the Executive spent too much, that was too bad but Congress would not approve the necessary taxes.

What should have been done in this stalemate? A possible course would have been for the President to provoke a political crisis by having his Minister of Finance resign because of the budget approved by Congress. The crisis would have served to put the country on notice about the fiscal and balance of payments problem. The President did not want to adopt this difficult course. The opposition in Congress was adamant. Moreover, the cash squeeze was not visible immediately, because the largest income and profits tax payments were to be collected by the end of the first quarter, and major public investment expenditures, especially for roads, did not arise until after the rainy season in the interior ended in April. For the time being, therefore, the urgency of the fiscal problem was not visible outside.

A high-level commission of parliamentarians, including leading opposition figures, and a few well-known civilians, most of them of a conservative bent, was named to study the tax reform proposals that Minister Mariátegui had submitted in his draft budget. Hopefully, the commission might arrive at recommendations that would have congressional support. The commission worked slowly during most of 1967. The slowness of its labors was not made up by the political weight in its recommendations, since the parliamentarians on the commission felt that their general acquiescence in the tax measures discussed by the commission was in no way a commitment to support those same measures in Congress.

The budget approved by Congress left the government the option of presenting new proposals to finance the officially estimated gap of S/. 1.5 billion. At the end of January the government sent the Senate a draft law to raise import-duty tariffs. There was some doubt among the Central Bank economists as to whether the new tariff schedule would indeed generate the additional revenue, since the high tariff proposed would have reduced certain types of high-duty imports considerably. The Central Bank, however, had very little say in the preparation of the proposal. The next word was up to Congress. For the next three months, the Senate, instead of speedily reaching a decision on the tariff proposal, spasmodically debated it and gave importers plenty of advance signals to begin accumulating a large stock of speculative imports. Members of the government coalition did not support the proposal: quite the contrary, at various hearings, reports of which quickly reached the public, they engaged in lengthy attacks on individual tariff changes. I recall the case of one Acción Popular Senator who spoke for a long time on his predilection for Parmesan cheese with his spaghetti; if the proposed duty were approved, he said, he would have to switch to local cheese, which could not be grated properly and was no good anyway.

As the debate in the Senate committee droned on, there

143

were signs that the fiscal problem was becoming more acute. Although the end of March income and profits tax payments temporarily swelled the Central Government's cash balances in the Banco de la Nación, the expected surplus did not materialize. Cash problems had appeared earlier, even before the tax collections, and in February the Banco de la Nación had borrowed U.S. $12 million from a Canadian bank: thinking that the operation was merely a short-term bridge until taxes were approved, the Banco management borrowed the money at the incredibly short term of ninety days. The dollars were sold to the Central Bank and the soles lent by the Banco de la Nación to the government. For the Minister, biding his time in the hope of getting his tariff increase through, the increase in the visible international reserves gave a respite until the foreign reserve increase that was expected to arise from the end-of-March mining company profits tax payments, which were usually made in foreign exchange. (See Table 27.)

TABLE 27. Summary Central Government Budgetary Cash Operations, First Quarter 1966 and 1967
(in millions of soles)

	January-March	
	1966	1967
Revenue and loan receipts (cash basis)	3,959	4,805
Expenditure commitments (total)	3,389	5,345
Surplus or shortfall	570	−540

Source: Controller General's Office.

Since no progress was made in the first two months of the year, the Central Bank decided to use public suasion. Lengthy public memoranda were sent to the Minister, to support him in his request to Congress for fiscal action. The economists of the bank had another vehicle, a periodic official economic newsletter put out by the bank. The *Reseña,* which gave a running but guarded commentary on economic events, was generally widely reviewed in the newspapers and on television. The January-February issue, which came out at the end of March, contained a special essay on taxation. It argued that the rapid rise in expenditures in recent years was a major cause of the budget deficit, but that an equally important reason was the relative lack of response of government revenues to a rapidly growing economy. Total tax revenues, including those collected outside the Central Government and also social security contributions, had stagnated at about 15 percent of GNP from 1960 to 1966. Furthermore, the tax load was relatively low in comparison to other major developing countries, except for Mexico. The report concluded that there was considerable room to increase tax revenues. As examples it pointed to the sharp fall in the effective taxation of profits, from 26 percent of profits in 1960 to 16 percent in 1965, the result of growing exemptions for manufacturing, and to the virtual absence of taxes on real estate and land.

The *Reseña* was greeted with indignation by much of the press and by Congress. Pedro Beltrán's *La Prensa* editorialized against "that damned little pamphlet" ("ese malhadado folletín") produced by the "hippies in the Central Bank." The Central Bank, it was said, was run by "Los sabios de Harvard" ("the wise guys from Harvard"), a reference to the graduate education of two of the advisers. What did the level of taxation in the Ivory Coast, *La Prensa* asked, have to do with the fiscal problem of Peru? Several speeches in Congress reflected the same point of view. Even the board of the Central Bank, which had reluctantly approved publication, wanted the staff to recant. However, the *Reseña* had at least made clearer the issues in the debate on taxes, which was to last for fifteen months until tax measures were finally approved in June 1968.

The month of April started out with a partial strike of public schoolteachers, who wanted the third annual 25 percent wage increase granted by Law 15215 in 1965. However,

145

the Minister of Education, Enrique Tola, stood firm: he was helped by the unpopularity of the teachers' demands among other civil servants and the Army. At about the same time, on April 5, the Finance Minister sent Congress a proposal to cut Central Government expenditures by S/. 1,500 million, including a sizeable reduction in the agrarian reform budget. In February the Cabinet had already approved the principle of a 10 percent across-the-board expenditure cut (or S/. 2.4 billion), but soon found that little could be achieved: certain items, such as debt service and pensions, could not be cut; the wage and salary bill could not be reduced significantly without dismissals of public employees; the only possible cuts were transfers to the rest of the public sector, although the bulk of these were for universities and hospitals, politically sensitive items. Public investment could of course be reduced, and was, but as the government's contribution to large projects fell, foreign loan disbursements also fell.

By the end of April, the import tariff increase proposal had not yet been approved by Congress. The official Central Government deficit had risen to almost S/. 800 million in comparison with a surplus of S/. 333 million in the same period of 1966, itself a bad year. The Central Bank's international reserves were down to U.S. $122.8 million, a loss of U.S. $30 million since the beginning of the year: hidden from public knowledge was the U.S. $12 million short-term loan obtained in February, which meant that the net reserve loss was already U.S. $42 million. A frank meeting with the President was necessary. The Minister and the Central Bank management marched up to the palace, determined to get the President to make a public stand on the fiscal issue. His popularity was at its pinnacle, after his return from the Punta del Este conference a few days before. The whole Cabinet would have to accompany the Finance Minister to Congress, and be prepared to resign "en masse" if the government did not get its way. But the President was reluctant. In that case, the head of the Central Bank hinted, put the measures in force by decree. But President Belaúnde would have none of that: he did not believe in illegally forcing the hand of Congress. The alternatives were explained. If tax measures were taken immediately, this would enable a gradual and orderly adjustment of the exchange rate; if no tax measures were taken, the country would be forced into a precipitous devaluation, jeopardizing the chances for tax measures and causing a financial crisis that would endanger the life of the government.

In the end, the President reluctantly agreed that the Minister would go to Congress by himself. The hope was that his presentation would galvanize Congress into passing the measures it had been discussing in various forms in the past year. The measures, it will be recalled, were the so-called tax reform package—which included a new and higher income tax, the introduction of a progressive tax on land and real estate, and of a tax on the share capital of businesses— plus the tariff increase and a cut of S/. 1,500 million in Central Government expenditures for 1967 proposed in the original budget submission. Before going to Congress, Minister Mariátegui was strongly urged by Fernando Schwalb, the president (or chairman of the board) of the Central Bank, and by Javier Otero, the director general of the bank, to put more pressure on Congress. Mariátegui thought that he might announce his resignation immediately after his presentation to Congress, as a means of putting pressure on Congress.

The presentation of the Minister to Congress on May 8, 1967, succeeded in being clear, but it failed in its main purpose. In view of his personal devotion to President Belaúnde, Minister Mariátegui did not resign. The government thus gave the impression that it would wait for Congress to make up its mind: in the meantime, the revelation of the size of the fiscal problem, which reasonably informed opinion had not suspected, led to increasing pressure on the foreign exchange reserves of the Central Bank. (See Table 28.)

147

TABLE 28. THE PROSPECTIVE 1967 CENTRAL GOVERNMENT BUDGET DEFICIT[a]
(in millions of soles)

Expenditures		Revenues	
1. Budget approved by Congress			
	24,640		24,64
2. Plus: required but		Less: overestimate in tax	
unbudgeted outlays	2,500	revenues	2,77
Min. of Education salaries	557	Suppression of pay-as-you-go	
Min. of Education pensions	300	income tax	70
Min. of Education, other	410	Tax reform presented to	
Tax office salaries	281	Congress but not	
Min. of Govt. and		approved	1,50
Police salaries	255	Overestimate in import	
Other unbudgeted items	697	duty revenues	57
3. Total projected		Total revenues without	
expenditures	27,140	new measures	21,87
4. Likely deficit without			
new measures			−5,2

[a] As presented by Minister of Finance Sandro Mariátegui to Congress on May 1967.
SOURCE: Central Bank, *Reseña Económica y Financiera*, March-April 1967.

The Minister stated to Congress that the 1967 budget deficit would be S/. 5,270 billion, or about 25 percent of projected current revenues, unless measures were taken. Recalling an old idea of President Belaúnde, he asked for authority to raise revenues and cut expenditures within certain limits. President Belaúnde's idea, discussed many times with the advisors, was to vary taxes each month in accordance with the deficit (or surplus) of the previous month: not without intellectual merit, the scheme was impractical from an administrative point of view.

Central Bank foreign exchange reserves fell sharply in the second week in May. Importers, fearing a tariff increase and seeing the possibility of a devaluation, stepped up their payments: the four-month long discussion in Congress about the proposed tariff increase had already given them plenty of time to sharply increase their orders abroad and accumulate a large inventory of imported goods. On the side of exports, too, foreign exchange earnings had begun to decline in February, as the price of fishmeal and of copper fell precipitously from the moderately high levels at the end of 1966. The decline in the value of exports was accentuated by a reduction in the exchange surrender of exporters. The Minister's speech sharpened these various speculative forces.

As a crisis appeared to be only days or hours away in the third week of May, a loan and some action by Congress seemed to ward it off for a few weeks. In the third week of May, the Banco de la Nación obtained another so-called "bridge" loan, a 60-day loan of U.S. $30 million to beef up the official foreign reserves in time for the end-of-the-month published figures. At the same time, on May 23, Congress approved two laws, one (Law 16567) giving the Executive a vaguely worded authority to raise import tariffs, and the other (Law 16568) granting a part of the existing stamp tax revenues to the armed forces for arms purchases. Both laws were signed by President Belaúnde, who wanted to avoid the turmoil of a confrontation with Congress. The military expenditures law obviously came at an inappropriate time, even though the military ministers had been pressing for such a measure since 1966 and it had been promised by Congressional APRA and UNO leaders for the 1967 budget. However, the time for Congress to withdraw tax revenue from the general fund to grant it for arms purchases was clearly not when Peru was passing through the gravest fiscal crisis in its recent history. The other law was left purposefully vague by Congress; its key provision (Article 13) authorized the Executive "to adjust import-[duty] exemptions, making them consistent with the Import Tariff and with existing tariff protection."[11]

[11] ". . . autorizar al reajuste de las exoneraciones a la importación,

149

The short-term U.S. $30 million loan and the legislation of the end of May marked the beginning of the last stage before devaluation; it was the last point at which the government still thought that "somehow this cannot happen to us."

THE DIFFICULTIES OF DEVALUATION

It may be well to reflect at this point on why devaluations are such traumatic events in many countries. The price of foreign exchange in most countries is perhaps the best-known and most easily identifiable price in the economy. Together with wage rates, of which there are many, the price of foreign exchange determines, for valid economic reasons as well as for psychological reasons, the greatest range of prices in the economy.

Poorer economies have no monopoly on the price effects of devaluations. But devaluations there are more frequent and larger.

The price effects of devaluation in many developing countries are perhaps more widespread and easy to identify than in more industrialized countries; for example, the prices of public services, the sale of which absorbs a larger share of urban working class incomes than in richer countries, usually rise because of their dependence on imported fuel or on domestically produced fuels with dollar-linked prices. Manufacturing tends to use a high proportion of imported raw materials and machinery. The inevitable increases in prices that this situation causes are augmented by the monopolistic position of many industries, sheltered behind high tariff walls or other restrictions. When a devaluation occurs, the protective barrier of import duties rises immediately in terms of domestic prices: tariffs, which are generally ad valorem, rise by the amount of the devaluation while other

---

concordándolas con el Arancel de Importaciones y con las protecciones arancelarias en vigencia."

protective devices, such as import licenses and import prohibitions, tend to be intensified in an effort to restore
depleted foreign exchange reserves. Inflation is intensified.

In addition, devaluation leads to a problem of income
redistribution that is sharper in the developing world than
in industrialized countries. In the latter, exports arise out of
output which is normally not exclusively for export. The
distinction between activities that benefit directly from a
devaluation because they export and those which do not
benefit or may lose in a devaluation is not a sharp one. In
most primary-producing countries, however, a few of them
advanced economies, the distinction between gainers and
losers in a devaluation is a much sharper one. Usually,
industries that export—such as mining, petroleum, agriculture, fisheries—sell by far the largest part of their output
abroad, whereas the manufacturing sector at best exports
only a small fraction of its production, and relies heavily
on imports. A sharp dichotomy arises between the loser and
the gainer, between the plantation and the city, between the
large—usually foreign—mining company and local industry.

The economic reasons that turn devaluations into major
events are magnified politically when they come after long
periods of exchange stability. Two dollars eighty to the
pound, five francs to the dollar, and *veintiseis ochentidos*
soles to the dollar become almost magic figures. A modifica-
tion of the exchange rate looks like a retreat for the government, and a personal defeat for the chief executive. The
longer the rate has stayed stable, the more likely it is to be
overvalued and the larger the required adjustment: the
greater, therefore, the domestic impact of devaluation and
the greater the resistance of the government to devaluation.

In Peru a number of special features sharpened the resistance to devaluation. The first was perhaps the feeling
of the government, and of President Belaúnde in particular,
that the budget deficit—which was seen as the cause of devaluation although, as noted above, it was in fact more an
accelerator of inflationary pressures already at work—was

151

the responsibility of the APRA-dominated Congress. With two more years to go before elections and a change of administration, why should Acción Popular devalue for the benefit of APRA, who would then win the 1969 election? President Belaúnde understandably felt a deep annoyance, which he occasionally expressed in private, at the thought of playing into the hands of the party that in his view had done its best to torpedo his land reform, popular participation, and the *Carretera Marginal* programs in Congress. A second important feature was the bond between the Belaúnde government and the income groups identified with the administration. These "middle income" groups (in reality within the top 3 to 5 percent of income recipients) had flourished in the sixties as never before in Peru. As described earlier, the growing share in total income of these groups, and the benefits of a booming economy and of rapidly increasing public education and health services for a large proportion of the population, were accompanied by a sharp increase in private financial savings, especially in holdings of mortgage bonds and in deposits in savings and loan associations, where there was a large number of small accounts. There was a genuine feeling in the government, and particularly in the mind of the President himself, that devaluation would wipe out these small savings and would put a halt to the gains of the domestic consumer and saver and instead channel wealth to the export sector. It was no use pointing out, as the Central Bank did repeatedly, that, in the event of devaluation, a temporary but substantial tax on exports would be needed to tap the windfall profits that would occur for some exports. In the mind of the president, such a proposal was abhorrent since it appeared to assume that devaluation was virtually a "fait accompli."

CONGRESSIONAL MANEUVERS, MIRAGES, IPC, AND OTHER MOVES

The demise of the exchange rate of S/. 26.82 per dollar was rapid, but if one considers the chain of events that preceded the withdrawal of the Central Bank from the exchange market on September 1, the remarkable thing was the resilience of the totally free exchange system, even with a substantially overvalued rate. The salient events were the repeal by Parliament in June of the authority it had given the Executive to raise import tariffs, the inability of the Senate to agree on a new presiding officer after an allegedly fraudulent election, the lack of a traditional inaugural session of Congress on July 28 to receive the President's annual state of the nation address, and, finally, the increasing public and press debate about the exchange rate. The debate was fueled by the government's repeated indignation against "speculators" and by the opposition view, proclaimed vociferously in *La Prensa* and on television, that devaluation was long overdue. In the middle of the crisis a disagreement broke out with the United States over the purchase of French *Mirage* jets by the Peruvian Air Force.

The first event was a speech by President Belaúnde towards the end of May. At the inauguration of the beautiful new building of the Marine Institute, facing the bay of Callao, the President departed from the expected speech and denounced any talk of devaluation as that of "traitors to their country." The result of this performance was twofold. First, by giving the distinct impression that the President would do just about anything rather than devalue, it was one more cause of capital flight since many business people felt that the free or black market rate in the event of some form of control being imposed would be much more depreciated than a possible official devalued rate. Second, and more important, the speech turned the word "devaluation" into a much greater political issue than it would have been otherwise. The President had unintentionally made the public aware that devaluation was obviously some sort of possibility, and had staked his prestige in fighting against what he regarded as an evil thing. It is not unusual and it is generally necessary for Central Bank governors and Ministers of Finance to deny categorically that there is any doubt about stability of an exchange rate; although these routine

153

denials usually merely succeed in changing the question from "whether" to "when?" they are obviously far different from a speech on the subject by the President of the Republic, as occurred in Peru.

At the end of May, the injection into Central Bank reserves of the U.S. $30 million from the short-term loans obtained by the Banco de la Nación appeared to give a temporary respite. A few days later, this feeling was reinforced when the government came out with the fiscal measures it had apparently been authorized to take through Law 16567. The main measure was the revision of the import tariff.[12] The tariff revision was intended mainly as a revenue measure for 1967 and 1968: it was to fail as such, and was important only in sharply cutting down imports of highly taxed items, thus holding back the growth of total imports a month or two before devaluation. The more important and long-term effect was a substantial increase in the level of protection; unfortunately, and against the opposition of the Central Bank, the increase was mostly in consumer durables, which were in any case assembled domestically out of imported components at tremendous cost and with few benefits for the economy. The bank made the obvious argument that consumption of durables would only be held back, and import growth of those items contained, if an excise tax was put into effect, so as to affect both finished imports and locally assembled products made out of imported parts. Politically, however, a tariff increase is generally easier to pass through a Congress than even the most modest excise or sales tax: Peru was no exception.

The higher level of protection of the new tariff was difficult to measure. In general terms, the new tariff was supposed to raise the ratio of import duties to dutiable imports (a concept very different from that of the level of protection, but the only indicator available) from 29 percent in 1966 to about 39 or 40 percent in its first full year, an increase of

[12] Decree 137-H of June 6, 1967.

one-third on average. In fact, because of the shift from imports of finished durables to components, and because of the effect of the devaluation upon higher-priced imports, the ratio of duties to imports *fell* in 1967.

Even the short-term effect of the new tariff was doubtful. Importers had been given such ample notice of the impending tariff increase that by the time it came after five months of parliamentary debate there was almost a sigh of relief, because importers knew that they would be able to sell at the new higher prices the large stock of consumer imports they had accumulated at the old prices. In view of the high level of stocks, almost any moderate tariff increase or excise would have had the same effect. Import orders of the goods affected by the tariff therefore fell off sharply, and, after a lag, customs revenue fell also. The right measure from a fiscal and balance of payments point of view would clearly have been an excise, not a tariff change.

Be that as it may, the new tariff at least gave the impression that finally something was being done. But Congress was not prepared to let this impression stand: a debate began immediately on whether the Executive was entitled to have passed the tariff increase on the basis of Law 16567 of two weeks earlier. As noted above, the law was not clear in its key clause, but the vagueness was assumed by many to have been a parliamentary tactic to dissociate Congress from a tariff increase they knew was coming anyway. After June 6, instead of letting stand what the bulk of opinion seemed to have accepted, the majority in Congress aggressively campaigned for a repeal of the new import tariff. Aware that the authority for it was not fully convincing, the government had in Decree 137 included a number of provisions about diminishing income tax and import duty exemptions,[13] in line with the requirements of Law 16567,

[13] Among these measures were stricter regulations for duty-free imports into the Amazonic region, the elimination of import duty rebates (*castigos*) for supposedly damaged merchandise, the tightening of regulations on investment tax credits in order to eliminate credits used

155

and had also decreed an expenditure cut of S/. 1.5 billion,[14] of which at most half (or about 3 percent of Central Government expenditure) was expected to be feasible, and even then with much drive and luck. But Congress was not satisfied, and on June 1967 it approved a law abolishing the tariff increase. The law was promptly vetoed by President Belaúnde. But the damage had been done by Congress. The events in Congress, which seemed to approve something one day and disapprove it the next, undoubtedly contributed to the sharp drain in the exchange reserves of the Central Bank.[15] (See Table 29.)

It was in the course of June that an old idea began to be revived. In 1966, after some remarks by a U.S. AID official, the Central Bank had thought of a "bridge" loan by U.S. AID to the Peruvian government. The loan, of the so-called "program" variety—a polite word for a general purpose loan that is used, within broad guidelines, for imports on the one hand, and for the government budget on the other hand[16]—

---

for purposes other than genuine plant expansions, and the establishment of a tariff commission to establish a list of minimum import prices for duty purposes.

[14] Decree 136-H of June 5, 1967.

[15] The reserve drain was to some extent offset by so-called "swaps." Peru had until then an active market in futures of foreign exchange. However, by June, as uncertainty had raised the cost of futures to 10 percent or more annually, exporters began to be reluctant to provide future deliveries of exchange. The Central Bank then stepped into the market, through a "swap": the bank would buy exchange, promising resale of the exchange 60 to 90 days later at a rate of S/. 26.82 per U.S. dollar. Several of us objected that this was an open advertisement for the lack of confidence in the exchange rate, when the problem did not seem to be merely a passing phenomenon—in which case "swaps" could have been useful. As a result, the bank deliberately held down the number of "swaps."

[16] As purchasers of imports pay for them by buying U.S. dollars, the amount available of the "program loan" goes down and holdings of local currency by the Central Bank or another similar agency go up; these "counterpart" funds of local currency are then re-used in the budget or kept for some other purpose. The question of the infla-

TABLE 29. CENTRAL BANK FOREIGN EXCHANGE AND GOLD RESERVES,
DECEMBER 1966 TO AUGUST 1967
(in millions of U.S. dollars)

End of Month	Gross Reserves	Liabilities Giving Rise to Increases in Gross Reserves (Cumulative)		Reserves Net of Liabilities
		Swaps	Other[a]	
December 1966	151.7	—	—	151.7
January 1967	135.7	—	—	135.7
February	133.8	—	12.0	121.8
March	140.2	—	12.0	128.2
April	122.2	—	12.0	110.2
May	110.6	—	42.0	68.6
June	109.3	15.1	42.0	52.2
July	109.3	16.3	52.0[b]	41.0
August	69.7	16.0	52.0	1.7

[a] These were not in the strict sense reserve liabilities of the Central Bank, since they represent borrowing by the Banco de la Nación; however, the short term of the loans and their balance of payments support nature made them virtually equivalent to Central Bank reserve liabilities.

[b] On the last day of July, the Banco de la Nación paid back the U.S. $30 million it borrowed in May, but the government obtained a U.S. $40 million five-year loan. Although the fact that the term of the loan was greater than one year excluded it from being counted as a reserve liability, the proceeds are shown here as a liability in order to show what the reserve drop would have been if the loan had not been obtained.

SOURCE: Central Bank, *Boletín Estadístico*.

was to help bridge the fiscal gap until new tax measures had produced their full revenue effect. At that time, the AID mission had made it clear that the loan would depend on taxes being approved first. Since there was little or no prospect of that in the immediate future, the idea was shelved. After the June 1967 measures, however, the idea revived, partly at the initiative of the AID mission director, Wil-

tionary impact of the use of these counterpart funds has been the subject of some controversy in the literature of development finance.

liam Dentzer, an activist who undoubtedly felt frustrated at the lack of operations of his agency in Peru. The suggestion came at an opportune time, because it was obvious that there remained a large fiscal gap even under the most favorable interpretation of the measures taken. In early June, several all-night sessions were spent by the Minister of Finance with the Central Bank team and the local representative of the International Monetary Fund to try to make ends meet, but, as usual in such cases, no amount of figuring could produce a viable plan. Even after allowing for domestic bond issues of dubious marketability, the "other" item always remained far too large. The trouble with the prospect of an AID loan—a sum of U.S. $40 million had originally been mentioned—was that it disappeared almost as soon as it was mentioned. The main reason was the purchase by Peru of 16 *Mirage* French supersonic fighter planes, which was revealed by the *Washington Post* in an article from its Latin American correspondent, John Goshko, who was based in Peru. The discussions of the program loan at that point became embroiled in U.S. politics. The episode was one of the less brilliant ones in foreign bilateral aid relationships.

The *Mirage* purchase had been made internally possible by the provisions of Law 16568, which had segregated existing general stamp tax revenues for military equipment. This financing existed only in a formal sense, however, since the country could not afford at that point to set aside general revenues for any expenditures other than those already budgeted. Moreover, the terms of the purchase took no account of the external debt servicing capacity of the country, despite warnings by the Finance Minister to the Air Minister. (The debt was one of the first to be refinanced in 1968, before most of the planes had even begun to be assembled.)

The *Mirage* purchase could not have come at a more difficult financial moment. The episode contributed, albeit not in a major way, to the crisis of confidence of mid-1967, and, paradoxically, may have led to President Belaúnde's loss of power over the armed forces, who successfully insisted that he allow the purchase. The U.S. State and Defense Departments also had an important role: by dilly-dallying in early 1967 with the Peruvian Air Force over the sale of F-5 jets, which were simpler and cheaper and were sold at longer terms, they caused a tide of national feeling among Peruvian officers, who felt themselves dependent on the existing old U.S. equipment. The pronouncements out of Washington, as reported in Peru, embittered these feelings further: when the *Mirage* purchase appeared certain, the U.S. spokesmen claimed they had been willing to sell the "supersonic" F-5 all along. When, a few weeks later, the U.S. House of Representatives passed the Conte-Long Amendment to the Foreign Assistance Act, withholding aid to countries that purchased "sophisticated" weapons,[17] U.S. spokesmen said the F-5 was not "sophisticated" (read "supersonic") whereas the *Mirage* was. The joke in Lima was that the F-5 was indeed supersonic, but only when it nosedived towards the ground. The various contradictory statements of the spokesmen from the various interested agencies in the U.S. government appeared to confirm to many people the view that the U.S. was not opposed to the purchase of war planes at all, but to the purchase of non-U.S. war planes.

An event later that year that definitely buried any hopes of the AID program loan was the passage by Congress of a law that reiterated the content of the laws of 1963 and 1964, stating that the sub-soil at La Brea y Pariñas was the property of the state (Law 16674 of July 26, 1967). The law was just about the only matter on which Congress was able to

[17] The text is as follows: "The president is directed to withhold economic assistance in an amount equivalent to the amount spent by any underdeveloped country for the purchase of sophisticated weapons systems, such as missile systems and jet aircraft for military purposes from any country, unless the president determines that such purchases or acquisition of weapons systems is important to the national security of the United States and reports within thirty days each such determination to the Congress."

159

agree in the midst of a turbulent period, which included a dispute on the election of a presiding officer of the Senate. The law gave the government authority for a period of thirty-one days to work out an alternative arrangement for IPC activities at La Brea y Pariñas and to expropriate any other IPC equipment and installations, "keeping in mind Article 29 of the Constitution, as well as the debts of the International Petroleum Company owed to the State" (Article 29 of the 1933 Constitution states that property can be expropriated only if there is a legally demonstrated public interest and once just compensation has been paid). The direct action taken by the government as a result of the law was to register the La Brea y Pariñas sub-soil as a property of the state, but no negotiations took place with IPC about a new arrangement. The charged political atmosphere of July-August 1967 would have made such a negotiation difficult. IPC was allowed to continue operating the La Brea y Pariñas fields under a temporary resolution issued by the Dirección de Petroleo. The impact of Law 16674 on the financial crisis of mid-1967 was that it made it even more difficult to obtain the necessary financial support. Its major importance for future history was that it mentioned possible debts of IPC to Peru, debts that had not before been the subject of legal discussion.

With the possibility of a U.S. AID program loan out of the way, the government began to look for other ways of refloating the reserves. A devaluation was necessary, it was reasoned, but should be held off for at least a few months until effective tax measures could be passed. But there was the constraint of the repayment of U.S. $30 million short-term loan obtained by the Banco de la Nación at the end of May, which fell due on July 31. There was no choice but to refinance the loan. It was decided by the Minister and the management of the Central Bank to obtain a slightly larger loan, of about U.S. $40 million, to buttress reserves a little so as to give time for a major offensive to get the tax reform package out of Congress when it convened on July 28. The task of obtaining the loan would be much easier if there was the support of the International Monetary Fund; in addition the announcement of a new stand-by credit from the fund would have a favorable effect.

WHY NOT EXCHANGE CONTROLS?

The strategy of the Minister was correct in the sense that a devaluation without correcting the key short-term factor in the balance of payments disequilibrium—namely the excessively large budget deficit—would not be effective. It was wrong in that the plan of staving off the day of reckoning and giving more time for the taxes to be passed assumed a degree of political enlightenment that was not to be. Two questions arise: was devaluation likely to mean that Congress would postpone the taxes "sine die"? and why not exchange controls?

The first question has an easy answer, as the events of the following twelve months were to show. A devaluation did in fact lead to postponing significant fiscal action for several months. The closer APRA came to the 1969 election, which it expected to win, the less likely it was to take a stand in Congress that would endanger its probable victory. It was only in June 1968, when the threat of a coup made APRA realize that it might lose all, that Congress allowed taxes to be passed, but even then not on its own responsibility but by letting the Executive take the measures by decree. In retrospect it was clearly over-optimistic to hope that such a Congress would in mid-1967 approve the tax reform package; the Executive would thus have had to by-pass Congress, a course President Belaúnde rightly considered to be contrary to everything his civilian democratic government stood for.

The second question is less amenable to easy answers. The term "exchange controls" covers a wide range of restrictions. The man in the street thinks of exchange controls as limits on the amount of foreign exchange that can be

161

purchased. This view was the generally accepted one in Peru in 1967—especially among industrialists, who saw that they would benefit from the additional protection that almost invariably accompanies payments restrictions—and there was much talk and writing about the fact "that this unrestricted freedom cannot continue forever." The other side of exchange controls, namely the obligation to bring back into the country all foreign exchange earnings, is understood less well[18] and was hardly considered outside the Central Reserve Bank. The bank in the first half of 1967 studied whether some form of exchange control should be put into effect at that time: the major tool proposed was the restoration of the exchange certificate system, which had been temporarily suspended by Pedro Beltrán in May 1960, but which had in effect been dormant since 1954. It could be restored by a simple decree, whereas other forms of exchange control would legally have required Congressional approval, a major bottleneck.

The main purpose of the exchange certificate system was to provide for full repatriation of all export earnings. On the payments side, it provided a limited means of control of the flow of import payments, and of profit and capital remittances abroad of foreign companies, a large item in the case of Peru.

The main objection to the restoration of the certificate system was not against the system itself, but against revising it before a new exchange rate—or at least a flexible rate—was established. The introduction of the certificate system at S/. 26.82 might convince some politicians that devaluation had been avoided, while the business sectors, especially the exporters and importers, would see the re-establishment of the certificate system as the sign that devaluation was just around the corner. As was to happen later, exporters would then hold back shipments and importers would speed

[18] See, for example, L. R. Morse (University of Minnesota), *The 1967 Peruvian Exchange Crisis: A Comment* (unpublished), which focuses almost exclusively on the question of the outflow of exchange.

up payments. The free or black market rate would rapidly depreciate below the official rate; each depreciation would make the official or certificate rate less tenable. Additional controls would therefore be required, but with the substantial amount of foreign financing outstanding for Peruvian exports (on average about U.S. $200 million during 1966-1968) and private sector imports (on average about U.S. $250 million outstanding at any point during the same period), small variations in the leads and lags of payments would wipe out foreign exchange reserves before any comprehensive control system could be organized and be made to work at the then existing rate of S/. 26.82.

A longer term difficulty stemmed from the fact that in theory exchange control systems tend to protect overvalued exchange rates. In practice this means that most forms of effective exchange controls, unless they are managed with a great deal of skill, provide a weapon to prevent or slow down exchange rate depreciation. In the political environment of Peru in 1967, with the problems of economic leadership and an opposition Congress, there was no doubt that this would occur. Indeed, it certainly occurred after the 1967 devaluation. Political management of the exchange system means that the controls end up causing the contrary of what they are intended for: "essential" payments swell while exchange earnings stagnate or fall. A caricature of how this happens might be somewhat as follows. Since consumer food prices must be kept low for the consumer, maximum prices are established, large-scale food imports are encouraged, domestic food output is thereby discouraged, and the food import bill grows rapidly. Since imports of raw materials and machinery are somehow considered essential for industry, they are generously allowed in, together with parts for local industries making appliances, which are considered "bad" when brought in finished and "good" when imported in bits and pieces enjoying tremendous duty-free subsidies. The result is that the import bill swells, while import duty revenue shrinks: a budget deficit is created, compounding the problem of overvaluation. In the meantime, the export sector clamors for rebates and subsidies, but the exportable volume does not increase, since the incentives to export cannot be borne by the government budget and it becomes less and less remunerative to export.[19]

These various considerations led the Central Bank to delay changing the exchange system. Introducing the certificate system, or some stricter variation of it, at S/. 26.82 per dollar would only have precipitated the devaluation.

DEVALUATION

In July 1967 negotiations by the government began in three fronts: domestically, to obtain some fiscal action when Congress reconvened later that month; with the International Monetary Fund, for a new stand-by credit; and with a group of New York banks to obtain a loan to accompany the Fund stand-by.

Negotiations with the Fund went smoothly. In fact, they went too smoothly because the Fund team that came to Lima did not officially do much to insist on tax and exchange rate adjustments that were necessary in the Fund's view. The Fund mission took a softer attitude on these issues than the Central Bank, which had hoped that the Fund visit would, on the contrary, help to support its point of view. Part of the reason was that Peru had been in very good standing with the Fund for the previous eight years: rapid economic expansion with a modicum of price stability

[19] There are many other side effects of the overvaluation cycle. An important one is the discouragement of domestic capital goods industries, which generally have a low rate of protection and which on average tend to provide more employment per dollar invested than industries making intermediate goods. See, for example, Chapters 12 and 18 of *Towards Full Employment*, Report of an International Labor Office mission to Colombia, headed by Dudley Seers, Geneva, International Labor Office, 1971.

had been achieved in most years, an exchange system totally free of restrictions had been maintained, and successive stand-by credits had been granted. Since Peru had not drawn under these arrangements and did not owe the Fund anything, it had a large margin to draw (U.S. $42.5 million, or half the quota) before it reached the so-called second credit tranche, at which point a program for a stand-by would have become much stricter. The head of the Fund mission did make a forthright lecture about policy to the Central Bank board, but since several of the directors were businessmen or commercial bankers, this only led indirectly to more leakages to the street, and consequent foreign exchange purchases. Since no special conditions were attached to the use of the stand-by, the program was rapidly negotiated.

It was clear from the beginning that the Fund would grant the stand-by credit up to U.S. $42.5 million without much difficulty and, therefore, negotiations were begun at about the same time to obtain a loan from the U.S. banks. Here again, the standing of Peru with the banks was good, although several of the eight banks in the group must have had doubts about a balance of payments loan at that juncture.[20] But, as often in the case of commercial bank loans to foreign governments, the doubts were outweighed by the need to do business with a country that had until recently, and might again have, large foreign exchange reserves to deposit abroad. Most of the negotiations were concerned with the rate of interest (1¾ percent over the "prime" rate, then at 7 percent), the term (5 years), and whether the Central Bank would maintain part of the pro-

[20] I remember that a colleague of mine and I, on a visit to a large New York bank, were confronted by one of its officers, who asked all sorts of cogent and embarrassing questions. After a while, he asked if we could excuse him for a minute. After he had left the office, my colleague commented that "this is not a friendly bank" and swiftly led me out to an elevator and onto the street.

ceeds with the lending banks (no such commitment was made).[21]

In the third week in July, once the government had obtained firm commitments from the Fund and from the New York banks, the package of U.S. $82.5 million was announced with some fanfare in Lima. The Central Bank threw a cocktail party in its stately old building with the International Monetary Fund mission in attendance. The head of the mission, Carlos Sansón, was depicted in an *El Comercio* cartoon as a giant and hairy Samson, strangling scrawny "speculators" in his iron grasp. Rather than the usual villain, the International Monetary Fund was shown by all the major newspapers as the saviour. However, as in the case of many other loan packages to defend currencies, its effectiveness would have been much greater if it had come at a time when fiscal and financial policies and the rate itself had been more defensible.

The success of the package was short-lived. A few days later a scandal broke out in the Senate over the election of a presiding officer for the legislative year due to begin on the national holiday, July 28. Usually, for a few weeks before the formal opening of Congress, the two chambers meet as separate preparatory committees (*Juntas Preparatorias*) in order to elect the officers for the coming legislative year and to hammer out legislative programs. It was at this stage that the government had planned to present again some fiscal measures to Congress.

The formal opening of Congress on July 28 cannot take place unless the officers for both chambers have been elected first. At the opening of Congress, the President delivers his traditional state-of-the-nation address. An unforeseen mishap was to interrupt this schedule of events in 1967, and precipitate the devaluation, despite the agreement with

[21] The so-called "best effort" clause in the agreement amounted to "no effort" since the reserves arising from the loan were almost entirely drawn down in four weeks and therefore hardly any deposits could be maintained with the lending banks.

the Fund, the loan from the New York banks, and the tariff increase of June. In mid-July the Senate was voting for a new president, to replace APRA's outgoing president, Luis Alberto Sánchez. There were two candidates, Julio de la Piedra, the colorful conservative leader of the Odriistas, and Daniel Becerra de la Flor, Senator from Tacna, a quiet Belaúndista doctor, who at that time was also Prime Minister. De la Piedra was expected to win, but as a result of the switch in the vote of three independents,[22] and to almost everyone's surprise, Becerra carried the vote. At this point, it is not completely clear what happened. Pandemonium broke out and the APRA-UNO coalition demanded a new vote; in the confusion, the government party went along with what they thought was a recount but in fact was a new vote. During the vote, someone in the APRA-UNO ranks, fearing a new defeat, cast a blank ballot, invalidating the vote. Inexplicably the government group agreed to a third vote, which they lost this time. At that point, the government spokesman declared the second and third ballots to have been illegal, and his group stalked out of the chamber.

These parliamentary shenanigans, shown to the public on TV, gave a very poor picture of the Senate which, in time of well-publicized economic crisis, was unable to agree even on a presiding officer. For the next two weeks the accusations went on, but without the presence of the government coalition. President Belaúnde did not want his party to go back into the Senate until the first ballot was recognized. By July 28, the problem had not been solved. There was therefore no spoken presidential message to Congress for the first time since the mid-fifties.

At 2 p.m. on July 31, a Monday, the Ambassador of Peru to the United States sat in the beautiful office of the former Chairman of the Board of the Manufacturers' Hanover Trust Company, then at 44 Wall Street, waiting to sign the

---

[22] Senators Arteta, Balarezo, and Burga. Their votes normally fluctuated between the majority Coalición and the government Alianza.

U.S. $40 million loan agreed to by the banks ten days before. The banks' representatives were gathered in the board room next door, supposedly finishing last-minute details in the loan agreement. But the week-end news from Peru had come in the morning, and some of the banks were now hesitant. Not only had the President been unable to make his annual state of the nation message, but there had been a new development in the International Petroleum Company case as the Peruvian Congress had declared the subsoil claimed by IPC at La Brea y Pariñas to be the property of the state. The possible attitude of Standard Oil of New Jersey, the owner of IPC, was obviously important to the banks, which were depositories of large Standard Oil funds. Some discussion followed with the Peruvian delegation, but the loan agreement had been negotiated two weeks before and could not be changed in Peru, where it had been approved by the Controller General. Finally at 4:45 p.m., as some of the bankers began to fear that they would miss their trains home, the loan documents were signed.[23]

The steady deterioration in exchange reserves that had taken place since the end of 1966 accelerated in August. The major contributing factor was the continuation of the parliamentary crisis, which lasted until the end of the month. In addition, the steady draw-down by the government of the soles generated by the U.S. $40 million loan, combined with the volatile political situation, was another important factor. In July, the government had again borrowed from the Central Bank and in August it drew down over half the S/. 1,073 million it obtained from the U.S. $40

[23] Immediately upon signing, the loan was credited to the account of the government of Peru in the banks. The government sold the exchange to the Central Bank for soles, and the exchange in the New York banks passed to the name of the Central Bank. At the same time, the Banco de la Nación bought U.S. $30 million from the Central Bank to repay its U.S. $30 million debt to two U.S. banks. These transactions all took place at the close of business on July 31. The increase in the gross reserves of the Central Bank arising from these operations was U.S. $10 million.

million loan. On August 18, the executive board of the International Monetary Fund formally approved the stand-by arrangement for U.S. $42.5 million, but this was barely noticed in Lima, where every day that passed without a solution to the parliamentary problem put additional pressure on the Central Bank's reserves.

In the first two weeks of August, the reserves fell by an average of U.S. $1 million to U.S. $1.5 million per day; the rate accelerated to about U.S. $2 million in the third week. By the last days of the month, the torrent had become an avalanche. On August 29, almost U.S. $7 million were lost. The following day, Wednesday 30, was the day of Santa Rosa de Lima, Peru's patron saint,[24] and a holiday. The board of the bank, against the advice of the staff, appeared to think that the bank could hold on. A board meeting on Wednesday was inconclusive. As a result, the bank opened for business on Thursday the 31st of August. By then, of course, rumors of devaluation were rife.[25]

Almost U.S. $8 million were lost on August 31. When the Central Bank window closed at its normal hour of 11:30 a.m., there was no longer any doubt about whether the bank could continue to intervene in the market on the following day. In the afternoon, one more in the long series of meetings with Minister Mariátegui took place. The papers that had been prepared in the last two months were examined. There was general agreement that the central bank could no longer support the rate of S/. 26.82. The next question was whether to set a new rate immediately or to let "the forces of the market set a new rate." The economists in the group were in favor of setting a new rate immediately, but the politically minded did not think they should

---

[24] Actually patron saint of the Americas and Philippines.

[25] One obvious lesson of these events was the obvious undesirability for a central bank to have an operating board made up of private citizens, since, even with the best intentions, they cannot conceal their views for very long, especially in a relatively small financial community.

bear the responsibility for setting a new rate. The immediate technical problems posed by a new rate—such as the effect on the budget and need for salary and public service price increases—were not insurmountable: a lengthy study had been prepared on the approximate level of the new exchange rate that might be appropriate (at least S/. 40 per U.S. dollar, since the unfinanced budget deficit was likely to go on for some months at least), on the domestic price effects of such a rate (between 15 and 20 percent over a period of six months to a year, depending on wage increases), and on the measures that would be necessary in the immediate weeks ahead. Some sort of compensatory public sector salary raise would be necessary, and so would increases in the controlled prices of gasoline, electricity, and public transport. In addition, and most important, a temporary and gradually diminishing export tax was recommended to diminish the inflationary pressures that would arise from windfall gains to the export sector, and at the same time to help reduce the budget deficit.

The staff considered that the plan should be announced immediately in an address to the nation (most of the measures were already in draft form), and that after a bank holiday on Friday, the Central Bank should reopen at a set rate on Monday. This was not to be, however. The President, dejected by the whole business, hoped that somehow the rate would stay at S/. 32 or S/. 33 if it were left to float. That night it was decided to withdraw from the market the following morning.[26] Early the following morning, all the banks received a note which stated:

Central Reserve Bank of Peru Communiqué:
The exchange market has in the last days faced a demand that exhibits an abnormal level of pressure.

[26] The board was advised that there would be a meeting the following day, but was not told what it was about, although most members must have guessed the reason. One board member could not be reached. His wife said he was "out for a walk." Several telephone calls later, after midnight, he was "still out for a walk."

170

This has occurred despite the stand-by agreement with the International Monetary Fund and other measures taken to maintain the stability of the nation's currency.

In view of this situation, the Central Bank has decided to suspend the sale of the official international reserves entrusted to it, until an exchange equilibrium level is attained that discourages operations of a speculative nature.

Lima, September 1, 1967.[27]

One more thing remained to be done. The night of August 31, the Minister approved the temporary tax on the windfall gain of exporters. Signed on September 1, the only article in the decree stated:

A Special Fund for Monetary Stabilization is hereby created within the Central Reserve Bank of Peru, said fund to be supplied by the retention at customs of 40 percent of the higher value (in soles) f.o.b. Peruvian ports, of exports as a result of the difference between the exchange rate registered at the close of business on August 31 and the average, as published by the Superintendency of Banks, of the day prior to customs invoicing.[28]

[27] The executive of a foreign bank who took my morning call reading the statement did not quite understand what it meant and was still selling dollars at S/. 26.82 hours after the other banks had stopped. He was not alone, however; El Comercio editorialized on the following day that the Central Bank withdrawal from the exchange market did not signify a devaluation. In his pamphlet on the devaluation, Ricardo Temoche, an APRA member of Congress, makes the point that the devaluation was "caused" by the withdrawal of the Central Bank from the exchange market. The pamphlet is a good indicator of the state of economic knowledge among many members of Congress at the time. See Ricardo Temoche Benitez, La Devaluación de 1967—Crónica y Análisis de una Catástrofe, Lima, 1969.

[28] The 40 percent difference worked out to a tax of about 13 percent at a new rate of S/. 40 per U.S. dollar, which was approximately expected. 40 percent of S/. 40 less S/. 26.82 is equivalent to S/. 5.27,

It may seem peculiar to establish an export tax at the time of a devaluation, which is presumably supposed to benefit exporters, who had suffered from a previously overvalued rate. The justification for an export tax at the time of devaluation stems from two facts, which have together been of importance in some Latin American countries, and possibly elsewhere. The first is the system of infrequent but large changes in the exchange rate. It is obvious that under such a system, where the fine tuning of frequent small changes in the rate does not take place, the rate will go from overvaluation to undervaluation, and then shift gradually back to overvaluation. It would be very difficult to establish an "equilibrium" rate after a devaluation, since by definition such a rate would mean no gain in international reserves, the previous decline of which was the very symptom that a devaluation was needed. If, therefore, some undervaluation of the new rate is inevitable, there is justification for taxing the "extra gain" of the export sector. Once the "extra gain" of the export tends to disappear, the export tax must of course be rescinded. Taxation will prevent exporters from yielding too easily to the higher costs following devaluation, especially because of wage demands. The durability of the new rate will thus, at least in theory, be better assured. The second reason is the redistributive one, so as to make less unpalatable to the losers in the devaluation (wage earners, domestic industry) the gains to the exporters.

Post-devaluation export taxes of the kind described above have been successfully implemented in a number of countries, including Mexico (1954), Argentina (1967), and Ecuador (in 1961 and again in 1970).

In Peru, the 1967 export tax decree was no doubt illegal: although it was careful not to mention the word "tax," but

---

or 13.2 percent of S/. 40.00. The reason that the formula was presented in this cumbersome manner was that the rate was to be a floating one.

to talk about a retention the proceeds of which were to be used against inflation, it was nevertheless establishing a tax that could be approved only by Congress. That the President had to resort to establishing a tax by decree was in large part the result of the negative attitude of Congress in the previous months. The measure was largely intended as a negotiating weapon with Congress, which would in the following weeks, it was hoped, pass some similar form of taxation, perhaps differentiating between the various export products. In the meantime, if the measure stuck and the exchange rate eventually reached the neighborhood of S/. 38 to 40 per U.S. dollar, it would yield about S/. 300 million per month, and thus cover over half the existing budget deficit.

CHAPTER VII

The Battle for Taxes

THE NINE months from September 1967 to May 1968 went
from one important event, a large devaluation for the first
time in eight years of increasing prosperity, to another, the
granting by Congress of authority to the Executive to pass
the basic tax reforms the latter had been requesting, sometimes vocally and at other times half-heartedly, since the
end of 1965.

Although one should resist the temptation to write history
in retrospect, it would not be a violation of that principle
to say that the two episodes that contributed most to the
October 1968 coup were the army intervention against the
guerrillas in 1965 and the events from September 1967 to
May 1968. The events of importance during this period were
not so much economic as political. The adjustment to a
44 percent devaluation[1] was surprisingly smooth: there were
few strikes, the post-devaluation domestic price increases
were moderate in relation to the size of the devaluation, and
export volume—against all expectations—rose. The devaluation can thus be said to have been moderately successful.
Although the fiscal problem persisted, and its solution continued to be the first priority of economic policy, its financial
impact did not increase, but rather was held back as government expenditures began to decline in real terms.

The more important aspect of the budget deficit was that
politically the Executive and Congress seemed unable to
come to grips with it. An atmosphere of increasing uncer-

[1] In terms of soles per dollar, the relevant comparison in order to
assess the impact on the domestic economy: in terms of the dollar or
gold value of each sol, the devaluation was from U.S. $0.037 to U.S.
$0.026, or close to 30 percent.

174

tainty was generated as four ministers of finance succeeded one another and Congress refused to move; rumors circulated of a new devaluation, of changes in the Cabinet, of a possible coup.

Each new Finance Minister would have to begin his term with two pilgrimages, one to Washington, D.C. and another to Haya de la Torre in his country retreat ten miles outside Lima. While the Washington agencies could not do much more than wish the Minister good luck in his efforts to bridge the budget gap, more could have been expected of the APRA leader, whose lieutenants in Congress were fully briefed and a few of whom were privately in agreement with the proposed tax measures. Nevertheless, Haya stuck to his slogan of "No más impuestos."

The response of the majority in Congress was tolerated in part by the attitude of the Executive. Neither of the two prime ministers of the period, Edgardo Seoane and Raúl Ferrero, who himself was Finance Minister for two months, staked his reputation or that of his Cabinet on solving the fiscal issue, which was generally recognized to be the overriding problem of the day. There was no deficit and the budget was "truly balanced," said the Prime Minister one day; a deficit had appeared, he would declare two weeks later, but could be solved; finally, he said, the deficit had grown in size from "a lemon into a watermelon." The President had difficulty in working out a strategy to bring the opposition Congress to heel. This difficulty was reflected in a speech to the nation on economic matters in November 1967.

By the time Congress finally gave the Executive power to pass tax measures in June 1968, Peru was suffering from an exacerbated political climate, the product of indecision, continuous Cabinet changes, and the beginning of an economic recession. In this atmosphere, rumors of a coup began to be heard. The rumors, it is true, were still muted, but were vocally encouraged by *La Prensa*. It should have been evident to the political observer that Peru in the first half

175

of 1968 urgently needed a solution to the budgetary problem and a period of political tranquility before the campaign for the June 1969 presidential and parliamentary elections. As time went by, of course, and 1969 approached, these requisites would be harder and harder to achieve.

A New Cabinet

On September 6, 1967, a week after the Central Bank had withdrawn from the market, the Cabinet resigned. President Belaúnde named an entirely new Cabinet; although some loyal Belaundistas who had been ministers in earlier cabinets were named again, the distinguishing feature of the Cabinet was the appointment of a non-political *técnico* as Finance Minister and of a reputedly strong general as Minister of War. The new Prime Minister was Edgardo Seoane, who had a reputation as something of a nationalist. Seoane, who was in his early sixties, was the younger brother of Manuel Seoane, who had been the chief lieutenant of Haya de la Torre and one of the most constructive influences within APRA until his death in 1964. Edgardo Seoane had devoted much of his life to the management of a small family-owned sugar estate, and had been elected First Vice-President of the Republic along with Belaúnde. Although a founding member of Acción Popular, his relations with Belaúnde became increasingly strained, partly because of personality differences but also because it was evident that Seoane wanted to give support to his presidential ambitions by shifting Acción Popular in a more activist and statist direction. In July 1967, Seoane had been elected Secretary General of Acción Popular in a hotly disputed race at the annual party convention in Cajamarca. The official candidate, Javier Alva Orlandini, had lost the election. To run for Secretary General, Seoane had returned some months before from his post as Ambassador to Mexico. He had chosen this position in 1964, when Congress had refused to give the Land Reform Institute that he headed the

176

Cabinet-level status that Seoane thought the agency ought to have.

Belaúnde's tactic in naming Seoane, whom he did not trust, was the obvious one of deflating Seoane's appeal in the party by putting him face to face with urgent problems. In fact, Seoane's actual steps when in office had little to do with his Cajamarca platform, which had concentrated on getting land reform moving. While Seoane's short tenure of office thus led to the result that Belaúnde was hoping for, and Seoane's presidential prospects dimmed considerably, it was a questionable tactic to place at the helm of the Cabinet a person with whom Belaúnde did not have an easy rapport, whom the APRA majority in Congress wished to antagonize, and who was not familiar with the urgent financial problems of the day. The very fact that Seoane assumed the Foreign Ministry portfolio rather than that of Finance already appeared to indicate that the Prime Minister was not going to immerse himself deeply in the central question of the day.

As Finance Minister, the President chose Tulio De Andrea, a bright engineer who had been very successful as head of the Industrial Bank. De Andrea had worked for a number of years in the 1950's in the U.N. Economic Commission for Latin America in Santiago de Chile. On his return to Peru he had helped to strengthen the technical side of the state-owned Industrial Bank, of which he later became chairman. The bank had successfully sought and obtained a minority private capital participation (partly at the urging of the World Bank), and had been notable for its high professional standards. De Andrea had also helped to organize the Lima water supply agency (COSAL), one of the few agencies of its kind in Latin America that provided an adequate water supply without a government subsidy to a city that stands virtually in the middle of the desert. De Andrea was not a political personality, but Belaúnde hoped that his high reputation as a technocrat would bring business and the APRA to believe the word

177

of the government in financial matters, changing their attitude to the previous Minister, Sandro Mariátegui, whom they had suspected of partisan motives.

Following tradition, President Belaúnde named the commanding officer of the Army, General Julio Doig, as War Minister. Doig was certainly an imposing figure, and was reputed to be one of the most forceful leaders in the armed forces. His role in the next nine months, however, was an ambivalent one. His support in the Cabinet for fiscal action was no more vocal than that of his ministerial colleagues, and he seemed to be acting like a politician. After January 1968, when De Andrea resigned, he was rumored to be preparing to lead a coup, but a few weeks later, whether out of genuine conviction or expediency, he seemed to take in public a completely contrary position. Asked at a press conference whether the Army would veto the election of APRA in 1969, he replied that "the word 'veto' no longer exists in the vocabulary of the Armed Forces."[2] Of the other two armed forces ministers, General José Gagliardi, the Minister for the Air Force, was vocal and particularly constructive. Gagliardi remained as minister until the October 1968 coup.

EXCHANGE ADJUSTMENT AND THE CERTIFICATE SYSTEM

The first task of the new Cabinet was to cope with the devaluation begun on August 31. In the first few days after the withdrawal of the Central Bank the reactions to the floating and depreciating rate varied from "Do you really

[2] Reportedly, the statement diminished the prestige of Doig in the armed forces. It was said at the time that at a gathering of top officers, the head of the Lima tank division, General Rodríguez Razzetto (el Machote) spoke out against Doig. Rodríguez Razzetto was a strong supporter of Belaúnde. Apparently, Doig tried to get him to resign his command. Reportedly pressed by Generals Doig and Velasco, Belaúnde compromised by sending Rodríguez to Washington, and thus lost the presence in Lima of one of his strong allies in the armed forces. It was said in Lima at the time that Doig had started plotting a coup.

178

think there will be a devaluation?" to "Why didn't you tell
me beforehand?" On Friday, September 1, there were in
fact no significant foreign exchange dealings as the commercial banks tried to take stock of the likely course of
events. Beginning on September 7, the rate began depreciating rapidly, and reached a low point of S/. 38.07 per dollar
on September 13. With the abolition of the special export
tax, the rate settled back to about S/. 36-37 for the next
week or so. The President of course wanted to limit the
depreciation as much as possible, to about S/. 32 or S/. 33
per dollar. The Central Bank argued that such a rate was
obviously unrealistic and its overvaluation would make it
of very short duration, with or without controls. You need
plenty of margin ("techo," i.e., roof) the economists would
say; with his flair for the political phrase, the President
would say he was less interested in a high roof than in a
solid floor ("prefiero piso que techo"). The upward climb
went on slowly without significant intervention of the
Central Bank. By September 26, however, the new Minister
of Finance, Tulio De Andrea, started to worry that the rate,
which was by then back at an average of S/. 38.07, was
depreciating too much.

What is an appropriate exchange rate to be established
after a long period of overvaluation? Although standard
formulas can of course serve as guidelines, taking into
account the past and prospective increase in domestic costs
and variation in the terms of trade, much depends on an
assessment of future government policies. If that assessment
is uncertain, two possibilities exist, at least in theory: an
undervalued rate, in the hope that it will outlast the inflationary pressures—usually brought on by a budgetary problem—or a system of frequent but small devaluations, provided of course that these begin from a base rate that is in
itself tenable. In Peru, the second alternative was not
politically viable. The sharp shift from the practice of stable
exchange rates for relatively long periods to one of periodic
small devaluations would have required a degree of sophis-

179

tication in economic decision-making that did not exist in Peru; moreover, and most important, frequent or periodic changes in the exchange rate would not have been feasible under the Belaúnde administration, which would in all likelihood have stopped the process after the first shift in the rate. It is only in a few countries, such as Colombia under the Lleras Restrepo administration, where outstanding managerial ability prevailed in public economic policy, that a gradual devaluation was made to work without disturbing political interferences. Moreover, in Peru, there was probably an economic case against a gradually devaluing rate since Peru had only a moderate rate of inflation: a frequently devaluing rate (say, every two weeks to a month) might have become in such a setting an inflationary force in itself.

In Peru, the Central Bank could only hope that the budgetary problem would be solved soon. Since this was only a hope, the staff of the bank decided that a new rate could be established only if there were adequate safeguards: the rate would have to be depreciated at least to a point where it could last for a couple of years, even with a continued although smaller budget deficit. Moreover, some form of control, especially over capital transactions,[3] would have to be established. The only form of control that did not require congressional approval was the reinstatement of the certificate system. During September there was an increasing demand from some newspapers, *El Comercio* in particular, for the re-establishment of the certificate system.

The certificate system derives its name from the issue by the Central Bank of negotiable dollar "certificates" in exchange for the obligatory sale to the bank of the whole of export earnings and of certain other less important foreign exchange inflows. The holders of the certificates—mostly

---

[3] The simplest way of controlling capital movements is, paradoxically, to supervise trade transactions, which comprise the bulk of exchange movements in most developing economies. Without such supervision, capital flight takes place out of export proceeds or by advancing import payments.

exporters—can then sell them within a prescribed time to purchasers—mostly importers—who are qualified by the Central Bank to purchase certificate exchange. A key feature of the system is the forced surrender of export proceeds; this is an important factor since in the period before a devaluation, as might have been expected, exporters repatriate a smaller proportion of their export earnings and borrow locally to make up for their cash shortage.

The other side of the system concerns the payments that can be made with certificates. These payments were defined by a 1948 law and included imports, the service on the external public debt, profit remittances, debt service of foreign companies, and certain other minor payments.

The analysis made in 1967 by the Central Bank of the likely operation of the certificate system showed that its success as a vehicle for holding down speculative purchases of exchange and for contributing to the recovery of exchange reserves would depend on the exchange rate established, on the balance between inflows and authorized outflows in the certificate system, and on the possible destabilizing pull of a separate free market rate. The free market would, under this system, take care of all non-certificate transactions. The advisers of the bank expressed many doubts about the viability of the system as constituted in 1948 and operated until 1954 if it were applied to the circumstances of 1967. The main reason was that in 1948-1954 profit and capital remittances of foreign companies through the certificate market were relatively small; in 1967 they were proportionately a very large part of foreign exchange payments. This was the result of the tremendous growth in foreign-owned mining production that had taken place in the meantime. Therefore, given the likely value of exports after the devaluation and the need to cover these foreign company payments, the certificate system would be in balance only if imports fell sharply and foreign capital investment came in at the certificate rate. Under the certificate law, investors bringing in new money had to bring it in at the certificate rate if they

181

wanted repatriation at the certificate rate, but then foreign investment was unlikely to be a major factor in 1967 and 1968, with the future of mining investments undecided and a presidential election scheduled for mid-1969. Thus it was likely that the volume of outflow items (imports, external public debt service, and remittances of foreign companies) would be larger than the inflow (exports and certain capital inflows).

In view of this imbalance, the advisers of the bank thought that the certificate system would not operate well if simply reinstated in its old form. Its main advantage, the obligatory surrender of export proceeds, could be obtained without imposing the rest of the system, which was out of balance. Furthermore, reinstating the system in its old form would likely create two exchange rates if the certificate rate was set at an overvalued level: the free market rate, although supposedly a "safety valve" in case of speculative pressures, would tend to depreciate at the slightest provocation. Such a trend, creating a growing margin between the free and certificate rates, would induce importers to accelerate their payments, a likely event in Peru because of the large amount—about U.S. $250 million—of foreign commercial credit outstanding for imports at that time.

It is important to understand that the certificate system is not an organized system of control of payments: importers are free to bring what they like and to pay for it at the certificate rate. Also in theory, foreign capital is free to remit profits and capital at any time, once local taxes have been paid. In these circumstances, if an unrealistic rate or some disturbing political or economic event would tend to accelerate import payments, the only countervailing mechanism available, aside from a tightening of credit,[4] would be a

---

[4] Credit measures, unless they are draconian, are rarely effective in a climate of high preference for foreign exchange, when importers accelerate their payments: of all the items in developing countries that commercial banks, whether private or state-owned, find it easiest to finance, imports are probably the main one. Credit measures, there-

"drop-by-drop" rationing of exchange, which would only intensify the speculative demand for exchange. The newspaper clamor during September, especially in *El Comercio*, for the imposition of controls was encouraged by the political problems during the months prior to devaluation, and also by the publication in the official gazette of the lists of all those who had purchased more than $1,000 in foreign exchange in the weeks before August 31. The decision to publish these lists, taken by Minister Mariátegui just before his resignation, was meant to show the public who the real culprits were. The Central Bank argued that to publish the lists would merely pillory people who had bought foreign exchange perfectly legally:[5] the Central Bank insisted, and got, that at least the list of sellers of foreign exchange should also be published. The lists were daily gossip for several days: General Odría had bought $10,000, a major newspaper had bought $150,000 on August 30, several Congressmen had bought unusually large sums in round numbers, etc., etc. Letters of explanation, recrimination, and accusation followed in the press. Everyone looked out for his favorite enemy.

By September 25, the Minister was pressing the Central Bank to re-enter the market at a fixed rate for certificate exchange, but no certificate system had yet been re-established. The bank held back until the Minister and the government could give convincing assurance that they would do something meaningful about the budget deficit. The battle went on until the first days of October, when the

---

fore, have to be draconian in the event of a foreign exchange crisis, since otherwise credit from other sectors is diverted to finance imports.

[5] The lists, paradoxically, gave the government in 1969 the idea, as part of a campaign to raise ethical standards in the government, of accusing Mariátegui and the chairman of the Central Bank of having willfully enriched the speculators by selling them exchange at S/. 26.82 which "should have been sold at S/. 44.00," an accusation that was rejected by the Supreme Court appointed by the new government itself.

bank yielded. On October 5 the certificate system was officially re-instated and on Monday, October 9, the certificate market opened at S/. 38.70 per U.S. dollar, a rate the Central Bank advisers did not consider depreciated enough in view of the uncertain fiscal prospects. The bank had, of course, received a public letter from the Minister stating that the fiscal deficit would be substantially eliminated in 1968, but this was only an intention. In view of the continuing budget deficit and of the time it took to bring it down to a manageable level, the new rate should probably have been depreciated to S/. 42 or S/. 43 per U.S. dollar.

The 1967 devaluation and the re-establishment of the certificate system was a success in more respects than it was a failure. Before that is established, however, it is worth stressing that the devaluation itself, although not its timing, was a wholly unavoidable event, regardless of whether or not there had been exchange controls before 1967 or of whether the Belaúnde government had checked the growth of public expenditures. To be sure, the fiscal policies of the Belaúnde government hastened the event, but, as analyzed earlier, the devaluation was in large measure the delayed result of the rise in domestic costs arising from sudden and rapid industrialization.

On the plus side of the ledger of the post-devaluation adjustment were the moderation of the increase in domestic prices that followed devaluation, the success of the certificate system in obtaining the full surrender of export earnings, and the resurgence—against expectations—in the growth of export volume, particularly fishmeal. The devaluation from S/. 26.82 to the certificate rate of S/. 38.70 to the dollar was the first devaluation since 1959. It was a large jump. In the six months following devaluation, however, the increase in domestic prices was kept down to 10.4 percent, thus assuring among other things a benefit for the export sector and a dampening effect on imports, which were crucial to the success of the exchange rate adjustment.

The main factor in holding down the price rise was the great restraint exercised by APRA on the unions that it controlled.[6] This attitude of APRA was clearly one of its few but most helpful actions toward the Belaúnde government. Most industrial wage settlements after September 1967 and into the first months of 1968 were held to a one-time increase of 15 percent or less. The public sector also contributed significantly to the restraint: two public sector salary adjustments that occurred in October and November meant a total increase in the government salary bill of less than 10 percent, with approximately a 10 percent increase in the lowest levels and lesser percentages at the higher levels.[7]

To success on the front of domestic prices and costs—an achievement not unrelated to the acquiescent nature at the time of the Peruvian labor force—was added success in the Central Bank management of export earnings. Unlike some other countries that seem to have interminable problems in the valuation of export earnings, some of which are therefore never surrendered to the Central Bank, the bank in Peru rapidly organized an efficient computerized system, which effectively ensured full export exchange surrender without interrupting the flow of foreign financing for export production. In 1968 exports recovered to U.S. $846 million compared to U.S. $755 million in 1967, largely as a result of a 30 percent increase in the volume of fishmeal output. This expansion, largely as a result of the incentive provided

[6] The APRA-controlled Confederación de Trabajadores del Perú had in the mid-sixties about 250,000 to 300,000 affiliated members, or 35-40 percent of the Peruvian labor force in mining, manufacturing, public utilities, and transportation. Its membership was about three-quarters of the trade union membership of the country.

[7] The portion of salaries above S/. 10,000 per month (or about U.S. $250 at the new rate) was not increased. Through some clever drafting by Luis González del Valle, the chief adviser in the Finance Ministry, the public salary adjustments at the lower levels appeared to be much bigger than they really were.

185

to production for export by the new exchange rate, was not expected by most observers, who thought that merchandise exports were limited by foreign market conditions. The negative aspects of the management of the devaluation included the creation of an unstable free or draft market and the fact that, on the political front, President Belaúnde was not able to take the opportunity to re-assert his leadership and to start with a clean deck after the storm. It was a clear omission for the President not to have explained to the country why the devaluation had taken place, and what measures had been taken to safeguard the new rate. After all, it would have been relatively easy politically to justify and explain the government program that surrounded the devaluation: the certificate system, restraint in public expenditure, and especially the introduction of a temporary tax on the windfall gains of exporters.

The Dispute with IPC over Gasoline Prices, October-November 1967

During the period of post-devaluation adjustments, the IPC question again came to the forefront of political debate. An event in November 1967, a few weeks after the devaluation, was probably of greater importance to the fortunes of IPC in Peru than the various laws and legal actions of 1967.[8]

[8] Among the main developments after Law 16674 was a request by Finance Minister Mariátegui, following the provisions of the law, to the Tax Court to assess the debt of IPC to the state after the company had allegedly enriched itself from a resource to which it was not entitled. The Tax Court, an arm of the Ministry of Finance, was not supposed to rule on the validity of the request, but simply on the amount. The court ruled, once Tulio De Andrea was Minister of Finance, that the amount should be retroactive 15 years, the period specified in the statute of limitations. The Minister of Justice, Luis Rodríguez Mariátegui, a Christian Democrat, disagreed and thought the amount should go back to 1924. In any event, the Ministry of Finance, using a period of 15 years and the volume of crude multiplied by Texas prices less an estimate for costs, in November 1967 announced that the amount allegedly owed by IPC was U.S. $144

It was the dispute between the government and IPC over the price of gasoline. The devaluation was clearly going to lead to higher wages and other domestic costs, while it had already caused an immediate 44 percent increase in the price in soles of imported crude. Imported crude was especially important to the state enterprise EPF (Empresa Petrolera Fiscal), which had just begun operating its 20,000-barrels-per-day refinery at La Pampilla near Callao, and also to the Conchán refinery south of Lima. The latter refinery was ostensibly owned in a fifty-fifty split by Standard Oil of California and the Prado family, although management was in the hands of Standard Oil of California; the refinery of about 3,500 barrels per day relied entirely on imports. On the other hand, the IPC Talara refinery of 64,000 barrels per day relied for only a part of its output on imports, with its major sources of crude being the so-called Lima concessions field near Talara—operated jointly with Burmah Oil of London—and the La Brea y Pariñas field.

The crude supply pattern of IPC meant the devaluation was unlikely to lead to a large increase in its costs because of imported crude, but would no doubt bring over time, probably after a few months, increases in the cost of labor and services. Shortly after the exchange rate began to depreciate on September 1, IPC drew the attention of the government to the need to raise the domestic prices of petroleum products, especially gasoline. Since IPC accounted for about 55 percent of gasoline sales, it was only natural that it should take the lead for industry petitions to the government. An important factor in the request was that gasoline prices had not been changed since 1959; without

---

million. At about the same time, Minister De Andrea ordered the embargo of S/. 50 million of IPC funds because of other back taxes. Relations thus deteriorated rapidly. The decision of the administrative tribunal was of great importance to the future of IPC in Peru and provided the background to the claim of the next government for the alleged debt of IPC of U.S. $690 million. See *International Legal Materials* 1969, pp. 301-304.

improvements in productivity, there would thus have been a tendency towards declining profit margins after inflation had worn off the effect of the relatively high gasoline and fuel prices established in 1959. IPC therefore felt that it was quite justified in requesting an increase in product prices in 1967: the problem was not the request, but the manner in which it was insistently pursued, and the particular time when this pressure was exerted.

In a large industrial economy, a company subject to public regulation for the prices of its products does not normally have to take significant account of political circumstances when it decides to request higher prices or tariffs. At the same time, the government and its regulatory agencies have sufficient power over privately owned public utilities to hold back price increases that are considered excessive or inopportune. On the other hand, price increases for regulated enterprises are accepted by the government with reasonable frequency, so that huge jumps in prices are unnecessary. While such a pattern approximates that of the United States, Canada, and most of the countries in Europe, in much of Latin America the balance of power between the regulator and the regulated is less harmonious. There are long periods when regulated prices are held down artificially so that large and apparently sudden increases become necessary. This feature exists even in a country such as Mexico, where inflation in the 1950's and 1960's, after the 1954 devaluation, was less than in most industrial countries. Another important feature in Latin American economies, at least until some years ago, was that the regulated enterprise was foreign, so that regulation contained potential diplomatic problems. It is only in the last ten years or so that foreign-owned public utilities have given up their position in most Latin American countries, and sold their ownership to state enterprises.[9] The only foreign-owned enterprises

[9] By 1973, the only major foreign-controlled public utilities remaining were Empresas Eléctricas Asociadas, serving the Lima area

188

subject to a substantial degree of regulation and still active in most Latin American countries are gasoline distributors and branches of foreign banks, but the clear trend in most countries is for local ownership of these facilities.

In Peru in October 1967, not only were these various elements present, but the potential conflict was enlarged by the dispute between the company and the government and by the weak political position of the government after the devaluation. Moreover, there was the by-election coming up for the Lima deputy seat left vacant by the death of Ciro Alegría, the famous writer, who had been a member of Acción Popular. The APRA-UNO candidate was Enrique Chirinos Soto, a hard-hitting journalist (see below for a description of this election). In these circumstances, it was hardly surprising that the government did not want an increase in gasoline prices. However, IPC kept insisting. Finally, in late October, only a few days before the election, IPC told the government that it could no longer supply gasoline in Lima at prevailing prices. News of the impending shortage got out, and queues of cars started forming at petrol pumps. Faced with the emergency, the president called General Doig, the War Minister, for a confrontation with IPC. Doig told IPC that their Talara facilities would be taken over unless IPC supplied Lima with gasoline immediately. Harsh words were exchanged. The exchange at the meeting confirmed the Army officers in their impression that IPC was an overbearing imperialist company. Thus the meeting served to strengthen the impression in the Army that IPC had to be taken over. In the end, although IPC won the battle—an increase of about 50 percent in gasoline prices was decreed shortly after the election—it was to lose the war.

---

and controlled by a Swiss group, and scattered distribution companies in Bolivia, Venezuela, Ecuador, and Brazil. As noted earlier, by 1974 Empresas Eléctricas Asociadas was controlled by the Peruvian government.

TULIO DE ANDREA

The first task of Tulio De Andrea, the new Finance Minister, was to find money: the Treasury was empty and by the time each fortnightly public salary payment ("la quincena") had to be made, the Minister had to scratch about desperately for non-existent funds. But De Andrea imposed a condition for the funds to be obtained: they must not come from the Central Bank, since the announcement effect of Central Bank lending to the government would create speculative pressures in the exchange market. Although this policy, which the Minister stuck to, severely limited his room for maneuver, it did after a time act as a brake on the approval of new expenditures, which was the result intended.

Minister De Andrea's quest for funds was complicated by the fact that on September 13 he had to rescind the export tax that had been put into effect two weeks before by his predecessor. Banner headlines in the press, especially in Pedro Beltrán's *La Prensa* and Luis Banchero's *Correo*—the latter naturally enough was sympathetic to the fishmeal interests of its owner—were combined with strong pressure from the exporters, especially the cotton and sugar producers, with the latter probably using their financial influence on some members of Congress. The natural animosity of exporters to the tax was reinforced by their belief that the tax would become permanent. Little that the government might have said—it said nothing—would have altered this belief or that voiced in some newspapers that the idea came from the "malefactors" in the Central Bank. Under these pressures, and with only five days' experience of the cash stringency in the Treasury, Minister De Andrea felt obliged to rescind the tax, much against President Belaúnde's views. The President saw correctly that De Andrea would soon regret his decision; he also felt that the exporters should pay for their gluttony (*gula*, the more descriptive term in Spanish).

190

A major reason for Minister De Andrea's abolition of the export tax was his belief that such a move would restore confidence to the export sector, and that in consequence exporters would respond to the Minister's request for a loan of upwards of U.S. $30 million, which would have come mainly from the major mining companies. De Andrea was rapidly disillusioned in this hope: having destroyed his main bargaining weapon, he was told by the mining companies and other major exporters somewhat arrogantly that they were in the "business of producing exports and not of making loans." De Andrea then tried the local bankers, hoping that they could put together a medium-term loan from their foreign lines of credit and the surplus local funds of some banks. As expected by the Central Bank, the banks' reply was that they would love to do it, but out of their legal reserves. The discussion embittered De Andrea, who had thought that the bankers would respond to his patriotic appeal. The dialogue with the bankers had its tragi-comic moments: when the Minister spoke of a "forty million loan," one aged bank director, in a mood to pull the Minister's leg, asked whether he referred to dollars or soles (forty million soles was one million dollars and a mere drop in the bucket).

Having failed with the businessmen, De Andrea began a tough apprenticeship and set out to talk to the politicians, first with his close friend Armando Villanueva, the president of the Chamber of Deputies and Haya's then heir apparent. A tough Aprista in his early fifties, Villanueva was the likely APRA presidential candidate for 1969 in case Haya de la Torre, who would have been seventy-four years old by then, did not run. Villanueva, who was a skillful political leader, did not commit himself to De Andrea but did not say no either. De Andrea told him that funds were needed urgently in order to bridge the gap in the remaining months of 1967, a cash deficit of about S/. 1 billion, after allowing for some increase in the "floating debt," the usual euphemism for unpaid bills.

As a second step, the urgency of buttressing whatever new exchange rate might be established with fiscal measures was stressed by the Minister and the Central Bank at innumerable meetings with other legislative leaders. Many attempts were made to explain the facts to Congress. De Andrea himself went twice to Villa Mercedes to see Haya, who had returned home some weeks before the devaluation after several months in Europe. There were more conversations with Villanueva, and with Luis Rodriguez Vildósola and Alberto Arca Parró, to name a few. Rodriguez Vildósola was a sensible and experienced parliamentarian, and the leading economic specialist of APRA. He agreed with De Andrea's proposals, but he did not have enough clout with the hierarchy. Arca Parró, an independent Senator who was close to APRA, had a large personal reputation in Congress as an economist, and had worked for many years in the field of statistics. The talks with Arca Parró were counterproductive, and rather tended to confirm his opposition to all kinds of fiscal measures except his own. He reasoned that since there was an International Monetary Fund, there was all the more reason for the creation of a National Monetary Fund, which would print money and lend it out with the "backing" of the nation's gold reserves. The National Monetary Fund, which was a Central Bank but with built-in inflationary features, would first buy all local gold production and pay for it in soles, and then lend soles—presumably to the government—"against" the gold. For months, the Central Bank tried to show Arca Parró very politely, and with lengthy memoranda, that his proposal had its problems, but the slightest criticism only made him more convinced that his solution to the fiscal problem was the only one. Throughout the following months, he used his prestige to delay most of the fiscal measures proposed by the government.

The parliamentary leaders, and Haya himself, were again briefed on the occasion of an informal visit by Pierre-Paul Schweitzer, the Managing Director of the International

Monetary Fund, when Schweitzer was returning in early October 1967 from the Fund's Annual Meeting in Rio de Janeiro. Very discreetly, Schweitzer made the point that the survival of the new certificate exchange rate depended on timely fiscal measures. Since expenditures were difficult to cut in most countries, and Peru was no exception, the measures would have to include taxes. Haya de la Torre, whom Schweitzer went to visit at the urging of the Central Bank, did not warm up to this message. Expecting to find a revolutionary, although mellowed by age, Schweitzer found, quite to his surprise, a defender of the major business groups. Haya pleaded for the exporters despite the fact that they were making a substantial income gain even after allowing for the 40 percent exchange differential tax and for the increased production costs arising from devaluation. Schweitzer also met with key parliamentary leaders of APRA and Acción Popular, to which he very tactfully gave the same advice.

The Schweitzer visit may have dented the thick armor of APRA's unshakeable public faith in expenditure cuts, but this was not apparent in the next weeks. The battle for the export tax was won only by strong pressure of the Executive on Congress and by a major concession to APRA. The pressure on Congress took the form of telling government employees that their wages could not be paid until Congress approved the needed funds, namely the export windfall gain tax. After a week of desultory discussion with the joint budget committee of both houses of Congress, on October 27, 1967, De Andrea faced them with a choice: either he would have to borrow from the Central Bank to pay the fortnightly "quincena" of salaries—due the previous day— and would then resign, or the tax would have to be passed as presented, immediately. A riot in front of the Ministry of Finance that afternoon lent weight to his position. APRA agreed to go along with the Minister, provided that the tax was turned into a forced loan from the exporters, repayable by the Treasury over a period of eight years. The 10

193

percent "contribution" would lapse at the end of the following fiscal year, i.e., March 1969.[10] The government proposal had excluded fishmeal and fish oil, and Congress rightly kept this exemption, since the price of fishmeal had been falling sharply and the industry needed a boost to recover from its financial crisis earlier in the year.

The approval of the 10 percent advance against future income tax payments—it had in fact the immediate effect of a tax, since the future value to an exporter of an interest-free repayment from the government over the following nine years was low—was an important step in tackling the government's fiscal problem. The fact that the 10 percent advance would be deductible as a cost in computing profits taxes in 1967 and 1968 meant that the net impact in those years upon the exporter was much less than 10 percent, but rather about 6 percent. Over half of the likely revenue from the measure, totalling about S/. 190 million per month, was to be taken up by the wage and salary increases in the public sector, which were approved as part of the export tax law. The law, which had cost so much effort to pass, turned out to be much less of a monster than the export sector had claimed. The 10 percent advance was lifted by Congress in March 1968 for cotton exports; in July 1968 coffee and petroleum exports followed under a clause that gave the Executive power to eliminate the 10 percent contribution for products facing high production costs. Finally, also in July 1968, the remaining exporters affected (minerals and sugar) were given the option, which most of them exercised, to pay the balance of the contribution in dollars, with this advance to be repaid to them in dollars by the government over three years at 7 percent annual interest.

Despite the export tax, a gap of at least S/. 600 million remained in cash terms for the months of November and December. The floating debt had increased by S/. 1 billion in the first ten months of the year and stood at the uncomfortably high level of S/. 1.7 billion at the end of October.

[10] Law 16710, of November 9, 1967.

Local suppliers, the main victims of the floating debt, were also being hit by a decline in private sector construction and were beginning to complain bitterly to the Minister of Finance. The Central Bank's gross international reserves, which had been fortified at the end of September by a U.S. $21 million drawing on the International Monetary Fund, had fallen in October by U.S. $11 million to U.S. $79 million. Importers were speeding up payments. The balance of payments burden of service on the external public debt, which had passed almost unnoticed under the free exchange system, was a major charge against certificate exchange income, which was almost wholly limited to export earnings. Moreover, the level of service on the external public debt was beginning to rise rapidly. The free exchange rate had departed from the certificate rate, and hovered at about S/. 40 per U.S. dollar, ready to depreciate at the slightest provocation. By the middle of November the financial picture was very bleak: the Minister, having given his commitment not to borrow from the Central Bank, saw no particular good will on the part of Congress and no prompt solution to the fiscal problem. He was near desperation.

As in many such cases of desperation, the way out was borrowing abroad. Against the opinion of the Central Bank—which advised that it would be better to bare the facts before the country and resort once and for all to a "maquinazo" (loan) from the Central Bank—the Minister probably rightly felt it was essential that he maintain his word of not resorting to Central Bank credit. In the end, it was exactly as if there had been borrowing from the Central Bank because, when the bulk of the foreign loans were repaid in mid-1968, the repayment was possible only through a Central Bank loan to the government. Altogether, somewhat over S/. 1 billion was borrowed (about U.S. $30 million), of which U.S. $17.5 million was borrowed from the Bank of Nova Scotia[11] at a renewable 90-day term: since

[11] Their Latin American representative, Edgar Felsenstein, had a good sixth sense and always seemed to time his visits with the moments when the government was most pressed for money.

the repayment period was so dangerously short, and so as to avoid turning this debt into a medium-term burden on external debt service, the Central Bank kept those dollars in a segregated account. The loan was paid back in mid-1968. The rest was borrowed by the government through Banco de Crédito, the largest local commercial bank, whose European majority owners—Banca Comerciale Italiana through Banque Française et Italienne pour l'Amerique du Sud—managed to place U.S. $11 million of Peruvian government three-year notes, mostly with Swiss banks. To top off the package, the Minister resorted to an old stand-by, an advance tax payment (of S/. 400 million) from the Southern Peru Copper Corporation.

The last two months of De Andrea's four-month ministry were taken up in a battle to get the 1968 budget, especially the tax measures, approved by the APRA-led Congress. It was an uneven struggle. APRA and their Odriista allies had received a big moral boost when they won by a sizable majority the by-election in Lima on November 12, 1967.[12] The seat had been held until his death by the author Ciro Alegría, who had sat as Acción Popular deputy for Lima. The APRA-UNO candidate, Enrique Chirinos Soto, was a polemic journalist who was not directly associated with APRA. For a month, in *La Prensa*—whose principal editorialist he was—and especially on television, Chirinos hammered away at the rising cost of living brought on by the devaluation. His appeal to the housewife was very convincing in the political climate of the time, so much so that the wives of educated upper-income professionals and businessmen did indeed believe that prices had risen 100 percent! In this situation, the government candidate ought to have been a very aggressive man. But Dr. Carlos Cueto Fernandini, who had impeccable credentials as an enlightened educator, former Minister of Education and international

[12] At the same time, APRA won a by-election in Trujillo. However, since this was APRA territory, this victory had much less impact than the one in Lima.

civil servant, had an almost impossible task. Moreover, his position and that of the government in general, was weakened by strained relations within the parliamentary alliance between the government and the Christian Democrats. The "DC's" had no particular program, but as a minority party in a period of an approaching presidential election, it was an obvious tactic for them to break away from a government that was in economic and political difficulties. Shortly after the election, the two Christian Democrats in the Cabinet resigned and their party announced that they were breaking away from the government coalition, although they would not necessarily vote against the government. In retrospect, the break did not make much difference since the Christian Democratic votes in Congress had certainly not been assured to the government even in the days of the alliance.

In addition to the strengthened position of APRA as a result of the election and to the departure of the Christian Democrats, De Andrea faced an equally important, if not a greater, obstacle within the Cabinet itself. In mid-November, after less than three months in office, Prime Minister Edgardo Seoane resigned without giving any public reason, although his reasons were probably the same ones that made the Christian Democrats leave. However, in his case, as a party colleague and vice-president under Belaúnde, he might reasonably have been expected to stay on board and face an uphill struggle. In his place, Belaúnde appointed Raúl Ferrero Rebagliati, who had dabbled in politics since his student days.

Ferrero, a lawyer who had never held major political office, had considerable personal charm. He always made it a point of being fully informed—from his vantage point in the decorously remote Club Nacional—about the latest doings in the political scene. From the beginning Ferrero genuinely thought that through his personality he would be able to hold the government together and avoid unseemly confrontations with APRA and Congress. He was thus not predisposed at all to Tulio De Andrea's schemes for

197

more taxes. He had an encouraging master in his tactics in the President himself, who disliked the idea of rocking the boat on a subject as controversial and seemingly hopeless as tax reform. Upon assuming the premiership, Ferrero brought in José Morales Urresti as Justice Minister, in the hope that Morales, who had a distinguished career in the Central Bank and was now vice-rector of the Catholic University, would soon replace Tulio De Andrea as Finance Minister.

Despite his doubts about it, there was little that Ferrero could do about the draft budget for fiscal 1968, since it had already been sent twice to Congress for approval. An earlier version had been sent by Mariátegui in August, but, because of the effects of devaluation on revenues and expenditures, it was withdrawn and a new version presented early in October. Although the totals were different, the tax proposals were quite similar. It was the presentation of this budget that had given the Central Bank the justification to re-enter the exchange market at the time the certificate system was re-established early in October. Although the tax measures were the issue on which the budget was fought, the deceleration in the growth of expenditures was projected to contribute almost as much to the solution of the budgetary problem (see table below). The main elements contributing to this real reduction of expenditures were in the two categories that had grown fastest in previous years: wages and public works. A fourth 25 percent annual salary increase for teachers had already been omitted in April 1967. The general salary adjustment after devaluation was extremely moderate and, combined with a limitation—the first effective one in several years—on overall numbers in the civil service, the wage and salary budget rose only by a little less than 10 percent. As for public investment, its stagnation was not so much the result of deliberate policy as of the gradual drying up of existing foreign loans, especially suppliers' credits. Although the De Andrea budget may have looked like a deflationary one,

198

the Central Bank thought that it would not turn out that way since it expected that it would be extremely difficult to control expenditures, as indeed turned out to be the case. Moreover, if the tax measures were eventually approved, a better basis was thought to exist to obtain large-scale project loans from the international lending agencies. (See Table 30.)

TABLE 30. CENTRAL GOVERNMENT EXPENDITURES AND CURRENT REVENUES IN RELATION TO GNP, 1965-1968

				1968	
				Budget	
	1965	1966	1967	Proposal	Actual
As percentage of GNP:					
Current revenues	17.4	17.3	16.9	18.7	17.4
Expenditures net of debt amortization	20.3	20.6	21.2	19.0	20.3

SOURCE: Central Bank, *Cuentas Nacionales* with 1968 estimate derived from *Reseña Económica y Financiera*, September-October, 1967, adjusted.

The tax package submitted by De Andrea was basically the same one that had been submitted two years running by Mariátegui, namely an increase in income tax rates, the introduction of a land and real estate tax, and of a levy on the share capital of enterprises.[13] In addition, there was the 10 percent export windfall gain tax—discussed above—and two measures proposed by De Andrea himself. One was the partial suspension for one year of some of the import duty exemptions: the main beneficiary of such exemptions, in addition to the government and the mining companies, was

[13] The basic economic proposals for these three tax measures was made in *Estudio Fiscal del Perú*, prepared under the auspices of the Organization of American States and the Interamerican Development Bank and completed in 1965 (published 1969, Organization of American States, Washington, D.C.). The report was requested in 1964 by Minister of Finance Javier Salazar Villanueva and was prepared by Professor Milton C. Taylor, with Robert A. Mundell, Wilfred Pine, Kenyon E. Poole, David I. Meiselman, and Gustavo Cañas Viana.

199

the manufacturing sector. The measure proposed was a very modest one, since it would not have affected exemptions under long-term contracts (the bulk of the mining companies, the car assembly plants, and some of the larger manufacturing plants) and those affected would still have had to pay only half the duty. The other measure was a small tax on diesel fuel, which was not then (and still is not) taxed, of S/. 1 per gallon (or U.S. $0.026 per gallon), to replace a 15 percent tax on electricity consumption in the Lima area proposed by Mariátegui. All in all, the tax package excluding the export tax was supposed to yield S/. 2.3 billion in fiscal 1968, or about 10 percent of 1967 current revenues. Perhaps the only source of support for the tax measures came from the Central Bank management —not exactly a political force!—who wrote in the issue of the Central Bank's *Reseña* which analyzed the budget:

". . . Regardless of the opinions which may exist on whether there is or not room for a heavier tax load—a debate towards which a recent issue of this publication contributed some background information—there is no doubt that the normal growth of revenues from existing taxes would not be sufficient to reach the budget proposal, even with the improved collection methods being implemented. For this reason, in order to provide financing for the budget it is necessary that either new sources of genuine revenues be obtained for a total of S/. 4.6 billion—of which about half has already been covered through the 10 percent surcharge against future profits of the export sector— or else that expenditure cuts be implemented for an equivalent amount.

"It is well to point out that the effect on the economy of achieving budgetary balance through higher domestic savings (i.e., through increased tax revenues) or through sizable expenditure cuts could well be different: the second measure might withhold income from segments of the population that tend to spend a large proportion of their total income—thus to some degree adversely affecting the market prospects for domestic industrial output—whereas the first method, consisting of higher fiscal revenues through direct taxes, would force a higher rate of saving upon the most favored sectors in the population, who tend to consume a relatively lower share of their incomes."[14]

If the Congress heeded one of these many warnings, it did not show it. Throughout December and early January, the joint committee of both houses on budget matters was busy working out a substitute proposal. The proposal followed the time-honored technique of the majority of inflating prospective revenues and systematically underestimating expenditures, even for such difficult items to cut as salaries and debt service. The main driving force behind the substitute proposal was the chairman of the budget committee of the Chamber of Deputies, the owner of a pharmacy in Trujillo, whose thesis was that the way to solve the Peruvian fiscal problem was to refinance the external public debt. It was simple, he said. If a debt of his pharmacy was due and he could not pay (or did not wish to), he would simply call the manager of the local bank, and say: "Pal, just renew this little note for another 30 days and it will be all settled."[15] The same, he suggested, could be done by Peru.

By early January, the APRA-UNO spokesmen were ready to discuss their proposal with the government. The Cabinet was in theory responsible for the government proposal, but De Andrea knew that several Cabinet members were unwilling to risk their ministerial jobs in a unanimous confrontation with Congress. This would have been the only way, he was convinced—after many unsuccessful conversations with APRA leaders and lengthy sessions with the budget committee in Congress—to get the bulk of the measures approved. In addition to the majority of the Ministers themselves, two others were firmly opposed to the idea of

[14] Central Bank, *Reseña Económica y Financiera*, September-October 1967, pp. 18-19.

[15] "Hermano, renuévame esa letrita por 30 días y asunto concluído."

201

a confrontation with Congress: President Belaúnde, who disliked the idea of having to go through another cabinet reshuffle, and Prime Minister Ferrero, who believed that with a combination of cajolery and diplomacy he might patch up the budget and emerge as a presidential candidate for 1969.

In these circumstances, De Andrea decided early in January 1968 to explode the balloon himself and cause a scandal that would force the Congress to back down after his resignation. It was essential for him to keep his plan confidential until the last minute—he told only the Ministers of Agriculture (Orlando Olcese) and of Health (Javier Arias Stella), and Chairman Schwalb of the Central Bank—since otherwise it was likely that Ferrero would use the pretext of the growing contraband scandal (see below) to get rid of him. De Andrea's resignation on the tax issue would morally put pressure on the Cabinet to resign—although he doubted if they would in fact do so—and would also certainly lead to the resignation of the whole Central Bank board, which had decided, when the Central Bank re-entered the exchange market in October, to remain only so long as there were firm and immediate prospects of action to resolve the fiscal crisis.

Despite the odds against him and the weakness of government leadership, De Andrea's stand came close to succeeding. On January 18 he went to the Chamber of Deputies to be present, as constitutional practice required, in the floor debate on the government budget proposal. Most of the Cabinet had no idea of what was going to happen, and no other Minister accompanied him.

A few days earlier, at a formal meeting of parliamentary leaders with the Cabinet about the APRA substitute budget proposal, De Andrea, who was officially receiving it for the first time (although he had secured a copy a few weeks before and had had time to go through it in detail), had merely said he would need time to study it. Thus when he stood up in the floor of the Chamber on that Thursday in January, it was only natural that he should begin by analyzing the substitute proposal he had received a few days earlier. For over two hours he tore it apart. His detailed analysis ridiculed the authors of the substitute proposal. The underestimation of essential expenditures together with the inflation of revenues were so large that the deficit under the substitute proposal would probably have approached S/. 10 billion out of expenditures of about S/. 30 billion.

Inevitably, De Andrea concluded his speech by saying that the substitute proposal was unacceptable and that he demanded a vote of confidence on his, the government's, budget and the tax package accompanying it. At the end, he launched a strong attack on the forces holding back the development of Peru, symbolized, he said, by Pedro Beltrán, whom he berated as "that senile standard-bearer of the Peruvian extreme right wing." Congress should no longer shrink the responsibility of the fiscal problem. If it rejected the budget proposal, it would be responsible for the second devaluation, which would inevitably come.

The APRA leadership was taken aback. They did not think that the government would go so far, and for a few hours they debated what to do. Some of De Andrea's ministerial colleagues were equally surprised when they got the news upon returning from a long lunch in Ancón, Lima's socialite beach resort, where a few of them had feasted Miss Peru. To make up for lost time, Ferrero rapidly organized a delegation made of Pablo Carriquiry, the Public Works Minister and an old friend of Tulio De Andrea, and Armando Villanueva, the APRA leader. During the evening recess in the debate, they went to see De Andrea, and asked him to resign in order to spare Congress and the Executive any further embarrassment. After telling Villanueva that he would not budge until Congress had clearly taken the responsibility for accepting or rejecting the tax package, he showed them both the door. General Doig, Minister of War, also intervened with Minister De Andrea,

203

asking him to back down. It was said at the time that Doig may have implied to his Cabinet colleague that there could be the danger of a coup.

The Minister knew that he would have to resign. A day later, after Congress approved the substitute proposal, De Andrea did in fact resign. The Chairman of the Central Bank, Fernando Schwalb, also resigned. The impact of his resignation would have been much greater if the whole Bank board had gone with him, as they had committed themselves to do a few months earlier in case the budget had no prospect of being balanced. But at the hour of decision, only five out of the ten Board members followed Schwalb.

De Andrea had come close to getting Congress to reconsider, but most of the rest of the Cabinet, by not supporting their own colleague, had decisively tipped the scale in favor of a postponement of the issue. During the following four months, Ferrero tried to continue a policy of compromise. The exacerbation of the political climate, the lack of clear leadership, and of course the economic crisis that ensued were the consequences.

It is interesting to reflect on the reasons for the adamant refusal of the Peruvian Congress to pass the tax measures. After all, it was not the first or the last Congress, in Peru or elsewhere, to take such a position. There were of course special factors, such as the recent devaluation, Chirinos' victory in Lima on a "No más impuestos" platform, and the doubts, some of them genuine, that existed among businessmen and some politicians about Belaúnde's spending programs. The question then is whether these factors were insurmountable, or merely meant the postponement of the approval of a tax package by Congress. The main reason for the APRA attitude was its electoral strategy for 1969, and the fact that President Belaúnde was not able to use his prestige in order to combat that strategy. The strategy was simply to use the APRA-UNO majority to keep the Belaúnde government discredited enough so that an APRA victory would be assured in 1969, but not so much that APRA would inherit a shambles. As far as the fiscal situation was concerned, the APRA position was also in part the result of disbelief in Central Bank data that showed that there was indeed a fiscal crisis. Belaúnde could have used another political weapon in addition to his own prestige: the progressive nature of the measures proposed. The income and land taxes could clearly have been described as "soak the rich" measures, but surprisingly this was not done: the fervor of the 1962 and 1963 election campaigns had been lost, and there were exaggerated fears of business reaction.

Less than five months after De Andrea resigned, APRA approved the measures it had so sternly rejected earlier but only when it looked as if there was a serious threat of a coup. The APRA position seemed thus not so much governed by the tax question itself, but by its ambitions for a presidential election that in the end never took place.

Raúl Ferrero Rebagliati

Rather than naming a new Finance Minister, Ferrero took over the Finance portfolio himself, under a system that allowed a Minister to keep his own portfolio while running another Ministry, for up to a month. When the month was up, Ferrero took over the Finance Ministry and stayed on as acting Foreign Minister. He was altogether at the Finance Ministry for two months because he genuinely believed that he could somehow settle the budget issue without a fight for major tax measures. During those two months he largely dispensed with the opinions of the existing advisers and brought in his own. One was his elder brother Rómulo, a conservative economic consultant widely respected in business circles who had been Finance Minister twenty years earlier. The other was Enrique Novak, the retired chief executive of Peru's largest commercial bank. Both advisers clearly told Ferrero that the

205

size of the deficit was such that it must have been obvious to him that tax measures were essential, since even a large expenditure cut, administratively and politically an extremely difficult undertaking, would not have been enough. For almost two months Ferrero maneuvered to get a little bit in expenditure cuts and a little bit in taxes, in a combination that would look credible. The end product was Law 16900, of March 6, 1968, called the "Law for the rationalization and reorganization of taxes." The law was put together with the help of Senator Miguel Dammert, an Acción Popular senator who had been Minister of Labor earlier in the government, and of Senator Alberto Arca Parró, who looked upon the law as a technical way of solving the fiscal problem.

The new law did have some good features. It included an increase of 10 percent in profits tax rates, from a maximum marginal rate of 52 percent to 55.5 percent;[16] the introduction of a 1.5 percent tax on unused urban land, and the application of municipal real estate rent taxes ("predios") to real estate trusts ("inmobiliarias") that had largely avoided payment of such taxes; the unification of real estate transfer taxes, which were raised slightly; and an authorization to revalue company assets (a practice not normally allowed in Peru) as a result of the 1967 devaluation, against payment of a 14 percent tax on the amount of the revaluation (a one-shot measure).[17] Also, the government was authorized to revise the ad hoc import duty exemptions given to industry under the industrial promotion Law 9140.[18] The trouble with the measures was that their

[16] The actual increase was from 35 to 38.5 percent, but in addition to this there was the existing complementary tax with a maximum rate of 26 percent on the profits after tax.

[17] The law did contribute to a sharp increase in direct tax revenue in 1968 although the largest element in the increase was from the so-called export tax, in actuality an advance payment by exporters of future profits tax.

[18] Exemptions granted under other laws (mining code, Law 13270 for industrial development, petroleum, car assemblies, etc.) were not

likely yield in 1968, a maximum of about S/. 600 million rather than the S/. 1,500 million envisaged by Ferrero, was too little to even begin to bridge the budget deficit. The budget, finally approved in mid-March, included an expenditure "cut" with which Ferrero completed the "balancing of the budget." As he said in mid-March, the budget was now truly and honestly balanced ("verazmente equilibrado"), without subterfuges or hidden leaks.

The major criticism of Ferrero's actions is that, while he recognized that there was an urgent problem, he supported measures that were inadequate in relation to the size of the problem. In defense of his attitude, he felt that the main priority was to calm the turbulent political climate. Otherwise, he said to his close friends, there would be a "bloody revolution." He was clearly right in his assessment that the government had to govern and to give a sense of clear direction, but his actions in fact served to prolong the climate of political indecision. When substantial tax measures were taken in June 1968 by a new Cabinet, the previous fears about a serious political reaction were shown to be largely unfounded, even in the case of the gasoline tax.

The Ferrero measures were in themselves good ones when seen as part of a long-term improvement in tax and financial administration. In addition to the measures in Law 16900, he introduced in the budget law a registry of all taxpayers ("registro del contribuyente"). If individuals or firms were not in the registry and did not have their taxpayer's card, they would not be able to enter into contracts, travel abroad, etc. Another useful innovation was a council, established early in February, to control the new external indebtedness and all purchases abroad of the public sector. Staffed by the Central Bank, the council had military and civilian members. Among the growing

---

affected. Exemptions under Law 9140 were the smaller part of such exemptions to the manufacturing sector, and the revision of such exemptions would obviously take time.

pains of the council were the reluctance of the military ministries to submit to council scrutiny; for reasons of national
security, they wanted an all-military council in the cases
of purchases by the armed forces.

The month of February was one of acute exchange
difficulties. As a result of the political uncertainty caused
by the handling of the budget problem, the free exchange
rate depreciated rapidly from S/. 39.10 per U.S. dollar at
the time that De Andrea had left the government to a
record of S/. 44.15 on February 23. The pressure on import
payments became enormous and Central Bank gross international reserves, which had recovered to U.S. $120 million
at the end of 1967 fell to U.S. $64 million at the end of
February. The Central Bank staff had prepared a prior
import deposit scheme in case it was needed. But the problem was more basic. Four months had gone by since the
Central Bank had re-entered the exchange market, but
nothing had been done to cope with the budget deficit.
A number of directors and the new Chairman of the Board,
José Morales Urresti, thought that if the political and fiscal
deterioration continued, a second devaluation would become inevitable. These worries were reinforced by doubts
about the level of S/. 38.70 at which the certificate rate
had originally been set in October 1967. However, with
export prices improving and domestic prices having risen
only moderately after the devaluation, the problem was less
one of costs than of lack of confidence in government economic policies. The board of the bank and some of the
advisers felt that a second devaluation would be the only
way to make Congress understand that serious fiscal action
was needed. Others felt that despite the possible technical
advantages of a small devaluation—expounded in a lengthy
study—such a move would gravely imperil the moderation
of the unions in their post-devaluation wage demands. The
end result of a second devaluation might be worse than
the original situation.

At that point Ferrero was called to the bank one evening

in late February 1968 and faced with a virtual fait accompli. The meeting lasted until three in the morning. Helped by his debating skill, perhaps also by the opinion of several of the advisers of the bank,[19] and by the directors' natural disinclination to accept responsibility for withdrawing the Central Bank once again from the exchange market, Ferrero managed to extricate himself from a predicament he had not expected. Fiscal measures would be taken; negotiations with Congress were advanced but, he said, the need for taxes was exaggerated. This last statement struck a sympathetic note in the private sector directors, who continued to cling to the notion that somehow the fiscal problem could be taken care of by eliminating waste. A few days later Ferrero passed two decrees to help with the exchange problem: one increased Central Bank reserves in a one-shot operation by reducing the volume of exchange certificates outstanding,[20] and the other prohibited imports of about 300 items of a luxury nature.[21] Although both measures were drafted in the Central Bank, the staff continued to have strong doubts about the second one, the idea of which had originated in the Foreign Ministry (of all places in the section supposed to enforce Peru's obligations under GATT). The trouble was that the U.S. $15 million or so of exchange to be saved through the import prohibition, about two percent of imports, would entail an estimated loss to the public sector of about S/.1 billion, or one-seventh of import duty revenues. This was obvious enough,

[19] For whom the author was the spokesman. A second devaluation would have been counterproductive, since it would have jeopardized the entire incomes policy of the government without bringing visible benefits so long as the fiscal problem was not resolved.

[20] This was done by reducing the period during which exchange earners (exporters) could dispose of their certificates (such as by selling them to importers) from five to three days.

[21] Another measure taken by Ferrero at the same time was a decree prohibiting sales in Peru by foreign mutual funds. Paradoxically, after he resigned as Prime Minister, Ferrero served briefly as Peruvian legal consultant to IOS, the mutual fund directed by Bernard Cornfeld.

since the items prohibited were the ones that paid the heaviest duties. As with the import duty increase of 1967, the prohibition was not likely to be very effective: the impact on reducing exchange payments would take time, smuggling would be encouraged, and in the end highly protected local assembly of these products, most of them with a high import component, would be encouraged, and the exchange savings would be sharply reduced or possibly even become negative.

One important measure that Congress approved during Ferrero's tenure as Finance Minister was a reform of Article 56 of the Mining Code. This long-delayed step opened the door to serious discussions with the major foreign companies holding concessions in Peru about the development of those concessions. Conversations with the companies began in March, once President Belaúnde, after Ferrero's fiscal legislation had been passed, selected Brigadier General Francisco Morales Bermúdez to be Finance Minister.

General Francisco Morales Bermúdez

The appointment of a general as Finance Minister was President Belaúnde's idea. He felt that the APRA majority in Congress would not dare to cast a vote of censure against a general. However, General Morales Bermúdez was relatively junior in the hierarchy of generals—he had made the grade just a few months before—and there was therefore a question of whether his status was that of a representative of the armed forces, chosen by them for the job, or simply an individual who happened to be a general and also Finance Minister. It was never quite clear to what extent Morales Bermúdez as Finance Minister had the official institutional support of the Army. Nevertheless, to President Belaúnde he had one important political credential: his father, also a distinguished army officer, had been murdered in 1932, it was believed by APRA orders. The

210

APRA majority, Belaúnde thought, would never dare to bring down the son in uniform of an APRA victim.[22]

Before his appointment as Minister of Finance, Morales Bermúdez had been the Director of Economy for the Army, a title that in practical terms means the chief of supply. He had also sat as a member of the external debt council established by Ferrero in January, and he had made a good impression there. Once in office, it did not take him long to understand that a massive injection of new tax revenues was needed, but that better control over expenditures was also required. Shortly after coming into office he made the ten percent increase in company profits taxes retroactive to fiscal year 1967, for which the final tax payment was due a few days later, at the end of March 1968. Later, in April, he established, with the help of a team of fiscal advisers from the International Monetary Fund, a system of centrally controlled fiscal delegates, one for each ministry and for major agencies, without whose approval expenditures could not be incurred. Although the schemes had many teething troubles—one of them being that the fiscal delegate found that his approval was requested at the time of payment, well after a commitment for the expenditures had already been made—the system at least established the principle of central control of expenditures.

To sell the tax package, Morales Bermúdez had González del Valle and the Central Bank advisers design a plan, which was a large, well-laid-out document presenting the case for the tax measures, summarizing them, and adding other measures that were considered essential, such as the negotiation of agreements for new investments in the copper sector. The bulk of the plan was made up of the same tax measures proposed by Mariátegui and De Andrea, namely the introduction of a real property tax, and of a tax on corporate capital, the reform of the corporate and

[22] General Morales Bermúdez subsequently became Finance Minister again in 1969 and then Prime Minister and President of the Republic.

211

personal income tax, plus the increase of gasoline sales taxes. In mid-April the plan was presented to the Cabinet in a lengthy session. Morales Bermúdez rightly wanted to get the Cabinet committed to every detail in the measures: after the provisions of each measure were read out by the Minister, one of the advisers was asked to explain the reasons for the measure and the likely results. The Ministers were somewhat bored by the disciplined presentation, and, in order to shorten the proceedings, they tended to approve everything, or, at least, Morales Bermúdez left with the distinct impression that the government was fully committed to the tax reform measures. He had every right to take away such an impression, but someone more accustomed to the ways of politicians would have taken with a grain of salt the assurances of Ferrero and some of his Ministers.

In fact, Ferrero was openly critical of his Finance Minister, a strange public attitude for a Prime Minister. Morales Bermúdez was still learning, he said, and needed to learn more economics—why, Ferrero would ask, was the Finance Minister reportedly insisting on deciding the IPC question? In order to show that he was the leading governmental Minister on economic questions, and also to steer attention away from the increasing economic crisis, Ferrero decided to present a "plan for national economic recovery." He asked his brother about the main topics for such a plan. Devalue and relax the credit squeeze being forced on the economy to maintain the 38.70 rate, he was told. This was hardly the advice Ferrero wanted. He turned to the Central Bank, and asked for a draft for the Finance Minister. Gonzáles del Valle of the Ministry and the author were seconded to help Ferrero with the draft. Charming as always, Ferrero invited us one evening to his office in the Torre Tagle Palace, and gave us a vivid historical sketch of the figures in the beautiful colonial paintings lining his office. Then he sat down at his very old personal typewriter (the keys had to be hit a couple of inches down before they struck the paper) and waited for his and our inspiration. Tax reform, copper investments, land reform and better prices for the farmer, encouragement of the construction industry, all flowed into the draft. The following morning, after the normal Friday Cabinet meeting, apparently without more than a vague mention of the subject to Morales Bermúdez, Ferrero released the "plan," a three-page document, to the press. The content of the document was laudable enough, but it seemed too much like a ploy to distract attention from the burning issue of the 1968 deficit and the need for tax measures. Rather than strengthen Ferrero's position, the plan weakened his credibility. It was further weakened a few days later, when he repeated his belief that the budget was "truly balanced." He qualified his statement in several ways, so that the bulk of opinion began to wonder whether the Prime Minister was telling the truth. The effect of speculative pressures on the free exchange rate was immediate: despite the fact that the Central Bank fed the free market, the rate depreciated rapidly from S/. 41.34 at the beginning of May, approximately the level that had prevailed since March, to S/. 45.54 at the end of the month, a few days after Ferrero's departure from the government.

The last days of the Ferrero cabinet, and the events leading to its demise, only heightened the political tension already so evident in Peru at the time. Unlike Tulio De Andrea, who got as far as facing the APRA Congress in Parliament itself, Morales Bermúdez did not reach that stage. The meetings of Haya de la Torre's lieutenants with the Minister took place in the Palace, with President Belaúnde in attendance. APRA would not budge on the tax issue. Morales Bermúdez could hardly meet the government's current payments, and he had to spend much of his time dealing with complaints about the rising amount of unpaid bills. The Central Bank, with a minimum level of international reserves and hoping to put pressure on Congress to grant the tax package, would not advance the government more than minimum sums. Understandably, Morales Bermúdez felt trapped. He was surrounded by impregnable *reductos* (bulwarks or fortresses): APRA, the Central Bank, the IPC problem. His major concern was the lack of progress on the tax question. Not only was the APRA leadership adamant, but the Executive was unwilling to confront Congress once again with the proposed tax measures. The President and the Prime Minister refused to submit the gasoline tax proposal. Faced with that refusal, Morales Bermúdez on May 23 fired off a letter to the President, announcing his immediate resignation.

"CONTRABANDO"

An episode that considerably weakened the moral image of the Executive and Congress was the smuggling scandal of the first few months of 1968. The importance of the scandal was not so much that anyone then in the government was discovered smuggling but that both the Executive and Congress adopted a rather lackadaisical attitude in the face of persistent newspaper stories about smuggling rings that were said to involve figures close to the government. In the end, two of the senior officials indicted, a police general and the director general of the Banco de la Nación, were convicted by the courts under the Belaúnde administration. A third trial, which was concluded with a conviction under the new government, was that of an admiral, who had allegedly used his position as Minister of the Navy in 1965 to organize a shipload of smuggled appliances on one of the cargo vessels of the Navy. None of the other major figures implicated by the newspapers, *El Comercio* foremost among them, was convicted by the courts of the following government, which had made the issue of uprooting corruption a major one when it entered into power.[23]

[23] See, for example, *Noventa Días Desputes, La Revolución Está en Marcha! Para un Perú Mejor para Todos los Peruanos*, Dirección General de Informaciones, Lima, 1969.

214

Yet for a period of three months, from March to May 1968, the "Contrabando" issue filled the newspapers. A relative of President Belaúnde was alleged to be involved (a charge never substantiated in a court of law). *El Comercio* said in a banner headline in mid-April that secret airfields had been discovered on the southern coast, where an airline aptly named RIPSA brought in regular cargoes of contraband. In his tract about the coup, Augusto Zimmermann insinuates[24] that Manuel Ulloa, the publisher of *Expreso* and close Accíon Popular friend of President Belaúnde, was involved with RIPSA. There was never any evidence that showed the alleged connection. The more sensational newspaper accusations against Accíon Popular leaders thus appear to have been baseless.

However, several important facts remain. Contraband was an almost established tradition in Peru. The issue was one of degree. Sometimes public officials looked the other way or sometimes they themselves did the smuggling, as occurred in the Navy case mentioned earlier. The bazars of the police (Guardia Civil), which imported large amounts of duty-free goods, were a channel for contraband, and two senior officials, including a police general plus other lesser figures accused, were convicted by the courts in 1968. How large the contraband was, no one knows, although a cross-check with exchange transactions suggests that the proportion of smuggling out of total imports was small,[25] although the possible fiscal loss would have been far greater because of the high duties applying to the types of goods smuggled. The second fact is that the Executive did not handle the issue effectively. It is true

[24] *El Plan Inca. Objectivo: Revolución Peruana*, Lima, Empresa Editora del Diario Oficial *El Peruano*, 1974, page 35. Zimmermann was in 1968 the chief editorial writer of *El Comercio*. He subsequently became Director of Information of the new government.

[25] In May 1968 an illustrative estimate was prepared for the President on maximum magnitudes of smuggled imports, which could have been up to two percent of dutiable imports. But there obviously was no way of being sure.

that the matter was up to the courts, and that the courts did convict some offenders, but the Executive did not adequately respond to the public need to know. And there were certainly events that were hard to explain. For example, a mysterious figure called Trachtman, who had been an Army officer several years before, was allegedly a large smuggler and had copious documents on others involved. The Trachtman papers, obtained by the Finance Ministry, were handed over to an investigating committee of Congress, headed by APRA Deputy Vargas Haya. The following day the papers had disappeared from the offices of the committee, which had apparently been broken into. Neither the Executive[26] nor the committee were apparently informed about the contents of the papers. The episode was in keeping with the treatment of the smuggling problem as a whole.

FERRERO DEPARTS

In the wake of the resignation of General Morales Bermúdez on the tax issue, the Chairman of the Central Bank, José Morales Urresti, and the government members of the board—who had publicly supported the measures proposed by the Minister—also resigned. They knew that their resignation would precipitate the fall of Ferrero, which was considered necessary in order to get moving on the tax issue. Ferrero managed to stay on for another few days. That period was one of acute financial difficulties. As the free rate depreciated, so import payments through the certificate market accelerated, and reserves fell rapidly. There was no Central Bank board to support action by the management, and only an interim Finance Minister, Pablo Carriquiry. Fortunately, Carriquiry, who was the Minister of Development and Public Works, was calm and took in stride the events of his short tenure at the Finance Ministry.

[26] Information obtained by the author from several Cabinet ministers.

The main economic action of those tense days was the imposition of a fifteen percent across-the-board tax on all certificate exchange purchases to pay for imports and for debt obligations arising out of imports. The measure, contained in Decree 178-68-HC of May 27, 1968, also included heavy excise taxes on cars and domestic appliances in order to discourage the heavy imports of parts for local assembly. Both the fifteen percent exchange surcharge and the excise taxes were illegal—since only Congress could approve new taxes—but they were the only temporary means available, especially in the case of the surcharge, to block the bulk of exchange purchases until a new Cabinet and Finance Minister were appointed. For the next four weeks, during which the fifteen percent surcharge was in operation, exchange sales by the Central Bank fell to about U.S. $25 million in comparison with the normal monthly rate—including public debt—of about U.S. $70 million, while the inflows from the surrender of export earnings continued at about U.S. $60 million per month, an apparent sign that the export sector did not consider a permanent fifteen percent devaluation likely. The Central Bank was therefore able to beef up its depleted international reserves.

When explaining the emergency measure to Carriquiry, the Central Bank told him that he ought to be under no illusions about the measure's solving anything. It was merely a desperate stop-gap because Congress had steadfastly refused to do what its leadership by then clearly knew was necessary. Carriquiry bravely marched up to the Palace with the decree and President Belaúnde signed it, but only after he had it retyped in the Palace in order to eliminate an article which he did not approve of. The following morning the text of the decree in the official gazette, *El Peruano,* omitted the key article, which made the fifteen percent payable at the time of the exchange transaction and not at the time of import. After some scrambling, the error was corrected. Otherwise, the measure would have been pointless.

217

The recriminations that arose in the private sector as a result of the decree were to be expected. Armando Villanueva, the APRA leader, denounced Ferrero on television and said that he ought to be replaced. Villanueva was reflecting the feeling in and out of government that Ferrero had to go. On the morning of May 29 the Cabinet agreed to hand in their resignations immediately to the President. The newspapers were already saying that Ferrero had resigned. Before going to the Palace, however, he suggested to his colleagues that they have an informal farewell gathering at his house. When the ministers got there, a sumptuous lunch awaited them. Ferrero used the lunch to attempt to convince his Cabinet to hold on. After lunch, Ferrero's nephew and his son in the adjacent library also urged him to hold on. The Cabinet members, in the living room, sat cooling their heels over after-lunch coffee. After some waiting, the three military members of the Cabinet, Generals Doig and Gagliardi and Vice Admiral Delgado, got up and left. The Ferrero Cabinet had ended.

CHAPTER VIII

Sixty Days

THE PERIOD from early June to October 2, 1968, was one of great importance in recent Peruvian history. With Congress having temporarily abdicated the center of the stage, a dynamic Finance Minister was able to put through the necessary fiscal reforms and a number of other key financial measures. The period of economic decline looked as if it was being sharply reversed, although only for a brief moment, for on October 3 a general and his associates overthrew the constitutional regime. The history of the last governing Cabinet of the Belaúnde presidency can be divided into two periods: the period of economic reforms and the last six weeks of political crisis prior to the coup. In this chapter we look at the first of these two episodes.

THE HERCELLES CABINET

It is sometimes hard to pinpoint in the chain of historical occurrences which was the event that markedly steered the future course of history in a decisive direction. The appointment of the new War Minister in the Hercelles Cabinet on May 31 was no doubt one of those events. For, following the tradition of naming the commanding officer of the Army to the ministerial post, President Belaúnde ought to have named General Juan Velasco Alvarado. However, for one reason or another,[1] he named his No. 2, General Roberto

---

[1] According to the President, the reason was his mistrust of General Velasco. Zimmermann, *El Plan Inca*, p. 40, gives a different explanation: General Velasco, Zimmermann claims, was already deeply involved in preparing a coup and did not want the job. According to Zimmermann, he prevailed on General Montagne to convince General Dianderas to accept it.

Dianderas, a mild-mannered officer who had been a successful Minister of Public Works of the Odría Junta, almost twenty years before.

Since this was the last functioning Cabinet of the Belaúnde regime, it may be useful to list its members:[2] Prime Minister and Foreign Affairs, Oswaldo Hercelles; Government and Police, Carlos Velarde Cabello; Finance and Commerce, Manuel Ulloa; Justice, Guillermo Hoyos Osores; Agriculture, Orlando Olcese; Education, José Jiménez Borja; Public Works, Pablo Carriquiry; Labor, Fernando Calmell del Solar; Health, Javier Arias Stella; War, Division General Roberto Dianderas; Navy, Vice-Admiral Jorge Luna Ferreccio; Air Force, Lieutenant General José Gagliardi.

Of these, Arias Stella, Carriquiry, Olcese, and Calmell had been in the previous Cabinet. Arias Stella was a doctor who had been active in Acción Popular and had been Minister of Health earlier in the Belaúnde administration. Carriquiry and Olcese had come in with Seoane in September 1967: Olcese, an independent, had been Rector of the Agricultural University and had a successful career as a promoter and owner of supermarkets in Lima. His year in office was highly productive. Among other things, he made a serious attempt to revise agricultural pricing policies. Calmell, a loyal Populista, had been mayor of Huancayo in the Central Sierra. He did well as Minister of Labor and took a greater interest in economic issues than most of his colleagues.

Of the new ministers, Carlos Velarde, a long-time personal friend of the president, had been with Grace and Co. and then Braniff in Peru for many years. The Minister of Government—who controlled the police and the Peruvian equivalent of the FBI ("La PIP")—ought to have been a personality with a knowledge of the burdens of his Ministry. José Jiménez Borja, a well-known man of letters,

[2] Second (i.e., mother's) family names have been shown only when commonly used.

hardly had time in his tenure in office to begin to cope with the huge administrative headaches of the Ministry of Education. The new Minister of Justice was a distinguished career diplomat and incisive journalist; he had been no stranger to political controversy and had been exiled by General Odría. In his seventies, Guillermo Hoyos Osores was safe and successful as Peruvian Ambassador in Caracas, and he was extremely reluctant to return to his tiny bachelor house in Lima and the discomforts of politics.[3] After much persuasion, he reluctantly accepted. The new Prime Minister, Oswaldo Hercelles, a well-known Lima surgeon with an interest in politics, was in his late fifties. He was named by Belaúnde because of his image as an independent moderate who had good relations with various of the APRA leaders. His appointment gave strength to the view that the Cabinet had been appointed after the advice and consent of the APRA, and that it was "un Cabinete conversado."[4] Rather, the tactic seems to have been that Belaúnde appointed a prime minister and a few key ministers whom he knew would have good rapport with the APRA leadership. Belaúnde's aim was to "des-Popularizar al Gabinete" (give the Cabinet an image less identified with Acción Popular).

The principal appointment was undoubtedly that of Manuel Ulloa as Finance Minister. Belaúnde later regretted that he had not appointed Ulloa to the post earlier. On the other hand, it is conceivable that Ulloa would have had much greater difficulty in achieving in 1966, for exam-

[3] The salary of a minister at the time was the equivalent of about U.S. $800.

[4] "A pre-arranged Cabinet." Zimmermann, in *El Plan Inca*, p. 40, states that "APRA and other sectors approved one by one each of the chosen (Ministers)." This statement is denied by several Acción Popular leaders. On the other hand, it seems that Arias Stella was to have gone to Interior but was ruled out for that Ministry because a militant Acción Populista was not acceptable to APRA in that sensitive post. The president's brother, Francisco Belaúnde, was an important influence in the selection of the various Cabinets from 1963 to 1968.

ple, what he did achieve in mid-1968, since APRA would probably not, even after the most persuasive arguments, have approved fiscal measures in 1966 and 1967. It only did so in mid-1968 when some of its leaders had finally convinced themselves that something had to be done, or else there might well be a coup that would wipe out APRA's good chances in the 1969 election. But even then APRA accepted the measures only on condition that it not be held responsible for them. Nevertheless, it is probable that if Ulloa had had the opportunity of running the Finance Ministry before mid-1968, he would have firmly convinced his own colleagues at Acción Popular that the measures were needed, and a good part, though perhaps not the decisive part, of the battle would have been won.

One of the reasons why President Belaúnde had not appointed Ulloa Finance Minister on previous occasions was Ulloa's past association with DELTEC. DELTEC, an investment banking house doing business principally in Latin America, was founded after the war by a group of enterprising young expatriate Americans based in Brazil, led by Clarence Dauphinot, a former partner of a Wall Street investment house. From selling pots and pans, DELTEC (the initials do not stand for anything in particular) quickly graduated to two-main lines of business. At the local level—especially in Brazil, Argentina, Peru, Mexico, and also Colombia and Venezuela—it acted as a lender to business beyond what the banks could do— charging the generally high interest rates to be expected in the market outside the banks—and financed these operations by selling local currency bonds to local residents. DELTEC could thus claim with some reason that it was helping to establish local capital markets. The other side of the business was international short- and medium-term lending, usually to the governments and some industries of the countries mentioned above. As Dauphinot widened the network of shareholders to include some well-known banks in the United States and especially in Europe, the international lending of DELTEC increased rapidly. With a small staff, DELTEC was very flexible and could mobilize large loans quickly, partly because it knew that its shareholders could help in disposing of the notes. For these rapid services, however, DELTEC charged more—although not always—than the large New York commercial banks and was regarded by some of them as the black sheep of the financial community. DELTEC was not licensed by the SEC to do business in securities in the United States, and it probably would not have wanted to for tax reasons, but this added to the slightly dubious image projected by some Bahamas-based financial operations.

Manuel Ulloa had risen to the top of DELTEC, and was President of the DELTEC Banking Corporation, the major operating arm, after he had spent many years with them, especially in Europe. With the election of Belaúnde, Ulloa became more active in Peru, and DELTEC became a relatively big participant in the earlier maturities of supplier credits to the government, especially for road equipment and for the purchase of merchant ships from Spain. By 1967, the part of the government's debt that had originally been arranged by DELTEC was probably of the order of U.S. $60 million.[5] The service on this type of borrowing from commercial sources contributed to the financial problems of 1968. More important, however, jealousies were fueled by Ulloa's cosmopolitan background and personal success in other ventures, especially the newspaper *Expreso*, which he built into the daily with the largest national circulation after having bought it in bankrupt condition in the early sixties. To attack Ulloa, some of the press, especially the sensationalist weekly *Oiga* ("Listen"), tried to show that DELTEC was really part of the

[5] DELTEC obviously promoted its own business rather aggressively. In May 1967, for example, it offered the Ministry of Finance a U.S. $20 million six-month loan to maintain the level of gross international reserves. The Central Bank refused. DELTEC insisted. However, upon the second refusal, they withdrew the offer.

223

Rockefeller interests,[6] a story that had little reason for existence other than the fact that IBEC, the International Basic Economy Corporation, an enterprise owned by the Rockefeller brothers, had apparently at one point had a small interest in DELTEC. Also, both names ended in "EC"! IBEC had played a pioneering role in developing the poultry industry in Peru and had established chains of supermarkets in various South American countries.

Even though there was little basis for linking Ulloa with Rockefeller, the story had a habit of sticking. In 1967, Ulloa left DELTEC, but that did not change the outlook of many Ulloa's press and business colleagues, who resented his rapid rise in the newspaper business. This setting contributed to Ulloa's difficulties in the last month of his productive four-month term as Minister of Finance.

A Strategy for Recovery

The first job of Hercelles and Ulloa was to get APRA to approve a tax package. To be sure of his figures, Ulloa immediately called González del Valle and the Central Bank. Several of the bank's advisers had been suspicious of the new Minister, thinking that he was going to be some sort of loan hustler. Quickly, however, a completely different impression appeared. The Minister was quick to grasp the issues, and did not need lengthy explanations. The problems were clear, but it was obvious that the fiscal gap and the resulting balance of payments problem were far greater than the Executive and Congress liked to

---

[6] See for example *Oiga*, October 25, 1968, cover story. As "proof" of its story, the periodical showed part of a picture of Ulloa and David Rockefeller sitting next to each other at what looks like a business conference. In fact, the author witnessed a meeting between Ulloa and Rockefeller at the latter's office in the Chase Manhattan Bank, at which the main subject of conversation was Ulloa's insistence that the banking system had to be "Peruvianized," a step that would adversely affect Banco Continental, in which Chase Manhattan was the majority stockholder.

imagine. Ulloa was not surprised to find that the Central Bank and his predecessors had been telling the truth to the politicians. The fiscal and balance of payments situation was as bad as the Central Bank, in its numerous communications to the Finance Minister (with copies to the leaders of Congress),[7] had said it was; indeed, it was by then worse. At the end of May 1968, the gross international reserves of the Central Bank were only U.S. $69 million, including the whole of the IMF standby credit of U.S. $42.5 million, the last portion of which had been drawn a month earlier. To look into the future: the burden of service on the external public debt for the remainder of 1968 and for 1969 was high—an annual amount of about U.S. $150 million—and particularly high if one considered the small size of the exchange surplus left in the certificate market after meeting import payments and profit remittances of foreign companies. The latter totaled about U.S. $150 million annually out of gross merchandise export proceeds of about U.S. $800 million. On the fiscal side, the gap was larger than had been expected by the Ministry of Finance at the beginning of the fiscal year, and the cash deficiency on an annual basis was of the order of S/. 5 billion.

As a result of these bleak prospects, Ulloa rapidly took two decisions: the original fiscal package (introduction of a real property tax, of a tax on share capital, and increases in the gasoline sales tax and in the income tax) would have to be modified to yield larger and more certain revenues in the immediate future, and a refinancing of the part of the payments on the external public debt would have to be obtained. Since the refinancing was only a last-resort temporary measure to roll forward a bulge in debt service

[7] For example, *Oficios* No. 1899 (September 15, 1967), No. 1914 (January 12, 1968), No. 1917 (February 23, 1968), No. 1923 (April 23, 1968), No. 1929 (May 15, 1968), and No. 1937 (June 17, 1968). Except for Nos. 1923 and 1929, copies of the others were sent to the leaders of the Budget Committees of the Senate and the Chamber of Deputies.

225

payments, a key part of the financial plan was to ensure the expansion of exports, especially through new investment in mining. The key elements of the financial plan were thus the fiscal measures, the refinancing, and the mining investments.

The negotiations of Hercelles and Ulloa with the APRA leadership (Haya de la Torre, Villanueva, Townsend, Prialé, Sánchez and Cox) were rapid. APRA was by then at last becoming convinced of the dangers of a coup if the air of political and economic instability was not quickly dissipated. The political arrangement arrived at was simple. APRA would give the Executive authority for sixty days to put into effect the needed measures, but APRA would not be responsible for the measures, since this would not require Congressional review and approval. Congress was merely to be informed or advised of the measures. On its side, the Executive undertook to do a thorough job, so that—hopefully—there would not be a need for further measures if APRA won the election and took over the Executive a year later. The question of IPC was obviously part of the discussion, but there was at that stage no firm commitment on the part of the government to do anything (see Chapter IX below).

On June 19, 1968, or less than three weeks after the Hercelles Cabinet had taken office, Congress passed a law with one article (Law 17044). The law stated:

"Single article. Authority is hereby granted to the Executive so that, within a non-renewable period of sixty days from the date of this law, in accordance with constitutional requirements, it take the emergency measures needed to solve the structural imbalance in public finances, to strengthen the balance of payments, and to encourage the integrated development of our economy.

"Authority is also hereby given to the Executive so that, in accordance with constitutional requirements, it take the measures needed to hold back the excessive rise in the cost of living, and specify the penalties applicable to those who speculate with the prices of the goods which make up the said cost of living. . . .

"The measures taken under the authority of this law will be in the form of Supreme Decrees approved by the Council of Ministers, with the obligation of advising the Congress of each measure so taken."[8]

Four days after the law was signed on June 20, the first two and the principal decrees under Law 17044 were issued. The speed of their issuance surprised most people, who did not think that the measures were really ready. Admittedly, there was a feverish effort for two or three days and nights to put everything together, since the Minister was determined not to lose any time. On the evening of June 24, Minister Ulloa was about to present the measures on television, but the appearance had to be postponed for an hour. As always, there was a last-minute political hitch—predictably enough—over the issue of the gasoline tax. President Belaúnde was adamant and resisted the increase in gasoline prices. The clock was running and he did not want to sign the decree: it was too much on top of the price rise that had followed the devaluation, there would be riots, the government would be endangered. In the end a compromise had to be worked out: the President accepted the increase for Lima and the coastal cities (where gasoline was cheapest), but for the Sierra—where transport costs to some areas raised gasoline prices to twice their level in Lima—there would be no increase. In fact, the President lowered the price in Cuzco and a few other Sierra cities. Since the Sierra accounted for only about ten percent of gasoline consumption, the revenue loss from the compromise and the rearranging of prices was not too large (the additional first year revenues were to be S/. 800 million instead of S/. 1 billion) but in the process the idea

---

[8] Spanish text in Central Bank, *Boletín Estadístico*, June 1968. There was thus no formal requirement for Congressional approval of the measures taken under Law 17044. However, Congress presumably could have rescinded some of the measures if it had wished to do so.

of a percentage ad valorem gasoline tax had to be abandoned since the tax increase (or decline) was now defined as the difference between the old and the new prices. The effects of the package of measures announced by Ulloa on June 24 were quick and somewhat unexpected. The forebodings about the gasoline tax simply did not materialize, despite the sharp rise in gasoline prices. The price of low-octane gasoline increased by 37 percent in Lima and other coastal centers, that of middle-range gasoline by 46 percent, and that with the highest octane by 66 percent.[9] The government simultaneously authorized the entry at reduced import duties of a number of taxis and "micro-buses." The dreaded effects of the increase in gasoline prices never came about. In the quarter following the measure, the cost-of-living index rose by less than two percent, or at an annual rate lower than in any year since the early sixties. While the relatively strong drivers' union staged a one-day strike, its plans for broader opposition to the measure did not meet with active enthusiasm on the part of the rank-and-file of the union. Within a few weeks, the measure was accepted and largely forgotten.

The reaction of the middle classes and the business groups to the tax package was equally unexpected. In the last days of June, the banks were flooded with dollar sales by individuals, a large number of them low-salaried employees who had bought small amounts of dollar bills in the preceding months. The draft market, where the Central Bank had intervened earlier in the year in order to present

---

[9] The respective price increases were from S/. 5.00 to S/. 6.95 per gallon, from S/. 6.86 to S/. 10.00, and from S/. 9.66 to S/. 6.00. The gasoline most commonly used by taxis and non-diesel buses was that of the lowest octane. The tax take in Lima at these prices was 40 percent of the price, 54 percent and about 70 percent respectively. The progressive rate of the tax was designed so that higher-income users, who usually bought the higher grades of gasoline because they had newer cars, would pay more. In comparison with U.S. prices, the new Peruvian prices were low to moderate, and about equivalent in the case of high octane gasoline.

too rapid a depreciation of the rate, now reversed itself as confidence in the sol improved. The rate appreciated from a low point of S/. 46.87 per U.S. dollar on June 13, to S/. 45.56 at the end of the month, and S/. 43.96 at the end of July. On July 26 and 27, the Central Bank bought a foreign exchange surplus of about U.S. $10 million from the draft market.

Despite their vociferous opposition since 1966 to any significant action on taxes, the business groups recognized that for once some real measures had been taken. The reserves of the Central Bank improved by U.S. $13 million in the quarter July-September, as the pace of import payments (not physical imports) slowed down. For the first time since the devaluation of September-October 1967, the substantial improvement in the trade balance that had occurred since then—largely through a decline in imports but also some expansion in the volume of exports—was reflected in the movement of actual payments as speculative pressure for faster import payments died down. True, a major factor in this improvement was the maintenance of the surcharge on import payments. The surcharge of 10 percent on import payments, introduced on June 24, together with the other measures in the tax package, succeeded the 15 percent surcharge established a few weeks earlier after the crisis arising from the resignation of General Morales Bermúdez as Finance Minister. The new surcharge was due to decline to 5 percent in December 1968 and be eliminated at the end of January 1969. The purpose was to encourage importers to re-finance their obligations abroad and thus give a breathing space for the reserves to build up. The measure worked because a large part of business opinion believed that it would really be only an interim measure. At the same time, import prohibitions on a series of luxury consumer items were continued temporarily, mainly for their political effect. The financial results of the prohibition of some imports were not important on the balance of payments side—a possible

229

annual foreign exchange saving of U.S. $15 million[10]—and were negative on the fiscal side—with import duty revenue losses of twice as much.

The import surcharge was of course a much less than perfect measure. In the first place, since food imports were not subject to the surcharge, it continued the long-standing practice of not protecting domestic agriculture. It would clearly have been politically difficult, on the basis of the temporary extraordinary powers bestowed by Congress, to depart radically from the agricultural price policy that Peru had pursued since the 1930's in favor of the consuming public in Lima. Payments for imports of basic foods (together with pharmaceuticals and newsprint) were therefore excluded from the surcharge. Secondly, the need for a flat virtually across-the-board surcharge implied that the certificate exchange rate had been set at an overvalued level. The draft market rate was after all at S/. 43 to S/. 44 to the U.S. dollar compared to S/. 38.70 for the certificate rate. It was true that political developments and fiscal policy since the devaluation had never really given the certificate rate a chance, but perhaps the intervening time had been irretrievably wasted and Peru would then in time pay the price by maintaining a politically fixed rate. However, few people seemed to have had these doubts in July and August 1968.

THE REFORMS

The tax measures put into effect in June 1968 (see table below) not only had the effect of providing revenue. Through the national real property tax, a decisive step was taken in the direction of making taxation more progressive and more dependent on direct taxation, which had declined in relative importance in the previous decade. It was also

[10] Possibly even less, if account is taken of the resulting higher imports of parts for local assembly of radios, TV sets, refrigerators, washing machines, etc.

230

the first organized attempt at taxing the largest form of wealth in Peru, land and real estate. Until then, there had been a number of taxes and fees based on the value of real estate, but only at the municipal level and applied in a very lax fashion in a few areas of the four or five main cities. They included the *predio*, a flat tax on the imputed rent supposed to be yielded by a property, and the *arbitrios* and *baja policía*, fees collected for public lighting, police protection, and garbage collection, but all based on the value of the property. If one assumes that these various taxes and fees were properly collected—a rare exception—in a prosperous urban area, they might have amounted to the equivalent of U.S. $250 annually on a house with a market value of about U.S. $40,000-50,000, obviously a very low rate indeed of taxation of real property.[11] Except for a small tax on unutilized urban land, there had been *no* taxes effectively levied on land as such. (See Table 31.)

The real estate tax was the part of the tax package most actively opposed by the older generation of wealth. *La Prensa,* in particular, was vociferous against it. The more sophisticated form of the argument against the real estate tax was that the tax in itself was not bad—as long as it was not applied to rural areas—but that there would be a temptation, since the tax was already established, to simply raise the rate if revenue was needed. But the same argument could be applied against most forms of taxation, and increases in rates would, in any case, in a democratic government, require the approval of Congress. Initially, property values as declared by the owner were to be the basis for taxation until up-to-date assessments could be developed. This method of self-assessment turned out to

---

[11] A sample made by the OAS-IDB *Estudio Fiscal del Perú*, in the two best residential areas of Lima, showed that the average *predio* paid was the equivalent of U.S. $35 annually per dwelling (p. 148, Spanish edition). The fiscal study provided the major elements needed for the fiscal measures of 1968 and is an excellent study of Peru's tax system prior to that date.

231

have serious implications for land holders who undervalued their holdings, since the 1969 Land Reform used their self-assessments as a basis for setting the value of properties.

TABLE 31. Principal Tax Measures Taken in June 1968 under Law 17044[a]

1. *Personal income tax*

   a. Elimination of schedular system that taxed different types of income at various scales.

   b. Elimination of bearer shares, in order to make all dividend revenue traceable and taxable at the level of the recipient of the income.

   c. Higher rates:

For taxable income	Old Rates	New Rates
to S/. 30,000	—	3%
S/. 30,001-S/. 100,000	7% to 25%	4% to 25%[b]
S/. 100,001 to S/. 1,000,000	30%	25% to 38%[b]
S/. 1,000,001 to S/. 5,000,000	30%	38% to 40%[b]
Above S/. 5,000,000	30%	42%

2. *Profits tax*

   a. Introduction of 40% tax on interest payable abroad.

   b. Rate changes
   Sharper progressivity of rates, but maximum rate reduced from 54.5% (38.5% basic rate plus 26% of after tax profits) to 52% (35% basic rate plus 26%).

3. *Tax on real estate property*

   a. New tax which did not exist before. It was combined with the old municipal "predio."

   b. Rates:

	Percentage	Value of property[c]
i. Urban	—	Up to S/. 300,000
	¼ of 1%	S/. 300,000-S/. 1,000,000
	½ of 1%	S/. 600,000-S/. 1,000,000
	¾ of 1%	S/. 1,000,000-S/. 2,500,000
	1%	Above S/. 2,500,000
ii. Rural	—	Up to S/. 500,000
	¼ of 1%	S/. 500,000-S/. 1,000,000
	½ of 1%	S/. 1,000,001-S/. 2,500,000
	¾ of 1%	S/. 2,500,001-S/. 10,000,000
	1%	Above S/. 10,000,000

4. *Gasoline tax*

	Old prices in Lima		New prices in Lima		Resulting tax as % of pre-tax price[a]	
Increase in tax					Old	New
low octane (66)	S/. 5.00	per gallon	S/. 6.95	per gallon	19	40
middle octane (84)	S/. 6.86	" "	S/. 10.00	" "	19	54
high octane (95)	S/. 9.66	" "	S/. 16.00	" "	30	70

5. *Selected increases in excises*

Higher percentage rates	Increase in tax	Percentage of retail price due to tax[d]
Cigarettes and tobacco	10%	15%[e]
Carbonated drinks	20%	7%
Alcoholic beverages (excl. beer)	20%	1-10%[e]

[a] Summary of main measures only. The changes in the profits and income taxes are substantially simplified in this table. For purposes of comparison, U.S. $1 can be taken as the rough equivalent of S/. 40 in 1968.
[b] Range of several categories.
[c] After allowable deduction of up to S/. 200,000 for outstanding mortgages.
[d] Approximate.
[e] Excluding import duties.

The criticism of the property tax meant that Ulloa had to proceed with caution. After all, the Executive was enacting legislation under a blanket authorization from Congress. Congress had to be advised of the legislation but it did not formally have to approve it.[12] Nevertheless, the President rightly wished to avoid a confrontation with Congress about an authorization that was intended to be used discretely.

The increases in the personal income tax rates, which made the tax more progressive, and especially affected the middle upper tax brackets, did not satisfy the advisers and fiscal technicians because the new range was not progressive enough. On the other hand, it was believed that a higher top bracket rate would encourage evasion. The principal

[12] All the decrees were prefaced by the title *Ley 17044* since Law 17044 was the enabling legislation.

measure in personal income taxation was the abolition of bearer shares (*acciones al portador*), which was a widespread form of ownership of banks, and enterprises in manufacturing, real estate, and agriculture. Although under the previous tax system dividends paid against bearer shares had automatically deducted from them a flat percentage tax, it was not possible to trace dividend income to the level of the recipient, who in most cases would have had to pay through income taxation a higher rate than the flat deduction. The abolition of bearer shares was, naturally enough, greeted by protest from the highest income groups and by enthusiasm from progressives. In fact the fiscal impact of the measure was not immediate, but it gave lawyers a lot of work as enterprises had to meet the November 1968 deadline to declare their owners. In order to discourage double-tier ownership—where the real owners would hide behind a holding company—the law established a significant tax on the incorporation of new companies of this type.

Aside from the change in the profits tax, the remaining tax measures were of the traditional variety and were designed to yield revenue as quickly as possible. The higher taxes on alcoholic beverages, soft drinks, and cigarettes were recognized to be regressive in their impact, at least on the basis of studies made in other countries (e.g., Colombia). But the rates of these taxes were low and more or less progressive according to the price range of the article.

The tax package made the decisive contribution in reversing the trend of increasing unmanageable budget deficits that became pronounced in 1965. In their first full year of operation, the tax measures were supposed to and did yield about S/. 2.2 billion (S/. 600 million net from the property tax,[13] S/. 800 million from the gasoline tax, S/. 300

[13] After the transfer to the municipalities of the amounts they would have received from the *predios*.

234

from the income tax, and about S/. 500 million from the various excises). Although the property tax had no effect on calendar 1968 revenues and the personal income tax had only a small impact because the preparation of the regulations took several months, 1968 Central Government current revenues, including the proceeds of the export tax, rose sharply (by 25 percent in the first six months of fiscal year 1968 over the same period of 1967 or by about 10-12 percent after allowing for inflation) while expenditures, especially salaries, increased only moderately, at a slightly lower rate than domestic prices. For the year 1968 as a whole direct tax revenue, buoyed by the export tax and the tax measures introduced by Ferrero (including the tax on the revaluation of company assets and the first increase in the profits tax) rose by 60 percent. The improvement was particularly noticeable in the third quarter of calendar 1968. Although there still remained a serious financing problem, it diminished as the additional tax collections increased in each of the months following the June 1968 measures. (See Table 32.)

TABLE 32. SUMMARY CENTRAL GOVERNMENT BUDGETARY CASH OPERATIONS, APRIL-SEPTEMBER 1967-1968
(in millions of soles, cash basis)

	1967			1968		
	Jan. to March	April to June	July to Sept.	Jan. to March	April to June	July to Sept.
Current revenues and long-term receipts	4,751	4,853	5,004	7,650	4,742	6,588
Total expenditures	5,843	5,592	6,725	7,413	5,752	7,564
Gap to be financed	1,092	769	1,721	(237)[a]	1,010	976

[a] Although there was a surplus on a cash basis, it was achieved through the accumulation of unpaid bills in a larger amount than the surplus.

SOURCE: Controller General's Office, as reproduced in Central Bank, *Reseña Económica y Financiera*, various 1967 and 1968 issues.

At the same time, the government began paying off the floating debt, which totalled about S/. 1.5 million of unpaid bills due in 1967 and 1968. The large backlog of unpaid bills was hurting suppliers and the construction industry in particular, although the main cause of the problems of the latter was the over-building of apartment houses in Lima in previous years. In order to provide about S/. 700 million to help to pay off the floating debt, the reserve requirements of the commercial banks were lowered[14] on the understanding that the banks would use the resources thus freed to purchase government bonds. The foreign banks immediately took up the bonds assigned to them, but it took several weeks to get the domestic banks to comply with the new regulations.[15]

The fiscal achievement, which greatly benefitted the government after the October 1968 coup, was not only important in a financial sense—after all, uncontrolled expenditures could again easily plunge Peru in a fiscal crisis—but because it relied partly on new forms of taxation, especially on real property, which had a large potential as a progressive source of revenue and as an engine of social change. At the same time, the tax system was made much more responsive to trends in income. By 1970, as a result of the combined effect of better enforcement in 1968 and subsequently, and particularly of the new tax measures themselves which were maintained by the new government, direct tax revenue was more than one-third of Central Government current revenues compared to about one-fifth four years earlier.

It was at the time argued by some press commentators, both inside and outside Peru, that the fiscal policies launched in June 1968 led the country into a recession.

[14] The basic reserve requirement was lowered from 28 percent to 24 percent on July 15, 1968.

[15] At the end of September, one respected local bank had not yet obeyed the regulations. Only after its owner was confronted with an unpleasant exchange at the Central Bank, did he "agree" to obey.

There is no doubt that 1968 was a year of recession, but this had begun well before the measures. The causes of recession were clear enough: a crisis in the construction industry because of past overbuilding of luxury apartments in Lima; a decline in public investment because of the lack of foreign development loans—a trend that also affected construction; the decline of output in certain industries hit hardest by the 1967 devaluation (such as the assembly plants of cars and appliances); and, foremost of all, the political turmoil during most of the year. The higher taxes in fact weighed heaviest in percentage terms on the export sector and therefore helped to contain the remittances abroad of foreign companies, especially mining companies. The containment of such payments abroad was hardly a cause for a domestic recession. On the contrary, it would in time have been a source of domestic investment. The government recognized, however, that the domestic economy needed a boost. Therefore, the other part of the economic program included the proposed mining investments, credit reform, incentives for new exports, for construction of low-cost housing, and for the domestic contracting industry, and a massive program of project preparation to reactivate long-term foreign aid.

The bulk of the non-tax measures approved during the sixty days were meant to lay the legal basis for this second effort. However, there were many both within and outside the government who felt that far too many decrees, on top of the strictly fiscal measures, were issued under the umbrella of Law 17044, and that many of these were related only indirectly to the purposes of the law. Law 17044 did contain a clause about authorizing measures "to encourage the integrated development of our economy," but many observers felt that several of the measures had little to do with this objective. This was particularly so in the case of the decrees reforming certain aspects of the banking system. Most critics felt that the majority of these measures would in all probability have been passed by Congress, although after the customarily long wait. The critics had a point especially in criticizing hasty drafting by some of the legal advisers brought in by Ulloa. On the other hand, the enthusiasm of the Minister in putting together a comprehensive package of economic legislation was understandable after several years of refusal by Congress to pass any but the least controversial economic measures proposed by the government.[16] (See Table 33 for a list of measures under Law 17044.)

The main non-tax legislative measures taken during the sixty days were the changes in the general banking legislation, the establishment of fiscal incentives for new exports and for the development of certain industries (petrochemicals in particular), and changes in the charters of a number of state institutions (the Agricultural, Industrial, Mining and Housing Banks, the state shipping line) in order to give them a legal basis for greater flexibility in their operations. The most important measure politically, and the one that got the most applause or generated the most opposition, required banks and insurance companies to have within one year two-thirds of their share capital owned by nationals (or foreigners with at least five years' residence). Banks that did not comply with this requirement would have the same status as branches of foreign banks,[17] which already

[16] Law 17046 of July 3, 1968 was a useful contribution by Congress to the package of fiscal reforms. It eliminated about 70 small indirect taxes that had high collection costs and that provided little revenue.

[17] The following were counted as branches of foreign banks: First National City Bank of New York, Bank of Tokyo, Royal Bank of Canada, Bank of London and South America, and Bank of America. There were four majority foreign-owned banks: Banco de Crédito (majority control of the Banca Comerciale Italiana-Sudameris Group), Banco Internacional (various foreign holders including Chemical Bank New York), Banco Continental (majority Chase Manhattan and associates), and Banco de Lima (large holding of Crédit Lyonnais). The measures of Ulloa (which were later expanded by the new government) started a trend of similar legislation in other countries,

were not allowed to obtain time or savings deposits. There were several motivations for the measure, all of them political. Foreign-owned banks or branches of foreign banks had after all not served Peru badly: they had brought capital in and repatriated very little (this was easily ascertained after the certificate system was introduced in October 1967); they had only a very small foreign staff and had trained a competent local management personnel; they tended to introduce more modern banking practices; and their lending was undoubtedly more "democratic" than that of some of the largest local banks, which flouted the law and tended to concentrate credit to their directors or their families.

What, then, was the reason for the attack on the foreign banks? For one thing, Minister Ulloa probably saw a way of building a nationalist platform that would not affect the economy very much. He did have a political basis for doing so, of course. The foreign-controlled banks altogether accounted for almost 60 percent of total banking system resources and credit. Demands were bound to increase for a banking system with a more visible Peruvian label. More important still, the largest foreign-owned bank—the Banco de Crédito—had in the 1960's built up an increasing lead over its immediate competitor, Banco Popular, owned by the Prado family and their associates. In 1968, Banco de Crédito accounted for one-third of commercial bank operations. Another bank that had grown rapidly was Banco Continental, originally a Peruvian bank in which Chase Manhattan bought a majority interest in 1965. However, both Banco de Crédito and Banco Continental were largely managed by Peruvians. The most patent case of foreign visibility was that of Banco Internacional. Banco Internacional—where various local and foreign non-banking business groups had a strong interest, including Felipe Beltrán

notably Venezuela. The branches of the foreign banks mentioned above continue to operate in Peru today.

(brother of don Pedro), W. R. Grace and Co., and La Fabril, which in turn was controlled by Bunge y Born of Argentina—had been a poorly run bank, which had accumulated large arrears to its foreign correspondents, in particular the Chemical Bank of New York. In 1966-1967, Chemical decided to obtain a controlling interest in order to collect and, as a by-product, to establish a network in a then rapidly growing Latin American economy. Chemical had a large exposure in other countries of the area,

TABLE 33. Principal Decrees Issued under Law 17044
(in the order of their appearance)

No. of Decree[a]	Summary Contents
202-68-HC	Cuts in 1968 budget, prohibited imports continued, 10 percent import surchange, Central Bank board composition changed, capital requirements for banks and insurance companies increased, new banking law authorized,[b] excises, higher gasoline taxes, readjustable mortgages for foreign-financed public housing.
203-68-HC[b] (287-68-HC) 227-68-HC	Reform of income tax, real property tax, and tax on capital of enterprises introduced, and elimination by November 1, 1968 of bearer shares. Incentives for manufactured exports; an official registry of importers established.
237-68-HC[c]	Established criteria for "outward signs of wealth" in assessing personal income tax.
248-68-HC	Reform of the Treasury, to control expenditures and centralize deposits of public funds.
250-68-HC	Exempts coffee exports from payment of 10 percent advance profits tax.
251-68-HC	Exporters still subject to 10 percent advance profits tax given choice of substituting remaining payments to March 1969 with purchase of 7 percent 3-year U.S. dollar bonds.
252-68-HC[d]	Introduces Central Bank approval of sale of banking shares to foreigners, eliminates banking sector representatives on Board of Central Bank, reforms Superintendency of Banks.

253-68-HC[b]	New basic law for Agricultural Development Bank.
284-68-HC	Modifies tax structure to encourage headquarters in Peru of multinational companies operating in at least three other Latin American countries.
297-68-HC	Banking and insurance reforms: two-thirds ownership by nationals required, increase in minimum capital, discretional limits on reinsurance abroad.
298-68-HC	New Mining Bank basic law.
299-68-HC	Reforms to Industrial Bank basic law.
085-68-FO	Special incentives for investment in petrochemical industries for enterprises with 30 percent or more national ownership.
344-68-HC[b]	New Central Reserve Bank basic law.
358-68-HC[b]	Authorization to establish domestic open-ended mutual funds.
360-68-HC	Reforms to Housing Bank basic law and widening of lending powers of savings and loan associations.
364-68-HC	Peruvian Steamship Corporation given autonomy in employment and financial and commercial operations.
367-68-HC[b]	Tighter requirements for branches of foreign insurance companies.

[a] In the numbering of decrees HC means a Ministry of Finance and Commerce decree, and FO a Ministry of Development decree.

[b] Decree subsequently corrected or replaces another decree also issued under the authority of Law 17044.

[c] Not issued under Law 17044.

[d] Decree subsequently corrected or replaces another decree also issued under the authority of Law 17044.

Colombia in particular, but for one reason or another it had not wanted, or been able, to get into actual branch banking in Latin America. With its network in the major cities of Peru, Internacional had obvious attractions. The problems of the purchase arose because the approach by Chemical came at a time when there was a growing political feeling against foreign control of banks. Still, Chemical went ahead, but without adequately informing the Peruvian authorities until after the event. In the small setting of

241

Lima, this omission caused resentment. The Central Bank management did not like the purchase because it felt that Peru was over-banked. Banco Unión had failed in 1966, and the Central Bank believed that the need was not foreign acquisition of existing institutions but rather the merger of weak banks with stronger ones. The local bankers did not like the entry into a small market of a potential competitor.

Sensing the discontent caused by the Banco Internacional episode, Ulloa decided from the beginning that the banking system had to be Peruvianized. During a visit to New York early July 1968 in connection with the refinancing of the public external debt (see below), Ulloa mentioned the matter to David Rockefeller, of the Chase Manhattan Bank. Legislation Peruvianizing the foreign banks was inevitable, Ulloa said, and Banco Continental ought to get used to the idea of becoming a majority Peruvian-owned bank again. Rockefeller was flexible and tactful in his answer, but he did not hide the fact he did not like the new policy. In any event, the law calling for the Peruvianization of the banks was decreed a few weeks later.[18] A useful by-product of the measure were much stricter rules governing lending to shareholders and directors, and a reorganization of the Superintendency of Banks, which had been lax in enforcing sound financial practices in a number of banks and was placed under the de facto control of the Central Bank.[19]

The changes in the basic laws of the four state development banks were more directly related to fulfilling the purposes of Law 17044 than the Peruvianization of commercial banks. The latter could scarcely be described as in tune with the purposes of Law 17044 and would in any

[18] The two-thirds minimum local participation was increased to three-quarters by the new government in December 1968. Subsequently, in 1970, the Banco de La Nación bought the majority of the shares of Banco Continental and Banco Internacional after the foreign shareholders of those banks had decided to keep their banks as foreign banks.

[19] The next government removed the control of the Central Bank over the Superintendency in December 1968.

case have been approved overwhelmingly by Congress. The changes in the laws of the four state development banks were economically significant: they were given autonomy to charge (and pay) more realistic rates of interest, to embark in new areas of lending (tourism in the case of the Industrial Bank, smallholder agriculture in the case of the Agricultural Bank), to create new financial instruments (readjustable mortgages in the case of lending for middle-income housing by the Housing Bank, leasing arrangements on the part of the Industrial Bank). The Mining Bank, which had until then played a small role in financing some of the smaller locally owned lead, zinc, silver, and copper producers, in particular emerged in a much stronger position as a result of its new law.

NEGOTIATIONS WITH THE MINING COMPANIES

In addition to the actual tax reforms and other decrees, the two other pillars of the recovery program were new investments in large-scale mining and the refinancing of part of the public sector external debt. The two were closely related. It had been increasingly obvious to the Central Bank, especially since the establishment of the certificate market, that the prospects for the balance of payments in the immediate years ahead were bleak. In the period 1964-1966, a combination of high export prices and an extraordinary volume of commercial foreign loans to the public sector had kept the balance of payments manageable in the face of a tremendous growth of imports, itself in part stimulated by rapid industrialization. Now the debts had to be repaid. The inflow of foreign loans was declining and could not be replaced in short order with long-term borrowing from international agencies, and the outlook for copper and fishmeal prices was uncertain. The only area where major additional export earnings could with certainty be generated within a predictable period was copper mining. In the best of circumstances, however, it would take four or five years before new investments in copper would actually yield export earnings. In the interval, some relief could be obtained by a reduction of profit remittances abroad—as the mining companies reinvested part of their profits to meet the local costs of the new investments—and by long-term development loans to the public sector, as a result of a concentrated effort to prepare development projects suitable for lending by the World Bank and the Inter-American Development Bank. However, for the immediate year or two ahead, when none of these favorable factors would have yet come into play, some form of special relief was needed: hence the idea of refinancing the largest part of the external debt payments of 1968, 1969, and, if possible, of 1970. The sequence of actions, as seen in mid-1968, was thus: (1) an agreement on new mining investments and partial refinancing of the external public debt; (2) a major effort at project preparation and a resulting increase in long-term external loan inflows which would begin to yield results in 1970-1971; (3) the reduction of profit remittances in 1970-1972 as major investments in copper mines were undertaken; (4) the repayment of the refinancing in 1970-1974/1975; and (5) a major increase in export earnings beginning in 1973.

The scheme was obviously very tight in its timing. On the other hand, several factors made prompt investments in new copper mines technically feasible for the immediate future. First, complete engineering existed for some of the major copper projects, and exhaustive mineral surveys were available for all of them. The two projects most likely to be undertaken first—the Cuajone concession of Southern Peru Copper[20] and the Cerro Verde Concession of Anaconda Copper—had final engineering plans ready. The total cost of Cuajone was then estimated at about U.S. $330 million, and that of the first stage of Cerro Verde at U.S. $70 million, with a resulting total output of 180,000 tons or U.S. $160

[20] As noted earlier, a consortium of American Smelting and Refining with Cerro Corporation, Phelps Dodge, and Newmont Mining.

million annually at very conservatively estimated price of U.S. 40 cents per lb.[21] Actually, this price was somewhat above the minimum price of U.S. 33-35 cents that the companies estimated as necessary, at the then prevailing costs and exchange rate, in order to pay back the investment and generate a profit. Cuajone and Cerro Verde were only the first of various other identified copper mining investments; although the ore content (about one percent) of these first two mines was low-to-moderate for open-pit operations, they both had the advantage of easy accessibility to the sea and, in the case of Cuajone, to the existing facilities at Toquepala (see map). The other projects included Michiquillay in the north (an open-pit mine with American Smelting and Refining as concessionaire), Antamina, Cobriza, and Tintaya in the Central Andes (underground mines with a high ore content, of which Cerro de Pasco Corporation was concessionaire), and Quellaveco in the south (an open-pit concession of American Smelting, near Cuajone and Toquepala). The full development of these five mines would have cost about U.S. $1 billion, and generated about U.S. $500 million annually in gross export earnings at an export price for copper of about U.S. 40 cents per pound, as it then was projected.

The fact that the proposed mines would enormously increase Peruvian exchange earnings and fiscal revenues in particular, and seemed within such close grasp of realization gave added urgency to the new investments. There had not been a single major mine opened in Peru since Toquepala began producing in 1960. This was stressed in an article on Peru's mining potential in the Central Bank *Reseña* of the first quarter of 1968.[22] Meanwhile, major projects for expanding copper output were being developed or considered

[21] The U.S. price in mid-1973 was about U.S. 60 cents per lb. Estimates of output and costs for the major mining projects were given in Central Bank, *Reseña Económica y Financiera*, third quarter, 1968, table XIII.

[22] Central Bank, *Reseña Económica y Financiera*, third quarter, 1968.

in Australia, New Caledonia, Zaïre, Canada, the United States, and next door in Chile.

Although mining investments have a long pay-back period, the decisions of investors are often influenced by short-term considerations: the prospect of a sharp decline in world copper prices, even for only a few years, could be enough to make the negotiation of new investments very difficult or postpone them altogether. The Central Bank therefore insisted that Peru had to get in before it was too late.

A second factor favoring the copper investments was the existence of a legal basis for agreement with the mining companies since the reformed Article 56 of the Mining Code had been passed by Congress in March 1968. Article 56 did not entitle investors to any special benefits above those granted by the Mining Code itself.[23] However, it did allow the government to enter into contracts with major investors, giving them the same privileges as under the Mining Code. The difference was that while the Mining Code might be changed at any time by Congress, a contract could not—at least legally—be altered unilaterally. With the prospect of the Chileanization of the mines just across the border, the major investors—American Smelting-Southern Peru, in particular—had insisted on the umbrella of these special contracts before considering major investments in Peru.

With a cabinet that was able to cope with the fiscal problem, the stage now seemed set for serious discussions with American Smelting-Southern Peru, Cerro de Pasco (Cerro), and Anaconda. Shortly after the Cabinet came in, the heads of the three firms (respectively Messrs. Tittmann, Koenig, and Parkinson) were invited to Peru for discussions with Minister Carriquiry. The Minister, taking his cue from Ulloa, told them that their concessions would be withdrawn unless some major projects got underway.[24] Then eliminate

[23] All of Cerro's investments were under the Mining Code, as were all the investments of Peruvian companies.

[24] The next government subsequently adopted this tactic in mid-1970, but substitute investors did not come forward at the time.

246

the ten percent "export tax," the companies said. Since Ulloa was convinced that the tax would have to go anyway, it was not difficult after a few days to establish the basis for a dialogue. On June 26, 1968, two days after the tax measures had been announced, *El Peruano* carried a banner headline stating that "agreement" had been reached on the new mining investments. A joint communiqué of the government and the companies was also published.

Of course, there was really no "agreement," but simply a basis for conversation. Nevertheless, this was substantial progress. The next step on the agenda was for the government to prepare a draft contract. In fact one already existed, since the government had begun some weeks earlier a negotiation for a small (U.S. $10 million) investment in the Madrigal mine by the Homestake Mining Company of San Francisco. As the negotiation with Homestake progressed in the following months, a preliminary but parallel negotiation with the other major investors took place, so that the Homestake contract in fact represented a virtually standard format.[25] The principal issue in the draft Homestake contract was the treatment to be given to the foreign exchange earnings of the company. Under the certificate exchange system, the mining companies had to surrender the whole of their export proceeds at the official exchange rate. The mining companies wanted to be able to dispose freely of their exchange earnings at the official rate ("libre disponibilidad de divisas"), a right they enjoyed, in theory at least, at the time in Chile. Of course, the companies could always go to the free market, although the differential between the official rate at which they sold their exchange and the free market made that possibility commercially unattractive. Moreover, if the companies had exerted any significant de-

[25] The contract with Homestake was signed by the next government early in 1969, and that for Cuajone in December 1969. Both were based on Article 56—subsequently repealed by the new government—and included the exchange treatment clause negotiated in 1968-1969.

mand in the free market, the difference between the two rates would have become unmanageably large.

It was obviously impossible to accept the companies' demand, since it would have created a glaring exception and loophole in the exchange system. The existence of such an exception would have been unacceptable. For several months, *El Comercio* had carried a number of articles emphasizing the toughness of the treatment by Chile of foreign investment in the mining sector.[26] The message was that Peru should do the same. However, there were some differences which *El Comercio* glossed over: the treatment of exchange earnings was tighter in Peru, and—a big difference —Chile had a few years earlier attracted a substantial volume of investment in copper expansion, whereas Peru had yet to do so.

It took several months in the second half of 1968 to hammer out a compromise formula. In fact, the final stretch of the negotiations with Homestake took place under the new government. However, by August 1968 there was a basis for saying that the main issue in the negotiation was close to resolution with bipartisan political support.

A more fundamental issue that was not faced at the time was whether in the future it would have been proper to develop all the major mines exclusively with foreign companies. In time some form of state participation was necessary, and the question was one only of degree. In 1968, however, thinking on the subject had only begun to evolve as the government became more aware of the very large potential for copper production and exports, and the first priority was to get the Cuajone project started.[27]

[26] This was in pre-Chileanization days. *La Prensa* predictably argued the contrary: Peru was too tough, and that was why there was no investment. It blamed the "hippies" at the Central Bank, who, it claimed, were encouraged by the "leftish exiled Paraguayan, Fernando Vera," who was in fact a long-time career official of the International Monetary Fund and its representative in Peru from mid-1966 to mid-1968.

[27] In fact the Cuajone project was developed under the new gov-

REFINANCING THE EXTERNAL PUBLIC DEBT

As soon as the tax measures and the basis for conversations with the mining companies had been hammered out, the Minister of Finance and the Central Bank devoted a major part of their energies to the refinancing of the external public debt. The Minister saw a clear need to reduce the burden of service of the external debt at a time of slowly expanding exchange inflows. But the enterprise was not begun lightheartedly. The Central Bank in particular warned public opinion that the refinancing was no panacea or easy undertaking:[28]

"The refinancing, either partially or totally, of the external debt of a country is not a simple task. In general a strong economy can easily obtain credit to finance its imports, especially given the interest of the exporter in selling his product to the importing country. The same is not true in the refinancing or in the rescheduling of already established repayment commitments, because such credits do not involve additional export sales for the creditor countries. While the refinancing or the postponement of payments is generally a common procedure in normal commercial life, a very different problem arises when a government (which by virtue of being a government qualifies for a higher credit rating) makes a request of this kind to its creditors, many of which are also governments.

"The moratoriums and massive financial collapses of the thirties led in the post-war period to a restructuring of the international payments system. Besides the creation of the International Monetary Fund and the strengthening of the Bank for International Settlements, other machinery for consultation has arisen. . . . These consultations (which

---

ernment through an exclusive agreement with Southern Peru Copper Corporation, but other smaller projects (such as Cerro Verde) began to be developed by the state enterprise Minero Perú.

[28] Central Bank, *Reseña Económica y Financiera*, third quarter 1968, pp. 2-3.

249

took place in recent years in the cases of Argentina and Brazil, for example) have established that the main reason to justify refinancing a major portion of the external debt of a country must be a balance of payments problem (i.e., a shortage of foreign exchange to meet scheduled payments) and that there must be a recovery program to justify the temporary relief granted by the refinancing. The shortage of domestic resources because of a fiscal deficit does not provide a convincing reason for creditors to grant a significant refinancing.

"In the case of Peru, the service on the external public debt has almost tripled in the last four years in absolute amounts, and represents in 1968 more than double the burden in 1965 in relation to merchandise exports. Another fact worth emphasizing is that this clear trend is taking place at a time when there are no immediate prospects for a sizeable expansion of export earnings, and when the inflow from foreign loans, largely channelled to the public sector, is well below the extraordinary level attained from 1965 to 1967.

"These various related phenomena (the unusual increase in the service on the external public debt, the decline in foreign loan disbursements, and the relative stagnation in the growth of export earnings) are the main reasons which have made it necessary to refinance a major part of the external public debt."

Peru had not until then had any significant experience with the rescheduling or refinancing of external debt. But it was obvious that the creditors would not consider a request unless a convincing case could be made. A prospectus was prepared in the Central Bank explaining the recent measures and showing with projections—for those who believed them—how the proposed refinancing would tide the balance of payments over until there were substantial capital inflows due to investments in copper and to a program of long-term foreign lending for development projects. There was initially no very clear idea of how much the refinancing ought to cover, or of what terms could be obtained. How-

250

ever, the aim was that there should be a grace period on the principal repayments of at least two years and the repayments of principal should thereafter be on a rising scale— if at all possible—so as to be tailored to the increasing foreign exchange inflows.

Several things became clear in the first two weeks of negotiation in early July 1968, first in New York with the main U.S. commercial banks concerned with Peru and then in Paris. First, despite the preparation made in Peru—the prospectus had been distributed in advance to major creditors— the process of refinancing would take much longer than expected. In the meantime, while arrangements were being negotiated, a patchwork of partial payments, postponements, and partial refinancings had to be arrived at. This was done not only because of the need to shore up international reserves, but also in order to put pressure on creditors to arrive quickly at decisions. The Central Bank management spent three difficult months, from late June to the end of September, working on the refinancing, from its most minute details to negotiations in the U.S., Japan, and Europe, while at the same time preparing some of the most important fiscal measures of the sixty days and negotiating a stand-by program with the International Monetary Fund. It was clear from the first day of negotiations that no refinancing agreements would be signed, and probably not even discussed, until there was an agreement with the International Monetary Fund.

A second feature that became apparent early was the difficulty and slowness of discussions in Europe and Japan. The debts to the United States were either to the U.S. government (AID or the Export-Import Bank) or to commercial banks. In the former case the concessionary nature of the terms and the relatively small amount of the debt did not justify a rescheduling. The major commercial banks had, despite their natural dislike of refinancings, an interest in going a long way towards meeting a Peruvian government request: they had a substantial "exposure" in Peru in loans to the government and the private sector. It was therefore in their interest to prevent a balance of payments crisis. Moreover they were the recipients of Peruvian Central Bank and commercial bank deposits, which had reached U.S. $120 million in 1965, and were still U.S. $80 million in mid-1968, with hopes of a future recovery. There were other features of the U.S. banks that were helpful. One was their concentration in New York (the San Francisco and Chicago banks, and also the Canadian banks, all have offices in New York). Decisions were made quickly, with only rapid reference to the top management of the various banks. The officers concerned with Latin America knew the area: preliminaries could be kept to a minimum. Another feature was the sheer size of major U.S. banks.[29] A U.S. $10 or $20 million international loan, which was then a major investment in Paris or London, was probably decided upon in a few minutes by a credit committee in New York.

The situation in Europe, and also in Japan, was quite different. The official Peruvian debts to those countries arose from suppliers' credits for equipment. Whereas in the U.S. only one decision-maker existed—namely the commercial bank involved—in Europe there were three: the bank that had made the financing available, the official export credit guarantee agency that had guaranteed that the bank or the supplier would be paid back, and the Ministry of Finance or Economy, which ultimately decides what the export credit agency can do. Add to this the number of creditor countries (Belgium, France, Finland, Germany, Italy, Japan, Spain, and to a lesser extent Great Britain), and one begins to see the complications of getting agreement among many

---

[29] This was a debatable point in comparison with European banks until it is realized that most of the largest U.S. banks have few branches (with the exception of the California banks), so that much of their resources is devoted to wholesale commercial operations. The large European and Japanese banks have national networks: a large part of their operations are at the retail level and international operations are proportionately less important.

parties. Moreover, it was not possible to tackle each one individually for, although the suppliers had fought with each other to make often indiscriminate and ill-conceived credits to Peru, they wanted to be sure that no one "got away" with giving tougher refinancing or rescheduling terms than they did. Hence the "Paris Club" or "Hague Club" informal arrangements used for debt renegotiations with developing countries.[30]

By the end of September, after three months of negotiations with banks, governments, and the International Monetary Fund, a package had been basically agreed with the creditors. It consisted of U.S. $68 million from the original consortium of U.S. banks,[31] somewhat over U.S. $60 million from other U.S. and Canadian banks, and about U.S. $70 million from European governments and banks and Japanese suppliers through their government. The most difficult negotiations were with the German and Japanese governments. The German government wished to maintain the fiction that no refinancing was really taking place; as a result, it arranged for a loan from the Kreditanstalt für Wiederaufbau, the government bank responsible for long-term loans to developing countries, with disbursements to the Peruvian

[30] The state of knowledge in Peru at that time about refinancing and debt problems in general is illustrated by the question of a senior diplomat in the economic affairs department of the Foreign Ministry. He called the Central Bank to say he was going to Europe and wished to stop in France and Holland to "leave his card" at the "Paris Club" and the "Hague Club." Did we by any chance know the addresses of their buildings?

[31] These were the banks that had participated in the loans of U.S. $40 million in 1965, 1966, and 1967. The lead bank was Manufacturers Hanover, whose then chief Latin American officer, James R. Greene, in 1973-1974 negotiated on behalf of the U.S. government an agreement with Peru for the compensation of various expropriated U.S. company assets. The actual net refinancing effect, including the added interest cost, during 1968-1969 of the U.S. $68 million operation was about U.S. $25 million with the final payments rolled backward from 1971 to 1973 on a schedule of increasing repayments of principal.

government every six months. The trouble was that the disbursements took place *after* the major six-monthly payments on the steel mill debt to Ferrostaal and other German suppliers. Nothing could be done to make the disbursement and payment dates coincide, so that the services of a German commercial bank—with the ensuing interest cost—had to be obtained to bridge the gap of a few weeks between each disbursement and the payments due. In the case of Japan, the difficulties stemmed in part from our ignorance of decision-making in the Japanese government. We received in the space of a month in Lima the visit of three different Japanese officials, who all asked the same questions and got the same answers. In the end, once they were presumably satisfied that we were consistent, we were invited to send a delegation to Tokyo, where two more rounds of talks took place before an agreement was finally reached in December 1968, after the new government had taken over. In fact, although a basic general agreement had been reached with the European creditors in London at the end of September,[32] individual loan agreements were negotiated and signed in December of that year. The majority of the loans from North American banks had been signed before the coup. (See Table 34.)

What was the effect of the refinancing? Was it worth it? In a sense, the question is academic, since there was no alternative to some form of refinancing in 1968: international reserves were very low, the outlook for the immediate expansion of export and other exchange earnings was bleak, and there was hardly any inflow from foreign development loans coming in. The next question is one of method. One

[32] The announcement on September 30 by Minister of Finance Ulloa that the refinancing was "completed" indirectly contributed to the timing of the coup. The incoming government was rather surprised to find that key legal arrangements still had to be worked out and that the refinancing was only partially operating. It took a major effort to get the European governments to maintain the agreement reached in London before the coup. See also Chapter IX, footnote 19.

TABLE 34. TRENDS IN PERU'S EXTERNAL PUBLIC DEBT 1962-69
(in millions of dollars; includes private debt guaranteed by the government)

	1962	1963	1964	1965	1966	1967	1968	1969
Total outstanding, excluding undisbursed amounts	180.1	243.1	317.3	435.1	592.8	704.9	801.2	927.1
of which from								
suppliers	47.8	87.3	124.6	149.7	216.0	249.4	261.4	301.4
foreign commercial banks	17.1	15.6	18.8	44.7	68.9	106.7	134.9[b]	197.5[b]
other[a]	115.2	140.2	173.9	240.7	307.9	348.8	404.9	428.2
Total service	40.7	41.2	47.4	49.0	93.4	99.5	135.2[c]	147.5[c]
Interest	9.3[d]	9.4	14.4	15.7	24.6	33.6	49.6	48.8
Amortization	31.4	31.8	33.0	33.3	68.8	66.0	85.6	98.7
Service as a percentage of f.o.b. merchandise exports[e]	7.9	7.4	8.6	7.1	11.8	13.3	16.0	16.7

[a] Largely IBRD, IDB, U.S. government, and the "old dollar bonds."
[b] Includes the refinancing of debts in 1968 and in 1969 by foreign banks and by foreign governments on terms similar to those of commercial banks.
[c] Before the refinancing.
[d] Estimate.
[e] Normally, exports of goods and (non-factor) services, less remittances abroad arising from reports, would be a more precise measure. Merchandise exports amount to about the same and are more readily identified.
SOURCE: Compiled from data from Central Bank, including *Reseña Económica y Financiera*.

possibility would have been to obtain one or two large free foreign exchange loans from banks in New York and London, avoiding the confrontation of a creditors' meeting in Europe, and the resulting if temporary ill effect on Peru's image as a debtor. This is the pattern that countries with an image of strength in their balance of payments have followed in recent years, with success in terms of avoiding a debt crisis. Peru's case was different, however. It was just beginning to emerge from two years of financial and political crisis. It is doubtful, therefore, if anything like the amounts of the 1968 refinancing could have been obtained without a full-scale examination with the creditors. The alternative of a publicly recognized refinancing exercise, therefore, was not so much chosen as imposed by circumstances.

The effect of the approximately U.S. $198 million of gross loans obtained in 1968 as part of the refinancing was a reduction of about U.S. $120 million in debt service in 1968 and 1969, after counting the interest cost of the new loans in those years. In addition, there was a postponement of various other payments due in 1971 and 1972 (see table below). The interest costs averaged about 7.5 percent at the time, but we projected the future interest cost at an average of about 8 percent because of the likely increase in Eurodollar rates.[33] The real cost of the refinancing, weighing the present benefit of a reduction of debt service against

[33] The annual interest rates ranged from a flat 5 percent in the case of the French Treasury refinancing of U.S. $4.5 million to 2¼ percent premium over the six-month Eurodollar deposit rate (then about 7 percent, plus the 2¼ percent premium) for two loans from London and Paris banks totalling U.S. $5 million. All the North American loans carried an interest rate of 1¾ percent over the "prime rate" (then 6 percent plus the 1¾ percent premium), with an upper ceiling on the total charge of 8¾ percent. It was not possible to obtain such a ceiling on the two small Eurodollar loans. The Belgian loan carried a flat 8 percent rate and the Spanish one a flat 7½ percent rate. The Kreditanstalt für Wiederaufbau loan carried a moveable rate of 3 percent above the Bundesbank discount rate (then 3¾ percent plus the 3 percent premium).

the future cost of additional debt service, was estimated at the time at 9 percent, certainly a modest amount in comparison with the opportunity cost of foreign exchange in an economy such as that of Peru. (See Table 35.)

One obvious criticism of the refinancing was the relatively high debt service burden that resulted in 1970 and 1971. This was the result of being unable, despite hard bargaining—including frequent breakdowns of the negotiations— to obtain a longer repayment period.[34] Therefore, a greater margin of safety was needed for 1970 and 1971. For this purpose, the Central Bank, at the initiative of Minister Ulloa, negotiated a stand-by credit with a group of North American and European banks. A subsidiary purpose of the stand-by was to open more contacts with European banks: the Central Bank had little knowledge of what European banks could offer.[35] Thus, the negotiation of the stand-by arrangement was a complicated affair, almost more so than the refinancing itself. The problems of negotiation had been largely ironed out by the time of the coup. The stand-by was to be usable up to June 1971, in proportion to drawings from the International Monetary Fund. In fact, it was never used. An interesting aspect of the negotiations was the large number of banks required to put together the U.S. $25 million provided by European banks; this was in part by design, so as to get an exposure to several banks in various countries, but it was also a reflection of the caution of European banks about Latin American loans. The German banks, for example, felt that they could not participate without a German government guarantee, even though the borrower was a Central Bank. In the end, 33 European banks agreed to put together U.S. $25 million, as against 11 banks for U.S. $65 million in the United States and Canada.

[34] Even after an ultimatum and stoppage of payments by the next government in 1969, the average term obtained in the 1969 refinancing was only one year longer than in 1968.

[35] The rapid growth of London as the center of the Eurodollar market had just begun a year or two earlier.

TABLE 35. EFFECT OF THE PARTIAL REFINANCING IN 1968 OF THE EXTERNAL PUBLIC DEBT (in millions of U.S. dollars)

	1968	1969	1970	1971	1972	1973	1974	1975
Original service due on debt as of mid-1968	135.2	147.5	141.0	139.7	125.9	118.4	83.8	73.6
Net effect, after interest charges, of refinancing	*−59.3*	*−58.4*	*22.2*	*30.6*	*41.5*	*50.4*	*19.0*	*0.5*
U.S. and Canadian banks	*−36.3*	*−28.8*	*16.0*	*16.0*	*25.9*	*34.8*	*3.7*	*0.5*
European and Japanese governments and banks (estimate)	*−23.0*	*−29.6*	*6.2*	*14.6*	*15.6*	*15.6*	*15.3*	—
New service on debt as of end of 1968	76.4	89.1	163.2	170.3	167.4	168.8	102.4	74.1
	Actuals				*Projected (as of 1968)*			
Merchandise exports	842.6	885.0	860.0	920.0	1,030.0	1,120.0	1,200.0	1,240.0
of which additional exports due to copper investments[a]	—	—	(10)	(30)	(100)	(150)	(200)	(200)
Original service as percentage of merchandise exports	16.0	16.7	16.4	15.2	12.2	10.6	7.0	5.9
New service as percentage of merchandise exports	9.1	10.1	19.0	18.5	16.3	15.1	8.5	6.0

[a] Assuming copper export price of U.S. 38 cents f.o.b.
SOURCE: Central Bank, *Reseña Económica y Financiera*, fourth quarter 1968, and material submitted to London meetings of creditors, July and September 1968.

CHAPTER IX

Coup

PRESIDENT BELAÚNDE was deposed from office by a military coup in the early hours of October 3, 1968. According to the semi-official history of the coup by Zimmermann,[1] General Velasco led the arrangements for the coup. He had begun the preparations in April 1968—according to the Zimmermann account—and by May, at the height of the political and economic difficulties of the Ferrero Cabinet, had expanded the group of collaborators to three Army generals besides himself, and five colonels.[2] Again according to Zimmermann, the team that entered into office on October 3, 1968 arrived with a complete blueprint—*El Plan Inca*—of all the major economic, social, and political measures that were taken later, in the period 1968-1974.[3]

The coup thus seems to have been in a state of latent preparation for about six months. It came at a time when Peru seemed to be starting a period of economic and financial recovery, but when President Belaúnde faced a serious political crisis. The crisis had several origins, including the uncertainties of the previous months, the increasing proximity of the 1969 presidential and parliamentary elections, and the growing division within Acción Popular. However, the detonating factor that brought the various forces together into a crisis was the sequel to the agreement of

[1] Zimmermann, Augusto, *El Plan Inca*, etc. *op.cit.* See complete reference, footnote 24, Chapter VIII.

[2] Zimmermann, *El Plan Inca*, p. 45, *El Equipo de Nueve.*

[3] Zimmermann, *El Plan Inca*, pp. 105-123, *El Plan de Gobierno.* No plan was divulged at the time of the coup. The publication of the plan came five years later.

the government with the International Petroleum Company (IPC) on August 12, 1968. The IPC affair also stimulated a speeding-up of the preparations for the coup.

WHY AN AGREEMENT WITH IPC?

During the period since the post-devaluation increase in gasoline prices in November 1967, the IPC issue had appeared to be dormant. However, on August 13, 1968, it burst into the headlines with the news that President Belaúnde had received from IPC that morning the formal transfer, in Talara, of La Brea y Pariñas. The President, a host of officials, and IPC representatives had flown to Talara in the morning of August 13, after an all-night negotiating session that had at least once been on the brink of failure. The U.S. Ambassador, J. Wesley Jones—an experienced diplomat who had been in Peru since 1962—had to be roused at 3 a.m. to intervene with the company. At Talara, Belaúnde said that the agreement settled all claims between Peru and IPC. Yet, seven weeks later Belaúnde was out of office, and a few days after that most of IPC was taken over by a military government. How is it that Belaúnde allowed himself to be drawn into a situation that developed easily into the setting for the coup?

Several issues stand out in an analysis of the agreement with IPC. Perhaps the least important is the agreement itself (actually, several separate agreements), which few bothered to read, then or now.[4] The key issues are why Belaúnde thought it was so important to reach an agreement with IPC; the political context of the agreement; and a series of circumstantial and coincidental events that were important in sealing the eventual fate of the agreement.

President Belaúnde had become convinced after five years in office that IPC was the millstone around his neck. The financial problems of his regime would be alleviated if AID

[4] English translations of the texts can be found in *International Legal Materials*, 1969, pp. 1217 ff.

could lend Peru the same amounts it made available to Chile or Colombia. Instead of relying on expensive suppliers' credits, loans from the IDB soft window and from AID would now become plentiful. Belaúnde was not wrong in his assumptions about AID funds. Immediately after the agreement with IPC, it became clear that the AID mission in Peru was working hard to put together a large lending program, including a possible "program" or general-purpose loan. There is thus little doubt, on the basis of the AID record in Peru before and after August 1968, that President Belaúnde was right about AID lending to Peru. Moreover, he was probably correct in thinking that AID financing would help Peru to overcome its fiscal and financial problems. This was so not so much because of the amount of possible AID financing, but because of the particularly opportune moment at which it would have come. A large tax package had just been passed, the rescheduling on longer terms of about one-quarter of the external public debt was virtually complete, and various important promotional measures had just been passed. Moreover, very important progress had already been achieved in the negotiations for large new investments by the mining companies. A complete turnaround in the fiscal situation was becoming clearly visible in the second half of 1968. While the effect of the mining investments would have been longer in coming, that gap could have been bridged by AID.

In fact, it is not far-fetched to speculate that Peru in 1968-1969 was set to enter a period of rapid economic growth. After the post-devaluation adjustment and with the period of fiscal and financial instability over, the domestic private sector was ready to start major investments in manufacturing. The trend would have been reinforced by the demands upon the domestic manufacturing and construction industries of the new mining investments. In 1970, due to the coincidence of high prices for fishmeal and copper, merchandise export earnings did in fact increase by 20 percent to over $1 billion. In an atmosphere of expanding pub-

lic and private investment, this record would have reinforced the psychological atmosphere of expansion. Events
in other countries in Latin America, such as Brazil and
Colombia, have shown that a period of rapid growth can be
ushered in and kept going even though one element of the
initial drive—such as exports—may lose momentum in a
particular year. In Peru there would have been a diversity
of possible elements, more or less coinciding in time: a large
increase in official external aid, the largest expansion in mining investment since the late fifties (the annual expenditures
on the three largest mining projects, about U.S. $120 million,
would have been equivalent to 2 percent of the 1970 GDP,
or 17 percent of 1970 gross investment), a jump in export
prices in 1970, and two years of good weather for agriculture in 1969 and 1970.

President Belaúnde had been right in seeing that some
agreement with IPC would unlock the foreign aid door. The
next question was what sort of agreement would be sufficient, and at what political price. This was the basic problem. The general public and political view of IPC was very
negative compared to five years earlier. Important groups
were against IPC: a majority of Congress, several of the
senior officers in the army, one of the two major dailies was
increasing its vociferousness against it, and a large part of
the president's own party was equally set against IPC. Any
negotiations with IPC, even though they might involve the
transfer of IPC facilities to the government, were thus
bound to provoke a strong reaction. Largely because of the
campaign by *El Comercio*, IPC had become for much of
Lima opinion a sort of national enemy; very few people
indeed were "for" IPC. In these circumstances, the only type
of agreement that would have been politically palatable—
or at least, against which active opinion would not have had
much to say—would have involved the end of any IPC involvement in Peru. Whether this could have been achieved
by an agreement between the Peruvian government and
IPC is unlikely; IPC would probably have insisted on mone-

262

tary compensation, which the Belaúnde government would have been in no position to offer, politically or financially.

Faced with the choice of nothing or some sort of agreement, the president chose the latter. Despite the opposition that an agreement of virtually any kind was bound to provoke, two factors were thought to be in favor of it: the prospect of external assistance, and the attitude of APRA. It was sometimes said that there was a "deal" between Belaúnde and APRA; the APRA-dominated Congress, according to this argument, approved the sixty-day authorization for financial measures by the Executive in exchange for a firm promise by Belaúnde and Ulloa that they would resolve the IPC issue. Such an agreement is most unlikely to have taken place: APRA would probably have insisted that the IPC part of the "deal" be done first; moreover, it is improbable that APRA would have insisted on a politically extremely difficult solution, which might bring on a coup, thus endangering APRA's chances in the 1969 elections. Nevertheless, there is no doubt that APRA was actively interested in some kind of agreement.

The ambivalence in the APRA attitude was reflected in a lack of clarity in the public pronouncements of the party on the IPC question. When the agreement came under strong attack in September 1968, the APRA leadership did very little to defend it, and thus helped to perpetrate the atmosphere that favored the demise of the Belaúnde government.

Background to the Agreement

A number of special circumstances surrounded the agreement: the rush to get it out before the expiration on August 19 of the sixty-day extraordinary authorization of Law 17044, the position and personality of the head of EPF, and the emergence of a coalition between those opposed to the tax reforms and those against the IPC agreement.

Why rush the IPC agreement? The Belaúnde administration still had ten months before the elections due in June

263

1969. Although an agreement reached after August 19 would have had to go to Congress for approval[5] there were strong political reasons for believing that an action of such importance should go to Congress anyway. The main reason for the rush was the desire of the Cabinet to show that in sixty days all the major problems could be solved. The ministers and the president went along with Ulloa, probably because of a "let's get it over with" attitude, understandable enough after the Congressional opposition of previous years. In any event, the speed with which the agreement was negotiated was a mistake, not because more time would necessarily have made much difference to the substance of the agreement but because it opened the agreement to criticism as an inside job on which there had been little consultation.

A major figure in the events surrounding the agreement was Carlos Loret de Mola. Then in his forties, he had been the government-appointed president (i.e., chairman of the board) of Empresa Petrolera Fiscal (EPF), the state oil concern, for several years. He was a prosperous engineer, from a family with large investments in mines; he was politically ambitious and had boosted his image by the expansion of EPF—especially the La Pampilla refinery outside Lima, inaugurated in 1967—and the advertising campaign with which the expansion was accompanied. In giving his advice to President Belaúnde about what ought to be done with IPC, Loret de Mola had been a moderate.[6] EPF had been given authority in January 1968 to "definitely resolve"

---

[5] Because the authorization for special financial measures under Law 17044 expired on that date. However, it was questionable whether Law 17044 gave sufficient authority for an agreement with IPC, since the agreement was not directly aimed at solving the fiscal and financial problem. Although Law 16674 of July 1967, in its third article, gave wide powers to the Executive to expropriate and to work out arrangements with IPC, Article 5 stated that these actions had to be undertaken within thirty-one days.

[6] In fact, according to President Belaúnde, early in 1968 Loret de Mola suggested a formula that was allegedly more favorable to IPC than the final arrangement.

the IPC issue.[7] Loret de Mola was therefore naturally apprehensive that the problem was now increasingly handled by Minister of Finance Ulloa, as part of the measures under the sixty-day authorization by Congress. Moreover, Loret's term as President of EPF was to expire before the end of 1968. With a lame-duck government, it was probably better for him to leave with a bang than to stay on an extra few months, especially if his reputed political hopes were to be fulfilled.

A key element in the events of August and September was the deterioration of the political position of the government, which stood in the middle, devoid of major allies. The business interests, never great supporters of the government, were being harangued into action by almost daily editorials in *La Prensa* attacking the recent fiscal reforms and banking legislation. In the center, the APRA, although it had given the sixty-day authorization, was not about to be overly friendly to a government it was hoping to defeat in the coming elections. Late in August, Armando Villanueva, the APRA leader who had been closely consulted on the main measures of the sixty days and had been part of a delegation that visited Washington D.C. in June, introduced a motion in the Chamber of Deputies to rescind a part of the gasoline tax increase, which was the main revenue-producing measure in the immediate fiscal program.[8] Worst of all, there were signs of an increasing division in Acción Popular. The division had of course been there for several years, sometimes overtly. But, as Belaúnde was getting near to stepping down, his unifying powers were bound to diminish; moreover the ascendance of Ulloa, who was said to be close to the Carlistas,[9] tended to alienate the *termocéfalos* or rad-

[7] Decree 7F of January 27, 1968.

[8] The move did not succeed, partly because of a strong Central Bank intervention with the leaders of Congress, but a similar reduction was in any case decreed by the new government a few months later.

[9] So-called because of the first name of their leading members,

icals in the party and those others who felt that they should be playing leading roles in the presidential contest. The split was to become public and violent in the following weeks, further weakening the government in the debate on the IPC agreement.

THE AUGUST 1968 AGREEMENT WITH IPC

The agreement with IPC reached in mid-August 1968 and declared null and void by the armed forces on October 4, 1968, in fact consisted of several separate documents, of which the main ones were the transfer of La Brea y Pariñas to the government, a ten-year contract for the sale of natural gas by EPF to IPC, and a similar six-year contract for the sale of La Brea y Pariñas crude to the IPC refinery at Talara. The last of these was the major cause of the subsequent controversy, in which the main agreement for the transfer of La Brea y Pariñas did not play a significant role.[10]

Carlos Ferreyros—a major industrialist, Carlos Muñoz—a personal friend of Belaúnde, and Carlos Velarde.

[10] The major legal documents involved in the agreements were: Supreme Decree 080-68-FO of August 9, 1968 (based on Law 17044—the sixty-day authorization) approving the draft agreement of transfer of La Brea y Pariñas and authorizing various officials to sign it; the notarized agreement itself, dated August 12, 1968, and signed by the Minister of Public Works and a senior Finance Ministry official, and the IPC General Manager in Peru, Mr. Fernando Espinoza; contracts of the same date for the sale by EPF to IPC of natural gas and of crude, signed by Carlos Loret de Mola (EPF) and the IPC General Manager in Peru; Supreme Decree 088-68-FO of August 13, 1968, establishing a transitional period until December 31, 1968, for the physical transfer of operations at La Brea y Pariñas from IPC to EPF; and three Supreme Resolutions (0020/1/2-68-FO/PE) of August 14, 1968 granting IPC 40-year concessions under the petroleum law for the operation of the Talara refinery, a plant in Callao, and various storage facilities and plants elsewhere in Peru. The *Acta de Talara*, a label sometimes used for the agreements with IPC, is in fact the official minutes of the transfer ceremony, attended

In the main agreement of August 12, 1968, between the government and IPC, "the government declares that, pursuant to the provisions of Laws Nos. 14696 and 16674, the La Brea y Pariñas oilfields belong to the state and are its property" and "International reiterates that it acknowledges the eminent domain of the Peruvian state, derived from its sovereignty over the surface and subsoil of the La Brea y Pariñas fields" (first clause). The third clause was the other major one; it stated "that the so-called pending matters regarding La Brea y Pariñas are hereby totally resolved and settled, making it a matter of record that . . . any debts that International may have owed the government derived from its occupancy and/or that of its predecessors of La Brea y Pariñas are considered definitely cancelled, as also those [debts] from the operations carried out such as the extraction of the products and/or the profits of said oilfields." The remainder of the clause made clear that this agreement applied to all debts, whether due to changes in the tax treatment of IPC, the profits from extraction, etc. The rest of the agreement defined the extent of the La Brea y Pariñas area and the facilities on it.

The second major piece were the agreements for the sale of natural gas and of crude from La Brea y Pariñas to IPC. Within the total operations of IPC, gas was not important. The price agreed for the gas was subject to upward adjustment depending on the price of fuel oil,[11] and the contract was for a long period of ten years.[12] The central document in the subsequent controversy was the crude contract, which had a life of six years. The most important feature of the crude contract—and the one over which negotiations nearly broke down on the night of August 12—was the price at which EPF would sell to IPC. The price implicit in the

---

by President Belaúnde and his Cabinet, at La Brea y Pariñas on August 13, 1968.

[11] 4th clause of the natural gas sales agreement.

[12] 2nd clause of the natural gas sales agreement.

agreement was adjustable upward, subject to government approval, during the six-year contract whenever the price of gasoline was raised by more than 10 percent. The price computation can be derived as follows:

Item	Clause in Contract	Soles per barrel
a. Base price received by EPF for crude 36.0°-36.9° API gravity	4th clause	89.00
b. Less discount because of guaranteed market	6th clause	−8.90
c. Less cost of storage by IPC	9th clause	−3.87
Sub-total		76.23
d. Less maximum cost of services (for water, gas, etc.) by IPC to EPF of up to 45 percent of sub-total	10th clause	−34.30
Total minimum price (Equivalent in U.S. $ at rate of S/. 38.70 applicable under Certificate Exchange legislation to petroleum transactions)		41.93
		$1.08

There are several important features in this price computation. First, the final minimum wellhead price of S/. 41.93 was not quoted in the agreement. It could be easily derived, as was done in the above table, from the various clauses in the agreement, but it was not specifically quoted. Why? Presumably because the cost of IPC services to EPF had not been worked out, although the fact that the cost of services was to be a maximum of 45 percent of the sub-total ought to have permitted a minimum price to be quoted. Second, the prices were all in soles, not in dollars. This became the subject of criticism, but in fact the quotation in soles was the correct procedure. The Peruvian commercial code does not recognize the quotation of prices in foreign currency for internal transactions; moreover, it was probably a good idea—in the light of the experience after the 1967 devaluation—to break the direct link between the exchange rate and gasoline prices, since Peru was still largely self-sufficient in petroleum. The third and probably most important feature of the computation was its complexity: why these various discounts and adjustments instead of a flat figure? When the government had to explain the agreement a few weeks later, the computation turned out to be, as might have been expected, a political liability.

The wellhead price of U.S. $1.08 equivalent per barrel was low by international standards. For example, Venezuelan crude, the most relevant for a comparison with Peru, in 1968 had a landed price at Peruvian refineries of around U.S. $2.80 per barrel,[13] varying up or down in relation to quality and gravity, a far distance from U.S. $1.08 per barrel. The fact that U.S. $1.08 was a wellhead price does not explain the difference between a wellhead price and the international price at the refinery.[14] The main reason for the big difference was the desire to keep domestic gasoline prices low, after leaving room for the gasoline excise tax. Still, one wonders whether the profit margin that the Empresa Petrolera Fiscal would have had at the U.S. $1.08 price would not have been less than that enjoyed by IPC. This of course cannot be proved without cost data of IPC for the period after the 1967 devaluation.

Another problematic issue in the various agreements was the forty-year concession the government granted IPC to continue operating the Talara refinery. While IPC could legitimately argue—as it did—that it needed a long concession in order to renovate and expand the aging plant, a forty-year period was well beyond the commercial require-

---

[13] For crude with a gravity of 31°-31.9°.

[14] Depending on distance, etc., the difference between cost at the wellhead and at a nearby refinery (as was the case at Talara) could normally be in the range of 10 percent.

ments to recover such an investment. Politically, of course, "forty more years of IPC" was scarcely a viable proposition in the political atmosphere of Peru in 1967-1968.

PAGE ELEVEN AND DÉNOUEMENT

For a couple of weeks after the announcement of the agreement with IPC, there was peace and quiet on the domestic political scene. Suddenly, however, on September 10, all that changed. Carlos Loret de Mola charged on television that the last page of the crude oil sale agreement between EPF and IPC was missing. He implied that the page had been deliberately mislaid, and that it contained an important part of the overall agreement with IPC, namely the sum that explained the price of $1.08.[15] Within a week, his allegations had become the center of a major political scandal, which sparked a formal split in Acción Popular and the downfall of the Hercelles Cabinet. Within a month President Belaúnde was out of office.

Several factors combined to give Loret de Mola's allegations prominence. First, *La Prensa* and *El Comercio* were for once united on an issue, *El Comercio* because of its traditional stance on IPC, and *La Prensa* because it saw a marvellous opportunity to embarrass the government after the tax reforms and increases that Beltrán opposed. Secondly, the government itself magnified the issue by trying to kill a fly with a sledge-hammer: repeated television appearances were made by Finance Minister Ulloa (substituting for the Minister in charge of petroleum questions, Pablo Carriquiry, who was in Europe when the controversy began) and various other members of the Hercelles Cabinet. The

[15] Zimmermann, *El Plan Inca*, seems to argue (p. 72) that this sum was secret until Loret de Mola revealed its existence. In fact, as was shown above, the elements of the sum were clearly set forth in the agreement. The actual content of the supposedly lost material, therefore, would have been of no importance, if the sum was what it contained, as Loret de Mola charged.

show on television only served to build up the image of Loret de Mola, whose term as head of EPF was in any case about to end (he resigned before then).

The highly polemical nature of the debate did not bring out clearly the main issues: (1) the principal agreement between the government and IPC was not under discussion, but only the six-year crude agreement between EPF and IPC; (2) since Loret de Mola (and not the government) had signed the crude agreement, he should have been responsible for seeing that a complete original of the agreement was duly kept; and (3) what Loret de Mola claimed was contained on the eleventh page, namely a "sumilla" (summary calculation) written by him in ink of the crude price equivalent to $1.08, in fact could be calculated from the first ten pages of the agreement, as was shown in the table above.

Was there in fact a page 11? Probably so. The government has never been able to show it, and neither has Loret de Mola. The number of the page was supposed to be 28160934, since the numbers of the two previous pages in the four-page folio of official paper were 28160932 and 3.[16] One plausible interpretation is that the main text ended at the bottom of page 10. Since Decree paper must be fully filled and must not be corrected (if a correction is necessary, the page has to be typed again), when in the rush in the night of August 12 to 13 it was discovered that the typist had ended the agreement at the bottom of the tenth page (page 28160933), leaving no room for final signatures, it was decided to have the agreement signed on a blank eleventh page (page 28160934). Loret de Mola claims that this is where he put down his interpretation of the price. This was of course a unilateral action on his part: he did not claim that IPC had signed the eleventh page. Since every previous

[16] Nevertheless, there is an apparent confusion about the numbering of pages. On p. 61 (footnote) of El Plan Inca, Zimmermann says that page 10, of which he shows a photostat (without the number of the official paper), is "the first page of the third folio." That would make it page 9, since each folio has four pages.

271

page had been initialled by him and IPC, and since the price was the result of various clauses in those first ten pages, he could scarcely claim that what he himself added in ink at the end of the agreement—without the signature of the other party to the agreement—had any legal value. Nevertheless, in the September debate Loret de Mola— probably with the advice of others, supposedly from *El Comercio*—picked on a fundamental political weakness of the agreement, namely the lack of simple clarity about the formulation of the price for crude. Loret de Mola also made much of the fact that the price should have been in dollars; however, as explained above, this was a less important point and was in any case probably not feasible from a legal point of view.

Why did Loret de Mola turn against an agreement that he himself had signed only two weeks before and that had been approved by the EPF board over which he presided? One possible guess is that it was a combination of personal factors—ambition, possibly of presidential dimensions in view of the visibility of the IPC issue; the rapid rise of Ulloa as possible presidential candidate of the Belaúnde wing of Acción Popular; and the evident cooling of relations between Loret de Mola and President Belaúnde. The general political situation—a lame-duck president with a divided party confronting various groups hungry for power— also may have given Loret de Mola extra encouragement. There is no way of knowing any of this.[17]

The challenge of Loret de Mola presented President Belaúnde with a very serious political problem. The credibility of his government was at stake. Page 28160934 could not be produced.

However, Belaúnde had one source of strength: the het-

---

[17] Zimmermann, *El Plan Inca*, p. 69, cites honesty and patriotism as Loret de Mola's main motives. Zimmermann was said at the time to be a close adviser of Loret de Mola. Zimmermann (p. 69) acknowledges that they were close friends.

erogeneity of the opposition, which consisted of elements as different as APRA, Beltrán, and radical groups. Nevertheless, his strength evaporated when his own party split, ostensibly on the IPC issue. The split in Acción Popular was not new. Since the party did not have the local grass-roots organization of APRA, there were no countervailing forces for cohesion when the leaders disagreed among themselves. The Seoane prime ministership had embittered relations between Belaúnde and the "termocéfalo" wing of the party. The IPC settlement widened the differences much further. However, in the end, personalities were probably more important than issues, and the rise of Ulloa contributed, despite his efforts at conciliation, to splitting the party further. With the "página once" scandal in full swing, almost daily editorials in *La Prensa* calling for an end to the Belaúnde government, *El Comercio* in a shrill campaign against the government, the split within Acción Popular became impossible to conceal. On September 20 Seoane issued a communiqué stating that he could no longer support the agreement with IPC and demanding its immediate abrogation. A few days later, a group of the anti-government wing of the party tried to take over the party headquarters in the center of Lima; the police had to be called in, tear gas was thrown, and the would-be assailants did not get in. The spectacle of the president's party split and demonstrating on one of the main streets of downtown Lima was, to say the least, most embarrassing to the government.

The political disarray following the IPC agreement masked genuine progress on the financial side. The refinancing package to be buttressed by a stand-by credit from United States, Canadian, and European banks was in the last stages of negotiation. The regulations for the implementation of the various tax reforms, especially the income and property taxes, were being prepared at a feverish pace. The USAID mission was working on a large package of loans, including a general purpose or "program" loan. The net

273

foreign exchange reserves, despite the jumpiness of the draft market as a result of political uncertainty, were recovering rapidly.[18]

Far from helping to cool political difficulties, the financial improvement whetted the appetites of those opposed to the government. In fact, a reason sometimes given for the timing of the coup was the statement by the Executive, just before his cabinet resigned at the end of September, that the refinancing arrangements were complete.[19] On September 30, Armando Villanueva of APRA once more (after bringing down the Ferrero Cabinet earlier in the year) went on television to call for a new government. The Hercelles Cabinet was at that point finished. President Belaúnde, who had in any case thought of the Hercelles Cabinet as an emergency fire brigade, felt that he could put in one more Cabinet before his term was up in July 1969. However, the reasons for changing the Cabinet were not clear to the public, for whom the impending change appeared as one more sign of instability. In any case, when the new Cabinet was sworn in at the presidential palace on October 2, the proponents of a coup had already decided that the moment had come to strike.[20]

The composition of the new Cabinet can only have given more courage to the proponents of a coup, although it probably had no influence on their decision. The new Prime Minister was Miguel Mujica Gallo, clearly a member of the old

[18] Central Bank reserves had risen from U.S. $69.4 million at the end of May to U.S. $91.0 million at the end of September.

[19] This was formally incorrect, since the Agreed Minutes with the European governments and Japan approved in London in the last days of September had to be followed by individual negotiations with each creditor government. The military government was quite surprised, a few days later, to find that work was still needed to complete the refinancing.

[20] See Zimmermann, El Plan Inca, p. 93. Earlier, on September 20, according to Zimmermann (p. 78), General Velasco had cancelled a trip to a conference in Brazil on hearing a rumor that he was about to be relieved by President Belaúnde.

Establishment. Mujica, a distinguished collector of Peruvian antiquities, had personally put together the most comprehensive and beautiful collection of Pre-Columbian gold objects, which was shown to the public in a wing of his house. He was also noted for his safaris to East Africa. His political credentials and experience were not apparent, however. In an effort to bring a non-controversial Prime Minister from outside Acción Popular, Belaúnde appeared to have brought in an outsider with little political clout. Some of the new Ministers had been in previous Cabinets, and some new faces were brought in, including, as Labor Minister, Alfonso Grados, a senior Interamerican Development Bank official who had in the past hoped for the Finance Ministry. Except for Ulloa, who was retained, the Cabinet did not give an impression of particular strength.[21]

In any event, the new Ministers did not have more than a few hours at their desks. At 1 a.m. on Thursday, October 3, an armoured column left the headquarters of the Tank Division and made its way to the presidential palace. Despite many rumors of a possible coup, no special precautions had been taken at the palace.[22] The presidential guard offered no resistance, and the chief military aide to the president was sleeping at home instead of at the palace. Belaúnde was roused out of bed at 2 a.m. and bundled off in his pajamas to a barracks, from which he was taken at 7 a.m. to the runway of the international airport at Callao. There an APSA[23] jet was waiting to take him to Argentina. Al-

[21] Some political figures of that period have alleged in conversation that the retention of Ulloa was like "waving a red flag" at the military leaders, thus leading to the coup. While there was undoubtedly animosity on the part of some military leaders to Ulloa, the thesis that his retention on October 2 led to the coup the following day appears to have no validity.

[22] According to very close friends of Belaúnde, he appeared for several weeks before the coup to be drugged, presumably by someone in the presidential palace.

[23] APSA was the privately owned international Peruvian airline. It has since ceased to operate. Its president at the time was Máximo

though there was much arguing in the morning between the Navy—whose commander refused to join the coup—and the Army leaders, by midday, despite a large demonstration and some shooting in downtown Lima, the coup was an event of the past.

Five years of constitutional government had ended.

Cisneros Sánchez, a lawyer, political figure, and, as legal adviser to the Navy, a Rear Admiral.

CHAPTER X

Epilogue

ALMOST eight years have passed since the end of the Belaúnde administration. Perhaps this is too short an interval
for history to be written. Nevertheless, some of the lessons
can probably be sketched.

The fact that the democratic regime was expelled through
a coup cannot but create a sense of failure, magnified by the
impression that Peru at present seems unable to return to
some form of democratic government. Yet there is no doubt
that the Belaúnde administration left a political legacy that
could be built upon in the future. The achievements were
important: the idea of popular participation in economic
development, a working system of democratic municipal
government, collective bargaining and peace in industrial
relations, a sense of the importance of the Sierra, and a shift
in the appeal of government from the center in Lima to the
provinces. On the economic front, while rapid modernization was inevitably enough concentrated in the largest urban areas, the government did make an effort through public health and especially education to spread some of the
benefits of growth much more widely than before. A new
area of Peru was opened up through the *Carretera Marginal*.
While the redistribution of income was mostly within the
"modern sector,"[1] a real widening of incomes did take place
in the main cities. The evolution of Peru was paralleled by
a shift in political power: the stereotyped vision of Peru as a
country controlled by a few landowning families was cer-

[1] See Richard C. Webb, *Government Policy and the Distribution
of Income in Peru, 1963-1973*, Discussion Paper No. 39, Research
Program in Economic Development, Woodrow Wilson School, Princeton University, June 1973.

tainly not at all valid at the end of the Belaúnde government, due to the combined effect of government policies and of the thrust of development away from plantation agriculture.

Yet, even at the time there was a feeling that more might have been done, that the economic crisis of the last two years of the government could have been largely avoided, and that the Belaúnde era, which had begun with great hopes and potential, ended in disappointment. Some of this frustration came from the view, described at the beginning of this book, that development ought to be a smooth process, patently an unrealizable dream. Still, there was a genuine feeling of unrealized potential.

Many far-reaching changes have taken place in Peru since October 1968. Any lessons that can be learned from the period 1963-1968 have been in some cases superseded by subsequent events. Still, there is some merit in reviewing some of these lessons as viewed from the perspective of 1968 rather than of the mid-seventies.

The institutional experience of 1963-1968 was perhaps not the most important one, but it left behind a number of lessons. One was that a specially designed political constitution is necessary if a government with a modicum of democracy is to govern and survive in a country at a level of development—social and political—similar to that of Peru. Of course, changes in a written constitution cannot by themselves be expected to go to the root of the question of balancing sufficient executive authority with a degree of parliamentary democracy. But such modifications can make a difference. A major needed point is the avoidance of a system of proportional representation in elections for Congress, which in the case of Peru under Belaúnde sharpened the fragmentation of parties in Congress. With the low level of political education of the electorate, proportional representation is bound to create strong centripetal forces. Political scientists and constitutional experts will always debate whether a parliament should be a mirror of political opinion in the country or whether there should be restraints, such as exist in the English and American electoral systems, where there is one representative per constituency or district. In Peru, under a modified system, Odriismo and the Christian Democrats would have had fewer representatives and the parliamentary battle would have become a clearer one.

Doing away with proportional representation by itself would not do much without a system of mid-term elections. The 1933 constitution of Peru does not provide the usual advantages of a parliamentary system (where the Prime Minister can call for elections under certain conditions) nor the safeguards of the U.S. presidential system, where Congressional elections take place half-way through each presidential term. A democratically elected Peruvian president with a minority position in Parliament at the beginning of his term cannot, under the 1933 constitution, do anything about it during his six-year term. If to this is added the right of Congress to remove a Minister by censure (a right exercised half a dozen times by Congress in the Belaúnde government), the system clearly had in it the makings of political instability.

A second area is that of economic management, where basic political institutions were antiquated. The constitutional system established in 1933—at a time when the idea of economic development was still incipient in many of the poorer countries—did not make room for a rational system of economic management and planning. Congress could initiate expenditures and conduct fiscal policy while paying little heed to the Executive. In the Executive, the Cabinet system in theory gave as much of a say to the Air Force Minister, for example, as to the Finance Minister on a tax question. The Ministry of Industry could be dispensing tax exemptions to industry at a time when the aim of the government was to raise revenues as much as possible. Clearly, many of these problems are typical of any government; nevertheless, a modern set of institutions could help.

279

One possible route would be an Economic Council (which is provided for in general language in the 1933 constitution) formally composed of the Ministers most closely responsible for economic questions: the Council would have specific powers (approve the initial draft budget, proposals for legislation in specified areas, foreign borrowing, for example) and a strong Secretariat. Ideally, Ministers would not attend all meetings of the Council, but send their deputies, who would thus create a coordinated network within the government. The Secretariat might be the planning office, although its nature would have to change radically—becoming akin to an economic management office, not exclusively concerned with long-range public sector forecasts, which should be handled elsewhere. A "primus inter pares" Minister would chair the Council, most probably the Minister of Economy and Finance. A system such as this was in fact attempted in 1975.[2]

As far as the balance with Congress on economic management is concerned, the experience under the Belaúnde administration showed that a clear shift was needed in favor of the Executive—in a reorganized form. There is no reason why this shift should be a permanent one, unchangeable under a revised political charter. There is no reason why a constitution in a country undergoing rapid change should not change also, or at least leave the door open for such change. A theoretical possibility—although possibly unfeasible in practice—would be an agreement that would gradually expand the economic powers of Congress over a long period, with a mechanism for altering the timetable if necessary.

Constitutional changes or alterations of political form will by themselves do little, unless they are accompanied by a clearer sense of nationhood. Nationhood is a vague concept, but it is perhaps easier to grasp through examples in which a national sense of participation is visible. Undoubtedly,

2 By General Morales Bermúdez when he became Prime Minister in 1975.

many of the efforts of the administration that began in October 1968 have as their objective the creation of a sense of nationhood. This is an extremely difficult task, and it thus should not be surprising that the means used for this purpose in many developing countries tend to rely on xenophobia. A more difficult approach, but in the longer run perhaps a more successful one, blends strong political leadership with popular participation. This approach may have more chances of success in countries at a stage of development broadly comparable to that of Peru than an approach that combines, on one hand, an appeal to insularity with, on the other, legislating from above complicated economic measures inspired from industrial countries.

Political leadership does not just depend on the President. The role of Congress is vital. In Peru from 1963 to 1968, the role of APRA within Congress was as important as the desires of Belaúnde and his party. On most initiatives by the Executive, the position of APRA was negative and offered no significant alternatives. Continuous opposition by APRA to significant land redistribution, to Cooperación Popular, and especially to a higher and more progressive rate of taxation, made it very difficult for the government to start the social reforms that it had genuinely wanted in 1963. The frustration of not being able to do much, and the financial problems that began in 1966, slowed down the original drive of the President and his government. The attitude of APRA was not only the result of personalities—its generation of senior leaders in particular—but also the result of past Peruvian history. For years, APRA had been ready to enter government with a progressive program, but it had not been able to realize its hopes. Frustration and disillusion set in, breeding a desire to make peace with the status quo. By the 1960's, some powerful business groups, who sensed a loss of political power, were only too eager to encourage the conservatives within APRA. As the elections scheduled for 1969 approached, the opposition role of APRA intensified. It was

281

only in mid-1968, when the threat of a coup was publicly felt, that APRA changed its attitude on the tax question. The financial recovery began soon afterwards. But by then various events were taking place—the jockeying for presidential position within Acción Popular, the split in the party, the ambivalent attitude of APRA to the financial measures already in force, and eventually the dispute over IPC—that provided the setting for the coup.

It is hard not to feel a sense of sadness at the way in which Belaúnde was forced to end his presidency. A progressive, a man of new ideas, a magnificent public speaker, a genuine believer in a democratic way of government, who was unwilling to short-cut constitutional procedures even in times of great crisis, he found himself for the last two years of his administration bedeviled by problems with which he was unable to cope. It was difficult for him to assert his leadership in the face of Congressional opposition when the main issue was public finance. He was just not interested enough in it to summon up sufficient enthusiasm and energy to devote himself fully to finding a solution. As an alternative, he could have delegated some of the responsibility to a strong Finance Minister with political strength of his own. Unfortunately, that did not occur until the very end of the administration. For the first years of his government, the President was surrounded, at least on the financial side, with party colleagues who were either not knowledgeable enough or candid enough to give the basic facts to the president. As a consequence, the palliative, the relatively easy answers were sought instead of more fundamental solutions. Perhaps a major criticism that can be made of the President was his choice of advisers in the initial years of his administration.

In this setting, the role of the financial "técnicos," who were mostly in a few financial institutions, was a difficult one. Advisers can be effective only if they have the confidence of those to whom they report. At the same time, they have to realize the limitations of the environment within which they work. Sometimes, advice will be listened to if it is presented in an exaggerated way. Technically ideal solutions are very rarely feasible, and this was so in the case of Peru, with an opposition Congress. It was not until 1967 that this group of advisers gained access to the President. This access generated understandable jealousy in other groups: the average age of the Central Bank team was only about thirty. Furthermore, the fact that during 1967-1968 there were seven Finance Ministers gave the Central Bank more power than it would have had in more normal times. The advisers, without really wishing to, allowed themselves to gain too much visibility. Eventually (in early 1969, a few months after the change of government) this fact cost them their influence and the Central Bank lost its position as the major institution of economic research and management.

The role of advisers in other areas, especially in land reform, also met considerable difficulties. Land redistribution was an even more politically contentious issue than taxation. The achievements in land redistribution, limited as they were by the very substantial amendments of the majority in Congress to the draft law proposed by Belaúnde, were largely due to the conviction and drive of the "técnicos" in the land reform office.

The history of the period 1963 to 1968 is not that of smooth progress, but of twists and turns and difficulties. But there was undeniable change and progress. The commonly accepted view that Peru was "run" by a few families until October 1968 does not fit with the record of the sixties. There was rapid modernization during that period. It is true that the modernization benefitted mostly the "urban and middle class" (which includes schoolteachers and salaried industrial workers). Nevertheless, there was a deepening effect of this greater prosperity through government policy in housing, health, and education. Although agricultural price policies hindered the growth of rural incomes (as was also the case before and after the Belaúnde administration), there was a deliberate effort on the part of the government to help the countryside through road-building, Cooperación Popular, the beginning of land redistribution and services to small farmers, and particularly the opening to the East through the *Carretera Marginal.*

The progress and difficulties of the period 1963-1968 took place in an atmosphere of freedom and public debate. Criticism flourished, although much of it was irresponsible and ill-informed. It is sometimes argued that freedom does little for the poor masses. That may be true in some cases, but it would certainly be hard to argue—in the case of Peru during the period 1963-1968—that lack of debate and freedom of public expression would have been necessary in order to generate faster economic and social change. The problem was not so much that public expression was misused, although it often was, but that the experience of Peru with a modicum of democracy was so limited that powerful forces in the country—such as some business groups, the majority in Congress, and also the President's own party—did not know how to refrain from abusing the power and freedom they enjoyed.

Appendix

SELECTED BASIC DATA FROM THE
NATIONAL ACCOUNTS

THE following tables reproduce material in Central Bank, *Cuentas Nacionales del Perú, 1950-1967*, Lima, 1968. The national accounts prepared by the Central Bank were the result of an exhaustive effort during the period 1963-1967 under the direction of Richard C. Webb, head of research of the bank, and with the advice of Charles F. Schwartz of the International Monetary Fund.

. GROSS NATIONAL PRODUCT AND POPULATION, 1950-1967

Years	GNP in current prices (millions of soles)	Index of GNP deflator (1963 = 100)	GNP in 1963 prices (millions of 1963 soles)	Population (thousands)	Per capita GNP in 1963 prices
1950	15,577	40.0	38,956	8,069.5	4,828
1955	28,947	55.6	52,065	8,890.8	5,856
1960	55,518	86.5	64,175	10,125.4	6,338
1961	62,294	89.7	69,411	10,420.4	6,661
1962	71,700	94.5	75,836	10,732.3	7,066
1963	78,710	100.0	78,710	11,059.2	7,117
1964	94,994	113.0	84,098	11,359.2	7,404
1965	113,000	128.1	88,146	11,750.4	7,502
1966	134,016	143.8	93,186	12,103.0	7,699
1967	153,807	157.8	97,467	12,486.0	7,806

II. GNP: Composition of Expenditure, 1950-1967
(in millions of soles at 1963 prices)

	1950	1955	1960	1961	1962	1963	1964	1965	1966	1967
Personal consumption	27,605	37,424	43,154	45,949	51,405	57,117	60,519	64,554	69,485	72,715
Government consumption	3,860	5,051	6,111	7,037	7,361	7,714	8,865	9,685	9,571	9,909
Gross investment	7,942	12,365	13,682	15,588	17,288	16,391	17,131	19,425	23,755	25,204
Machinery and equipment	*3,147*	*4,099*	*5,482*	*7,083*	*8,676*	*9,051*	*8,269*	*9,982*	*11,443*	*12,210*
Construction	*3,900*	*6,316*	*5,210*	*6,452*	*6,962*	*6,060*	*6,394*	*7,540*	*8,286*	*8,706*
Increase in inventories	*895*	*1,950*	*2,990*	*2,053*	*1,650*	*1,280*	*2,468*	*1,903*	*4,026*	*4,288*
Exports of goods and services	5,915	8,634	14,195	16,567	17,556	16,897	18,225	18,422	18,579	18,799
Less: Imports of goods and services	6,366	11,409	12,967	15,730	17,774	19,409	20,642	23,940	28,204	29,160
Total: GNP	38,956	52,065	64,175	69,411	75,836	78,710	84,098	88,146	93,186	97,467
Memorandum item: Real GNP adjusted for changes in the external terms of trade	39,802	52,324	62,997	67,771	74,748	78,710	86,741	90,272	98,069	101,551

III. GNP: Sector Composition, 1950-1967
(in millions of soles at 1963 prices)

	1950	1955	1960	1961	1962	1963	1964	1965	1966	1967
Agriculture and forestry	8,790	11,190	13,386	13,940	14,612	14,275	14,946	14,875	15,089	15,195
Fisheries	160	333	1,041	1,356	1,599	1,510	1,838	1,513	1,783	2,048
Mining	1,768	2,667	4,585	4,850	4,590	4,995	5,130	5,325	5,293	5,653
Manufacturing	5,286	7,681	10,642	11,694	12,912	13,839	15,071	16,330	17,935	18,957
Construction	2,000	3,218	2,671	3,280	3,579	3,091	3,419	3,864	4,207	4,422
Public utilities	218	252	480	596	621	660	706	838	895	987
Home ownership	3,404	3,784	4,345	4,474	4,611	4,754	4,901	5,054	5,210	5,372
Government	3,432	4,187	5,046	5,702	6,109	6,562	6,936	7,323	7,769	8,243
Commerce, transport, banking, and other services	13,898	18,753	21,979	23,519	27,203	29,024	31,151	33,024	35,005	36,590
Total: GNP	38,956	52,065	64,175	69,411	75,836	78,710	84,098	88,146	93,186	97,467

IV. Composition of National Income in Current Prices, 1950-1966
(in millions of soles)

	1950	1955	1960	1961	1962	1963	1964	1965	1966
Wages and salaries	5,518	11,153	22,260	25,338	28,781	32,319	38,705	46,217	53,850
"Blue collar"	3,025	5,873	11,274	12,951	14,622	16,087	18,571	22,943	26,413
"White collar"	2,493	5,280	10,986	12,387	14,159	16,232	20,134	23,274	27,437
Self-employed income	5,075	8,741	14,151	15,829	18,323	18,996	23,439	26,514	31,015
Farmers	3,059	4,857	6,575	7,461	8,623	8,094	9,805	10,955	12,561
Others	2,016	3,884	7,576	8,368	9,700	10,902	13,634	15,559	18,454
Property rent	1,115	1,867	3,457	3,819	4,052	4,253	4,732	5,583	6,144
Corporate profits	2,334	3,447	7,378	7,607	9,633	10,263	12,651	15,709	19,693
Profits taxes	903	1,098	2,375	2,588	2,778	3,196	3,296	3,457	3,583
After-tax profits	1,794	2,612	5,445	5,237	7,311	7,765	10,057	13,566	17,023
Inventory valuation									
adjustment	−363	−263	−442	−218	−456	−698	−702	−1,314	−913
Net interest income	153	399	920	1,094	1,242	1,626	1,651	1,788	2,053
Total national income	14,195	25,607	48,166	53,687	62,031	67,457	81,178	95,811	112,755

V. SAVINGS AND INVESTMENT IN CURRENT PRICES, 1950-1967
(in millions of soles)

	1950	1955	1960	1961	1962	1963	1964	1965	1966	1967
Gross savings	2,721	6,658	12,292	14,223	16,725	16,391	18,111	21,370	27,499	32,669
Enterprises	1,367	2,655	6,359	6,435	8,028	8,752	12,369	15,858	21,410	28,054
Depreciation	652	*1,410*	3,282	3,574	4,121	4,724	5,175	6,370	7,846	
Retained earnings	715	*1,245*	3,077	2,861	3,907	4,028	7,194	9,488	13,564	
Personal savings	1,058	1,678	4,921	6,006	6,299	4,649	6,329	2,683	1,657	
Government sector current account savings	484	722	1,511	1,557	1,427	824	−154	−408	−492	−2,133
External current account (− = surplus)	−188	1,603	−499	225	971	2,166	−433	3,237	4,924	6,748
Gross domestic investment	2,721	6,658	12,292	14,223	16,725	16,391	18,111	21,370	27,499	32,669
Gross fixed investment	2,336	5,488	9,541	12,293	15,141	15,111	15,389	19,210	22,563	26,808
Government sector	177	954	659	1,228	1,545	993	1,775	3,047	4,250	5,101
Enterprises	2,159	4,534	8,882	11,065	13,596	14,118	13,614	16,163	18,313	21,707
(of which state enterprises)	*na.*	*na.*	583	1,640	1,254	2,100	2,805	3,131	3,732	2,866
Change in inventories	385	1,170	2,751	1,930	1,584	1,280	2,722	2,160	4,936	5,861

Bibliography[1]

STATISTICAL

Banco Central de Reserva del Perú (Central Bank).
Boletín Estadístico (statistical bulletin, monthly).
Cuentas Monetarias (annual, limited circulation).
Cuentas Nacionales, 1950-1967, Lima, 1968.
Reseña Económica y Financiera (periodic economic survey, published quarterly or bimonthly 1966-1969).
International Monetary Fund, *International Financial Statistics*, Washington, D.C., monthly.
Organization of American States, *Latin America's Development and the Alliance for Progress*, Washington, D.C., 1973.
United Nations Economic Commission for Latin America (ECLA) *Annual Economic Survey of Latin America* (annual), United Nations, N.Y.
United Nations Food and Agricultural Organization *Report on the 1960 World Census of Agriculture*, Rome, 1971.
United States Government
a. Agency for International Development
Summary Social and Economic Indicators, 18 Latin American Countries, 1960-1971, Washington, D.C., June 1971.
Latin America: Economic Growth Trends, May 1972.
U.S. Overseas Loans and Grants, periodic publication, Washington, D.C., various issues, 1972.
b. U.S. Department of Agriculture
Indices of Agricultural Production for the Western Hemisphere, Economic Research Service, April 1970 issue.
c. U.S. Department of Commerce
Survey of Current Business, monthly, various issues.

[1] This list does not attempt to be a general bibliography on Peru in the 1960's. It only includes material consulted or mentioned by the author.

BIBLIOGRAPHY

GENERAL

Astiz, Carlos and Garué, José Z., *The Peruvian Military; Achievement Orientation, Training and Political Tendencies,* Western Political Quarterly, Vol. 25, December 1972.

Belaúnde Terry, Fernando
El Perú Construye, Annual Presidential Messages, Lima, July 1964 and July 1965.
La Conquista del Perú por los Peruanos, Ediciones Tawantinsuyu, Lima, 1959.
Pueblo por Pueblo, Lima, 1959.

Bourricaud, François, *Power and Society in Contemporary Perú,* Frederick A. Praeger, New York, 1970 (translation—original in French, published by Librairie Armand Colin, Paris, 1967).

Dunn, W. E., *Perú—A Commercial and Industrial Handbook,* U.S. Department of Commerce, Washington, D.C., 1925.

Einaudi, Luigi R. and Stepan, Alfred C. III, *Latin American Institutional Development: Changing Military Perspectives in Peru and Brazil,* Rand Corporation, Santa Monica, 1971.

Hirschmann, Albert, *Development Projects Observed,* Brookings Institution, Washington, D.C., 1967.

Hunt, Shane J., *Growth and Guano in Nineteenth Century Peru,* Discussion Paper No. 34, Research Program in Economic Development, Woodrow Wilson School, Princeton University, February 1973.

Kozub, Jacques, *Agricultural Development Priorities in Peru,* Unpublished, Washington, D.C., 1968.

Peruvian Times, weekly news magazine published in English in Lima.

Pike, Frederick B., *The Modern History of Peru,* Frederick A. Praeger, New York, 1969.

Roemer, Michael, *Fishing for Growth: Export-Led Development in Peru, 1950-67,* Harvard University Press, 1970.

Romero, Emilio, *Historia Económica del Perú,* Editorial Sudamericana, Buenos Aires, 1949.

FISCAL AND FINANCIAL

Banco Central de Reserva del Perú (Central Bank), *Reseña Económica y Financiera* (periodic economic survey, published quarterly or bimonthly, 1966-1969).

Banco Continental, *Quarterly Economic Report*, published in English in Lima.

Morse, L. R., *The 1967 Peruvian Exchange Crisis: A Comment*, unpublished, University of Minnesota, 1968.

Organization of American States and Interamerican Development Bank, *Estudio Fiscal del Perú*, Organization of American States, Washington, D.C., 1969. Prepared by Milton C. Taylor with Robert A. Mundell, Wilfred Pine, Kenyon E. Poole, David I. Meiselman and Gustavo Cañas Viana.

Temoche Benítez, Ricardo, *La Devaluación de 1967—Crónica y Analisis de Una Catástrofe*, Lima, 1969.

Thorp, Rosemary, *Inflation and Orthodox Economic Policy in Peru*, Bulletin of the Oxford Institute of Economics and Statistics, Volume 29, No. 3, August 1967.

Webb, Richard C., *Tax Policy and the Incidence of Taxation in Peru*. Discussion Paper No. 27, Research Program in Economic Development, Woodrow Wilson School, Princeton University, September 1972.

INCOME DISTRIBUTION, LAND REFORM

Carroll, Thomas F., *Land Reform in Peru*, unpublished, prepared for the spring 1970 review of the U.S. Agency for International Development, Washington, D.C., 1970.

Handelman, Howard, *Struggle in the Andes: Peasant Mobilization in Peru*, University of Texas Press, Austin, 1975.

Malpica, Carlos, *Los Dueños del Perú*, Fondo de Cultura Popular, Lima, 1970.

Organization of American States, *Perú—Tenencia de la Tierra y Desarrollo Socioeconómico del Sector Agricola*, Organization of American States, Washington, D.C., 1968.

Strasma, John
Financiamiento de la Reforma Agraria en el Perú, in *El Trimestre Económico*, Volume 32, No. 3, July-September 1965, Mexico, D.F.
The United States and Agrarian Reform in Peru, in Daniel A. Sharp, editor, *United States Foreign Policy and Peru*, University of Texas Press, Austin, 1972.

Webb, Richard C.
The Distribution of Income in Peru, Discussion Paper No. 26, Research Program in Economic Development, Woodrow Wilson School, Princeton University, September 1972.
Government Policy and the Distribution of Income in Peru, 1963-73, Discussion Paper No. 39, Research Program in Economic Development, Woodrow Wilson School, Princeton University, June 1973.

THE IPC ISSUE, U.S. ASSISTANCE

Basadre, Jorge, *Historia de la República del Perú*, Volumes 12 and 13, Editorial Universitaria, Lima, 1970.
Levinson, Jerome and de Onis, Juan, *The Alliance that Lost Its Way*, Quadrangle Books, Chicago, 1970.
Furnish, Dale B., *Peruvian Domestic Law Aspects of the Brea y Pariñas Controversy*, Kentucky Law Journal, Volume 59, 1971.
Goodsell, Charles T., *American Corporations and Peruvian Politics*, Harvard University Press, 1974.
Goodwin, Richard N., *Letter from Peru*, in *The New Yorker* magazine, May 17, 1969.
Pernitz, Jessica, *Expropriation Politics*, Lexington Books, Lexington, Mass., 1974.
United States Senate, *Hearings before the Subcommittee on Western Hemisphere Affairs of the Committee on Foreign Relations*, April 14-16, 1969.
Zimmermann, Augusto
La Historia Secreta del Petróleo, n. pub., Lima, 1968.
El Plan Inca. Objetivo: Revolución Peruana. Empresa Editora del Diario Oficial "El Peruano," Lima, 1974.
The American Society of International Law, *International Legal Materials*, 1968, Volume VII, pp. 1203-1254, Washington, D.C.

A reader who wishes to gain a view to Peru in the 1960's from a different angle than that of social scientists ought to read some of the literary works by contemporary Peruvian authors, such as: Bryce Echenique, Alfredo, *Un Mundo para Julius*, Barral Editores, Barcelona, 1970; Vargas Llosa, Mario, *Conversación en la Catedral*, Barral Editores, Barcelona, 1970.

Index

Names cited in footnotes are included in the index, but authors cited only in the bibliography are not repeated in the index.

Acción Popular, government political party, 27, 32, 122, 142, 193, 215, 282; alliance with Christian Democrats breaks up, 197; split within, 265-266, 272-273
Acta de Talara, 266
Adelman, Irma, cited 19
Aerolineas Peruanas (APSA), 275
agrarian reform, *see* land reform
agrarian unrest, 64-65
Agricultural Bank (Banco Agropecuario), 14, 58, 69, 238, 243
agricultural incomes, 71
agricultural prices, 11, 15, 230, 280
Agricultural University, 93
agriculture, *see also* land reform; general features, 10-11; 48
Air Force, 36, 153, 158-159
Alegría, Ciro, writer and member of Congress, 189, 196
Algeria, 107
"Alianza" of Acción Popular and Christian Democrats, *see under* each
Alianza Popular Revolucionaria Americana (APRA), *see also Coalición*, Congress; 24, 210-211; past history, 30-31; alliance with Odriístas (*see Coalición*), 26, 40-41; and

elections of 1962 and 1963, 38-41; and *Convivencia* with Prado, 41; and *Carretera Marginal*, 54; and Cooperación Popular, 62; and guerrilla issue, 66; and IPC, 120; and taxes, 161, 175, 193, 201-203, 204-205, 213, 265; and wage policy after devaluation, 185; and 1967 elections, 189, 196-197; and Gen. Morales Bermúdez, 213-214; and Hercelles Cabinet, 221-222, 226; and Law 17044, 226-227; and IPC, 262-263; assessment of role, 281-282
Alliance for Progress, 45
Alva Orlandini, Javier, Acción Popular leader, 1976
Amazon, Amazonic region (also called *Montaña* or *Selva*), 3, 52-54, 64, 74, 126; petroleum in, 9; special tax status, 81, 155
American Smelting and Refining Co., 8, 244, 246
Anaconda Mining Co., 244, 246
anchoveta (fish), 6, 7, 128
Ancón, 203
Andes, 3, 5, 53
Antamina mine, 245
APRA Rebelde, 65
Arbitration Tribunal of 1922, 114

arbitrios, 232
Arca Parró, Alberto, statistician
    and Senator, 192, 206
Arequipa, 63
Argentina, 104, 172, 222
Arias Stella, Javier, Minister of
    Health various times,
    1963-1968, 202, 220
armed forces; political attitudes
    of, 36-37, 39; role in 1962
    elections, 39; junta 1962-1963,
    39, 44-48; expenditures on,
    88, 90, 96; and guerrillas,
    102-103; and IPC, 110, 262;
    1967 expenditures, 149; and
    APRA, 178
army, 36, 276; and guerrillas,
    66, 102-103, 174; and IPC,
    189
Arteta Terzi, Oscar, General
    and Senator, 167
Ashworth, Jack, former IPC
    official, 117
Astiz, Carlos, cited 30, 36
Australia, 246
automobiles, in Lima, 20, 55,
    73; assembly of, 12, 81-84

baja policía, 232
balance of payments, *see also*
    exchange rate, 127-137
Balarezo Lizarzaburu, Teodoro,
    Senator, 167
Bambarén, R. P. Luis,
    bishop, 35
Banca Comerciale Italiana,
    196, 238
Banchero Rossi, Luis,
    industrialist and newspaper
    publisher, 190
Banco Central de Reserva,
    see Central Bank
Banco Continental, 224, 238,
    239

Banco de Crédito, 196, 238, 239
Banco de la Nación, 98-99,
    144, 149, 154, 160, 169, 214
Banco de Lima, 238
Banco Internacional, 238-242
Banco Popular, 239
Banco Unión, 242
Bank for International
    Settlements, 249
Bank of America, 55, 238
Bank of London and South
    America, 238
Bank of Nova Scotia, 195
Bank of Tokyo, 238
banks, banking reform, *see*
    commercial banks
Banque Française et Italienne
    pour l'Amerique du Sud
    (Sudameris) 196, 238
barriadas (*pueblos jovenes*),
    see Lima, slums
Basadre, Jorge, cited 107
Becerra de la Flor, Daniel,
    Prime Minister, 1965-1967,
    167
Bedoya Reyes, Luis, politician
    and mayor of Lima, 55
Belaúnde, Rafael, father of
    President, Prime Minister,
    1945-1946, 24
Belaúnde, Victor Andrés, uncle
    of President, diplomat, 24
Belaúnde Terry, Fernando,
    President of Peru, 1963-1968;
    early career and major
    attitudes, 24-27; elections
    1962-1963, 38-41; takes office
    July 28, 1973, 41; and public
    works, 27, 51-59, 94; attitude
    to economists, 51; *Carretera
    Marginal*, 52-55; Cooperación
    Popular, 25, 60-62; land
    reform, 62, 67-70; guerrillas,
    65-66; attitude in 1963 to

IPC, 49, 118-120; at Punta del Este, 126-127; international financial schemes of, 126; relationship with Central Bank, 140-141; and tax question, 142, 147; and Congress on fiscal issue, 146, 147, 149, 161, 175, 198, 202, 205; devaluation, 151-152, 153-154, 170, 179; blames APRA for deficit, 151-152; general attitude to Congress, 161, 233; and 1967 Senate conflict, 167; names Cabinet, Sept. 1967, 176-178; relations with Seoane, 177; and export tax, 190; and gasoline tax, 214, 227; financial emergency of May 1968, 217; appoints Hercelles Cabinet, 219-221; agreement with IPC, 260-273; and U.S. aid, 260-261; coup against, 272-276; assessment of, Chap. X

Belaúnde Terry, Francisco, brother of above, 221
Belgium, 252
Bellido, Enrique, Central Bank chairman, 76
Beltrán, Felipe, 238
Beltrán, Pedro, newspaper publisher and Prime Minister, 1959-1961, 34, 48, 52, 77, 98, 118, 240; helps create savings and loan system, 34; tenure as Prime Minister and Finance Minister, 41-44, 142; and exchange rate 1959-1961, 129-130, 162; and devaluation of 1967, 138; and tax issue, 145, 190, 203; and IPC agreement and coup, 270, 272, 273
Benavides Correa, Alfonso, 118

Benavides, Oscar, Marshal, President 1933-1939, 117
Blanco, Hugo, peasant leader, 65
Bolívar, Simón, 111
Bolivia, 53, 54, 189
Bolo, Salomón, priest, 35
Bourricaud, François, cited 24, 26
Braniff Airways, 220
Brazil, 54, 189, 222
British government, and IPC, 114
budget (of central government), see also fiscal policy, government expenditures, taxation; "program" budget 1963, 47; composition and role of, 14-15, 75-78; and money supply, 79; budget deficit and financing, 95-102; size in early 1900's, 113; 1967 budget, 139-143, 147-150; relation to exchange rate, 133-134, 180; 1968 budget, 198, 207, 213; 1968 compared with 1967, 235
Burga Puelles, Manuel, Senator, 167
Burmah Oil Co., 187
business groups, attitude to public sector service, 15-16; and Carretera Marginal, 54; and exchange rate, 127, 128; and De Andrea, 191; and Belaúnde, 284
Bustamante y Rivero, José Luis, President, 1945-1948, 31, 118

Cabinet, 176-178, 220-221, 274-275
Caja de Depósitos y Consignaciones, see Banco de la Nación

Cajamarca, 53, 176
California banks, 252
Callao, 187
Calmell del Solar, Fernando,
    Minister of Labor, 1967-1968,
    220
Canada, 245
Canadian banks, 249, 256
Caracas, 221
Caretas newsmagazine, 33
Carretera Marginal de la Selva,
    52-56, 68, 152, 284
Carriquiry Maurer, Pablo,
    Minister of Public Works and
    acting Finance Minister, 1968,
    76, 120, 203, 220; as acting
    Minister of Finance, 216-217;
    and mining companies,
    246-247; and IPC, 270
Carroll, Thomas F., cited 63,
    67, 70
Castro, Fidel, 65
Catholic University of Chile, 30
Ceja de Montaña, western edge
    of Amazonic region, 26, 64
censure of Ministers, 279
Central Bank (Banco Central
    de Reserva), 16, 160; staff of,
    28-30, 42, 75-76; and Planning
    Office, 77, 91; role in early
    1967, 138-141; on tax issue,
    98, 101, 133, 144-145, 146-147,
    200-201, 211-213; and
    Congress, 133, 147, 156, 225,
    265; devaluation and exchange
    system, 152, 162, 168-172,
    176, 179-185, 208-209; 1967
    import tariff, 154; and USAID,
    156-157; and IMF, 164, 166,
    225; and De Andrea, 190-193,
    195, 202, 204-205; and
    Carriquiry, 216-217; and
    Ulloa, 223, 224-225; and
    external debt, 243, 249-257;

and mining, 245-246; and
    La Prensa, 145, 248;
    assessment of role, 282-283
Central Highway, 52-55
Central Railway, 45
Centro de Altos Estudios
    Militares (CAEM), academy
    for armed forces, 37, 48
Cerro Corporation, 8, 244, 246
Cerro de Pasco, 45
Cerro de Pasco Corporation, 8,
    245, 246; sheep farm, 69
Cerro Verde mine, 244, 245, 249
certificate exchange, *see*
    exchange system
Chamber of Deputies, *see*
    Congress, *Coalición*
Chan Chan, 30
Chase Manhattan Bank, 224,
    238, 239, 242
Chemical Bank, 238-242
Chicago, 249
Chiclayo, 57
Chile, 30, 104, 107, 245, 248,
    261
Chira-Piura irrigation, 63, 67
Chirinos Soto, Enrique, journalist
    and politician, 189, 196
Christian Democrats, 27, 55,
    142; break with government,
    197
Church, political role of, 35
Cisneros Sánchez, Máximo, 275
Coalición, see also APRA and
    UNO; formed 1963, 40-41;
    and *Carretera Marginal*, 54;
    and Cooperación Popular, 62;
    and guerrilla issue, 66; and
    land reform, 67, 70; and fiscal
    policy, 95-97; and IPC, 120;
    and foreign aid, 123; and 1967
    budget, 141-142; and military
    expenditures, 149; and 1967
    election of Senate officers,

167; and by-elections 1967, 189, 196-197; and De Andrea tax proposals, 201-203, 204-205; assessment of, 281, 284

Cobriza mine, 245

Colombia, 54, 104, 180, 222, 234, 241, 261

commercial banks, domestic, 59; and De Andrea, 191, 236; foreign, 95, 134, 165, 182, 195-196, 236, 238-241; list of, 238; and debt refinancing, 251-254, 273; stand-by credit from, 257; regional, 23; banking reform 1968, 237-243

Comptroller General, 75, 78

comunidades, in Sierra, 60

Conchán, 187

Confederación de Trabajadores del Perú, 185

Congress, see also Coalición; 118, 145, 156, 173, 195, 238, 279-282; composition of, 1963-1968, 40; and fiscal policy, 95, 97, 138; and 1967 budget, 141-142; election of officers, 166-167; and export tax, 194; and tax measures, 204-205; and emergency measures of May 1967, 217; passes Law 17044, 226-227, 234; and IPC, 262-263

Constitution, of 1823, 111; of 1933, 160, 279-280

Conte-Long Amendment to U.S. Foreign Assistance Act, 159

Contrabando scandal, 1968, 214-216

Cooperación Popular, and Inca past, 25, 60, 281, 284; achievements, 60-62

copper mining, see mining

Cornfeld, Bernard, 209

Correo newspaper, 190

COSAL, 44, 56-57, 177

cotton farms, 128

coup, 175, 254; origins and October 3, 1968 coup, 259-276

Cox, Carlos Manuel, APRA leader, 226

Crédit Lyonnais, 238

Cuajone mine, 8, 244-245, 247

Cuba, and guerrillas, 65

Cueto Fernandini, Carlos, educator and politician, 196

Cuzco, 64, 65, 227

Cyprus Mines Co., 8

Dammert, Miguel, Senator, 206

Dauphinot, Clarence, 222

De Andrea, Tulio, Finance Minister, 1967-1968, 76, 120, 211, 213; tenure as Finance Minister, 177-205; tax reform proposals, 199-201; confronts Congress and resigns, 202-205

de Lama, José, 111

de la Piedra, Julio, UNO leader and Senator, 94

de la Puente Uceda, Gonzalo, guerrilla leader, 65-66

Delgado, Raúl, Vice-Admiral, Navy Minister, 218

DELTEC Banking Corp., 222-224

Dentzer, William, USAID official, 157-158

de Onís, Juan, cited 107

de Quintana, José Antonio, 111

Deutsche Bundesbank, 256

devaluation, see exchange rate

Dianderas, Gen. Roberto, War Minister, 1968, 219-220

Dirección de Petróleo, 160

Doig Sánchez, Gen. Julio, War
Minister, 178, 189, 203, 204,
218

economic growth, 48-50,
261-262; compared with Latin
America, 50
economic reforms of 1968,
237-243
economics, study of, 17
Ecuador, 53, 54, 63, 110, 172,
189
education, 57, 74; comparison
with other countries, 73; cost
of public education, 88-91
Einaudi, Luigi, cited 36, 37
El Comercio newspaper (see also
Miró Quesada), 33, 88, 91,
129, 166, 171, 180, 183, 214,
215, 248; and IPC, 108-109,
270, 272, 273
elections, municipal (1963), 25;
presidential elections (1962),
31, 38-39; 1963, 25, 31, 38;
by-elections (1967), 189,
196-197
El Peruano gazette, 217, 247
employment, 21, 23, 64, 71, 73
Empresas Eléctricas Asociadas,
188, 189
Empresa Petrolera Fiscal, 187,
264, 266, 270-271; price
agreement with IPC, 268,
270-272
Espinoza, Fernando, IPC
official, 266
Eurodollar loans, 256
European banks, 252, 256
exchange controls, see exchange
system
exchange rate, 42, 127, 213, 230;
in 1959-1961, 129-130;
purchasing power of sol,
1959-1966, 130; devaluation

of 1967 (Chap. VI), 164-173;
difficulties of devaluation,
150-152; adjustment to
devaluation, 174, 179-185;
effects of devaluation,
184-186; possible second
devaluation, 208-209; effect of
tax measures on, 228
exchange system, certificate
exchange system, 140, 161-164,
180-185, 209, 217; controls,
161-164, 180; draft exchange
market, 228-229
excise taxes, 217, 234
exports, general trends, 4-10,
49, 131, 135, 137, 262
export tax, 171-172, 190-191,
193-194, 247
Expreso newspaper, 33, 215, 223
external borrowing and debt,
134-135, 144, 150, 160, 182,
195, 208, 225, 243; refinancing
of, 249-258, 274; and coup,
254, 274

Falk, David, cited 107
Felsenstein, Edgar, banker, 195
Ferrero Rebagliati, Raúl, Prime
Minister, Foreign Minister
and Finance Minister,
1967-1968, 76, 175, 202, 204,
209, 211, 214, 274; appointed,
197-198; tenure as Finance
Minister, 205-210; attitude
towards Gen. Morales
Bermúdez, 212; leaves office,
216-218
Ferrero, Rómulo, economist and
former Finance Minister, 205,
212
Ferreyros, Alfredo, Central Bank
chairman, 76, 98
Ferrostaal, 254
Finance Ministry, see Salazar,

Morales Machiavello,
Maríategui, de Andrea,
Ferrero, Morales Bermúdez,
Ulloa and González del Valle
Finland, 135, 252
First National City Bank, 238
fiscal policy, see also government
expenditures, and taxation;
role of, 75-79; 1962-1963 junta
and, 76
fishing and fishmeal industry, 5,
44, 128, 136, 138, 141, 194
Fishlow, Albert, cited 19
floating debt, 191
Fondo Nacional de Desarrollo
Económico, 61
food, production and imports, 48
Ford Foundation, and Central
Bank, 29
France, 252, 256
Frei, Eduardo, President of
Chile, 127
Furnish, Dale B., cited 107

Gagliardi, Gen. José, Air
Minister, 1967-1968, 178, 218,
220
Garué, Jose Z., cited 36
gasoline prices, 56, 186-189,
228, 269
gasoline tax, 227-228
geography of Peru, 3; Humboldt
current, 6, 128; territorial
waters, 6; Ceja de Montaña,
26; Lake Titicaca, 45;
Amazonic region, 52-54, 64,
74; map, 46
Germany, 252, 253
González del Valle, Luis; Finance
Ministry official, 28, 76, 185,
211, 224
Goodwin, Richard N., cited 106,
107, 109, 119, 123

Gordon, Lincoln, U.S. Asst.
Secretary of State for
Interamerican Affairs, 121
Goshko, John, of Washington
Post, 158
government expenditures, see also
budget, 78, 88-95, 199; cuts
proposed in 1967, 146, 157;
special outlays for armed
forces, 149; 1968 proposals,
198-199; performance 1968,
235
government revenues, see budget,
taxation
W. R. Grace & Co., 220, 240
Grados Bertorini, Alfonso,
Minister of Labor October,
1968, 275
Great Britain, 252
Greene, James R., U.S. banker,
253
Grieve, Jorge, Minister of Public
Works under Prado, 44
Guardia Civil (police), 215
Guatemala, 110
guerrillas, in Sierra, 37, 64-66,
174
Gutiérrez, German Tito, 118
Guyana, 107

Haiti, 110
Hague Club, 253
Harvard University, and Central
Bank, 29, 145
Haya de la Torre, Victor Raúl,
APRA chief; see also Alianza
Popular Revolucionaria
Americana, 33, 176; in
elections of 1962 and 1963,
38-41; in Colombian embassy,
1948-1955, 40; and tax ques-
tion, 175, 192-193, 226
Helguero, Genaro, 112

Hercelles, Oswaldo, Prime Minister, 1968, 219-221, 224, 226, 270, 274
Hickenlooper Amendment, 122
Hilliker, Grant, cited 30
Hirschman, Albert, cited 69
Homestake Mining Co., 247, 248
hospitals, 57
Hoyos Osores, Guillermo, diplomat and Minister of Justice, 1968, 220, 221
housing, 56
Housing Bank (Banco de la Vivienda), 44, 238, 243
Huancavelica, 65
Huancayo, 220
Hudson Institute, 126
Humboldt current, 6, 128
Hunt, Shane J., cited 5

imports, 131-134; income and price elasticity of, 133-134; "autonomous" imports, 133, 136; trends 1962-1967, 136; prohibition of, 209-210
import tariff, 48, 217; trends 1963-1968, 85-86; 1967 tariff, 143, 149, 154-155, 229-230
income distribution, 17-19, 23, 70-74
income tax, 86-87
Industrial Bank, 14, 58, 68, 77, 238, 243
industrial parks, 22, 81
Instituto de Reforma Agraria y Colonización (IRAC), 52
Inter-American Development Bank, 54, 124-125, 127, 199, 231, 244, 275
International Basic Economy Corporation, 224
international commodity prices, 49, 128, 245

International Court at The Hague, 117
International Monetary Fund, 77, 104, 171, 211, 248, 249; and 1967 stand-by arrangement, 164-167, 169, 192-193, 225; and refinancing of debt, 249, 253, 256
International Petroleum Company (IPC), 48, 49, 95, 160, 168; political context of, 106-109; and U.S. Embassy, 108-109; and El Comercio, 108-109; and armed forces, 110; early history, 110-121; 1963 and 1968 arrangements compared, 119; and U.S. Government, 120-125; gasoline prices, 186-189; August 1968 agreement with, and political consequences of, 260-273; price agreement with EPF, 268, 270-272
international reserves, 135, 138, 156-157, 168-169, 195, 208-209, 225, 274
International Telephone and Telegraph (ITT), 13
investment, see private investment and public investment
Investors' Overseas Services (IOS), 209
Iquitos, 3, 81
irrigation, 57-58
Israel, 100
Italy, 252
Ivory Coast, 145

Japan, 252, 253, 254
Japanese banks, 252
Jiménez Borja, José, Minister of Education, 1968, 220-221

Jones, J. Wesley, U.S.
  Ambassador to Peru in
  1962-1969, 260
Junín, 65

Kahn, Herman, 126
Kennedy administration, 104
Keswick, William, 114
Koenig, Robert, Cerro Corp.
  chairman, 246
Kozub, Jazques, cited 64
Kreditanstalt für Wiederaufbau,
  253, 256

labor force, 21, 23, 70-71, 185
La Brea y Pariñas, 111-121,
  159-160, 168, 187, 260,
  266-267; see also International
  Petroleum Company
La Convención, 64
La Oroya, 45
La Pampilla refinery, 187, 264
Lake Titicaca, 45
land reform and distribution,
  18-20, 62-70, 283
land reform law, of 1964, 62,
  67-68; of 1969, 63, 69
land use and availability, 63, 69
La Prensa newspaper, see also
  Pedro Beltrán, 33, 42, 43, 98,
  145, 153, 175, 190, 196,
  248, 265; and IPC, 270; and
  coup, 273
Law 3016 (La Brea y Pariñas),
  114, 115
  7511 (La Brea y Pariñas), 116
  9140 (industrial incentives),
    81, 206, 207
  13270 (industrial incentives),
    206
  14695 (La Brea y Pariñas),
    120
  14696 (La Brea y Pariñas),
    120, 267

14863 (La Brea y Pariñas),
    120
  15037 (land reform), 62
  15215 (Escalafón Magisterial
    —teachers' salaries and
    status), 89, 145
  16567 (import tariff), 149,
    154, 155
  16568 (defense equipment),
    149, 158
  16674 (La Brea y Pariñas),
    159-160, 186, 267
  16900 (taxes), 206-207
  17044 (extraordinary powers),
    226-227; measures under,
    227-243, 263-264, 266
  17046 (fiscal reform), 238
Leguía, Augusto B., President,
  1908-1912, 1919-1930, 116
Letts, Ricardo, 62
Levinson, Jerome, cited 107
Lima, capital city, 4, 26, 189;
  economic concentration in,
  20-22; slums in, 22, 55; in
  elections of 1963, 25; literary
  in, 33
Lindley Pérez, Gen. Nicolás,
  head of provisional
  government, 1963, 36
literacy, 32
Lleras Restrepo, Carlos, President
  of Colombia, 1966-1970, 180
London, 252, 256
London and Pacific Petroleum
  Co., 113, 114, 122
Loret de Mola, Carlos, President
  of EPF, 264-266, 270-272
Luna Ferreccio, Adm. Jorge,
  Minister of the Navy, 1968,
  220
Luna Victoria, R. P. Romeo,
  priest, 35

Madre de Dios, 54

Madrigal mine, 247
Majes irrigation, 63
Malpica, Carlos, cited 18
Mann, Thomas, U.S. Assistant
  Secretary of State for
  Interamerican Affairs, 121
Mantaro hydroelectric project, 78
manufacturing industry; general
  features, 11-13, 48; tax
  treatment of, 82-83, 86
Manufacturers' Hanover Trust
  Co., 167
Marcona Mining Co., 8
Mariátegui, Sandro, Finance
  Minister, 1965-1967, 76, 140,
  143, 158, 160, 169, 178, 183,
  186, 198, 200, 211; and
  Congress, 147-148; resigns, 178
Marine Institute, 153
Martin, Edwin M., U.S. Assistant
  Secretary of State for
  Interamerican Affairs, 121
Maryknoll missionaries, 35
McNamara, Robert S., cited 26
Mesa Pelada, 65
Mexico, 30, 100, 172, 222
Michenfelder, Joseph, Maryknoll
  missionary, 35
Michiquillay mine site, 245
middle class, 70-71, 73
military, see armed forces
Minero Perú, 249
Mining Bank, 59, 238, 243
Mining Code, 135, 210, 246
mining industry, 5; general
  features, 7-10, 43-44, 129;
  profit remittances of, 131, 135;
  1968 negotiations with mining
  companies, 243-248
Ministry of Development and
  Public Works, 75
Ministry of Finance, 75-77, 225;
  see also Salazar, Morales
  Machiavello, Mariátegui,

De Andrea, Ferrero, Morales
  Bermúdez, Ulloa and González
  del Valle
Mirage aircraft, 153, 158-159
Miró Quesada, Francisco,
  Minister of Education, 88
Miró Quesada, Luis, newspaper
  publisher, 33, 109, 117
monetary policy, 79-80, 98-103,
  182-183, 195, 236
Montagne, Gen. Ernesto, 219
Montaña, see Amazonic region,
  map p. 46
Montesinos, Alfonso, 118
Morales Bermúdez, Gen.
  Francisco, Finance Minister,
  1968, 76; tenure as Finance
  Minister, 210-214; tax
  proposals and resignation,
  211-214
Morales Machiavello, Carlos,
  Finance Minister, 1964-1965,
  76, 77
Morales Urresti, José, Justice
  Minister, 1967-1968 and
  Central Bank Chairman, 1968,
  198, 216
Morris, Cynthia Taft, cited 19
Morse, L. R., cited 162
Moscoso, Teodoro, U.S.
  Coordinator of Alliance for
  Progress, 123-124
Mujica Gallo, Miguel, Prime
  Minister, October 1968, 274
municipal elections, 25

national income, shares in, 71-73
nationhood, 280-281
Navarrete, Ifigenia M. de,
  cited 19
navy, 36, 214, 276
New Caledonia, 245
Newmont Mining Co., 8, 244
newspapers, see press

New York, 252, 256
Nigeria, 104
Novak, Enrique, banker, 205

Odría, Gen. Manuel A., President, 1948-1956, 26, 117, 183; in elections of 1962 and 1963, 38-41; leads coup in 1948, 40
Odriísmo, see Unión Nacional Odriísta
Oficina Nacional de Reforma Agraria (ONRA), 67-68, 176
Oiga Magazine, 223, 224
Olcese, Orlando, Minister of Agriculture, 1967-1968, 202, 220
Oliver, Covey T., U.S. Assistant Secretary of State for Interamerican Affairs, 121
Organization of American States, 199, 231
Organization of Petroleum-Exporting Countries (OPEC), 109
Orrego, Eduardo, Acción Popular politician, 62
Ostertag, Fritz, 114
Otero, Javier, Central Bank official, 29, 147

"page 11" controversy, 270-272
Panamerican Highway, 52
Paris, 251, "Paris Club," 253
Parkinson, Charles J., Anaconda chairman, 246
Pássara, Luis, 62
Pastor de la Torre, Celso, Ambassador to U.S., 39, 120, 167
Payne, Arnold, cited 39
pensions (of government), 93
Pérez Godoy, Gen. Ricardo, head of provisional government, 1962-1963, 36

Pernitz Einhorn, Jessica, cited 107
Peru, see also separate entries for agriculture, geography, income and wealth distribution, labor force, manufacturing industry; as a nation, 280-281; "El Peru Construye," 50
Peruvian Corporation, railway co., 44-45
petroleum law of 1952, 118
Phelps Dodge Copper Corp., 8, 244
Pike, Frederick B., cited 24
Piura, 57
Planning Office (Instituto Nacional de Planificación), 22, 75, 91; and Central Bank, 77; 1966-1970 Plan, 105
population, 64, Appendix Table I
ports, 56
poultry industry, 224
Prado family, 187, 239
Prado, Manuel, President, 1939-1945, 1956-1962, 31, 69, 117, 142; deposed 1962, 38-39
predios, 231, 234
presidential messages, 60-61, 70
press (see also El Comercio, La Prensa), 17, 32-34, 134; and IPC, 262-270, 272, 273; role in coup, 270
Prialé, Ramino, APRA leader, 226
prices, see also agricultural prices, gasoline prices, domestic prices, 10, 59, 196; trends in, 102; export and import prices, 128; regulation of, 188; effect of tax measures on, 228
Princeton University, and Central Bank, 29

private investment: stagnation
1962-1964, 49, 58, 128; private
foreign investment, 134
profits tax, 86-87
property tax, 55
proportional representation
(*cifra repartidora*), 27,
278-279
protection from imports, *see*
import tariff
public enterprises, 13-14
public housing, 56
public investment, under
Belaúnde, 51-59
public sector, role in economic
life, 13-17
public utilities, 188
public works, under Belaúnde,
51-59
Púcuta, 65
Punta del Este: 1961 Charter of,
50; 1967 Conference of
Presidents, 126-127

Quellaveco mine, 245

railways, 45
"Ranger" troops, and guerrillas,
66
Ravines, Eudocio, journalist, 138
real estate tax, 206, 230-233
recession 1968, 237
Rio de Janeiro Annual Meeting
of IMF, 193
RIPSA airline, 215
road network, 52
Rockefeller, David, 224, 242
Rockefeller interests, 224
Rodríguez-Pastor, Carlos,
Central Bank official, 29
Rodríguez Mariátegui, Luis,
Justice Minister, 186
Rodríguez Razzetto, Gen., "el
Machote," 178

Rodríguez Vildósola, Luis, APRA
leader & economist, 192
Roemer, Michael, cited 5
Royal Bank of Canada, 238

Salazar Villanueva, Javier,
Finance Minister, 1963-1964,
76, 199
Sánchez Cerro, Gen. Luis M.,
President, 1931-1933, 116-117
Sánchez, Luis Alberto, author
and APRA leader, 66, 89, 167,
226
Sandoval, Clara Elsa de, cited 19
San Francisco, 252
San Lorenzo irrigation, 57, 69
Sansón, Carlos, IMF official, 166
Santa Rosa de Lima, 169
savings and loan system, 34, 73
schools, 57
school teachers, 72; as political
force, 89; salaries of, 88-92;
strike of, 145-146
Schwalb, Fernando, Prime
Minister, 1963-1965, chairman
of Central Bank, 1966-1968,
28, 39, 66, 116, 147, 202, 204
Schwartz, Charles F., IMF
official, 285
Schweitzer, Pierre-Paul,
Managing Director of
International Monetary Fund,
192-193
Seers, Dudley, cited 164
Selva, *see* Amazonic region
Senate, *see* Congress, *Coalición*
Seone, Edgardo, First Vice
President of the Republic,
1963-1968, Prime Minister,
1967, 175, 220; and land
reform, 67-68; Prime Minister,
176-177; resigns, 197
Seone, Manuel, APRA leader,
176

shipyard (at Callao), 84
Singapore (industrial parks), 81
Sierra, 3, 5, 53, 64, 227
Sierra Maestra (Cuba), 65
smuggling, *see Contrabando*
social security, 73, 78
Southern Peru Copper Corp.,
    8, 9, 43, 107, 129, 196, 246
    249
Southern Railway, 45
Spain, 135, 252
Sri Lanka, 122
stamp tax, 48
Standard Oil of California, 187
Standard Oil of New Jersey, 113,
    168
state enterprises, 78-79
Stepan III, Alfred C., cited 36
Strasma, John, cited 63
strikes, 71, 102
sugar farms, 128
Superintendency of Banks, 242
suppliers' credits, 100-101
swaps, 156

Talara, 109, 110, 187, 189, 260,
    269
Taylor, Milton C., cited 199
taxation; *see also* export tax;
    general features, 15; tax
    concessions for industry, 11;
    APRA attitude to taxes, 41;
    under Beltrán, 42-43; under
    1962-1963 junta, 48; trends
    1963-1966, 80-87; exemptions
    from, 84-87; of imports,
    85-86; of manufacturing,
    82-85, 86; regressivity of, 86;
    income and profits taxes,
    86-87; tax proposals for 1967,
    141, 155; export tax, 193-194;
    De Andrea tax proposals,
    199-201; Law 16900 measures,
    206-208; measures proposed

by Gen. Morales Bermúdez,
    211-212; measures under
    Ulloa, 230-236; fiscal impact
    of measures, 234-236
Tax Court, 129, 186
teachers, *see* school teachers
Temoche Benítez, Ricardo, APRA
    member of Congress, cited
    171
territorial waters (200-mile
    limit), 6
Thorp, Rosemary, cited 44
Tinajones irrigation, 57-58
Tintaya mine, 245
Tittmann, Edward M., American
    Smelting Chairman, 246
Tola, Enrique, Minister of
    Education, 146
Toquepala mine, 7, 9, 42-43,
    127, 136, 245
Torre Tagle palace, 212
Townsend, Andrés, APRA leader,
    226
Trachtman, Capt. (ret.), 216
Trujillo, 196
Tumbes, 110
Turkey, 104
Tweddle, Herbert, 112

Ulloa, Manuel, newspaper
    publisher and Finance
    Minister, 1968, 33, 76, 215,
    220-221; and DELTEC,
    222-224; tenure as Finance
    Minister, 224-242, 249-258;
    tax measures, 232-233; other
    measures, 240-241; and
    mining companies, 246-247;
    and external debt, 249-258;
    role in IPC issue, 270, 273
Unión Nacional Odriísta (UNO),
    see also Coalición, APRA,
    and Odría, 40-41; and
    Carretera Marginal, 54; and

Unión Nacional Odriísta (*cont.*)
Cooperación Popular, 62; and
guerrilla issue, 66; and IPC,
120; and 1967 elections, 189,
196-197; and taxes, 201-203
United Nations Economic
Commission for Latin America
(ECLA), 47, 77, 177
U.S. Agency for International
Development (AID), 95; and
IPC, 121-125; assistance to
Peru, 121-125; program loan
discussion, 156-160; and IPC
settlement, 260-261
U.S. Department of Defense, 159
U.S. Department of State, see
U.S. Government
U.S. direct investment in Peru,
10
U.S. Embassy; and IPC, 108-109,
117
U.S. Export-Import Bank, 8, 42
U.S. Government; and IPC,
108-109, 117; assistance to
Peru, 120-125; compared to
other countries, 125; and
defense purchases, 159
U.S. mining industry, 246
U.S. Treasury, 104
U.S. universities, 30
universities, 78; expenditures on,
92-93
upper income groups, attitude to
public service, 15-16, 70-71
Urrutia, Miguel, cited 19
Utah Construction Co., 8

Valdivia Morriberón, Col. and
then Gen. Angel, 47
Vargas Haya, Hector, APRA
member of Congress, 216

Vaughn, Jack H., U.S. Assistant
Secretary of State for
Interamerican Affairs, 121
Velarde Cabello, Carlos, Minister
of Government and Police
1968, 220
Velasco Alvarado, Gen. Juan,
178, 219, 259, 274
Velasco, Mariano, 119
Venezuela, 100, 107, 189, 222
Vera, Fernando, IMF official,
248
Villa Mercedes, 192
Villanueva, Armando, APRA
leader, 191, 192, 203, 218,
226, 265, 274
Vuscovic, Pedro, Chilean
economist, 47

wages and salaries, 71-73, 102,
185, 194
War of Independence, 110
Washington, D.C., 265
Washington Post, 158
water and sewerage authority,
see COSAL, 56-57
wealth, distribution of, 18, 22
Webb Duarte, Richard C.,
Peruvian economist and
Central Bank official, 19, 29,
285; cited 18, 71, 87, 277
World Bank, 69, 104-105,
124-125, 127, 244

Zaïre, 245
Zarak, Alex, Finance Minister,
1961-1962, 43
Zileri, Enrique, newspaperman,
33
Zimmerman, Augusto, 215; cited
106, 219, 221, 259, 270, 272,
274

Library of Congress Cataloging in Publication Data
Kuczynski, Pedro-Pablo, 1938-
  Peruvian democracy under economic stress.

  Includes index.
  1. Peru—Economic policy.   2. Peru—Economic
conditions—1968-   3. Peru—Politics and government—1968-   4. Belaúnde Terry, Fernando, Pres.
Peru, 1912-   I. Title.
HC227.K83   330.9'85'063   76-24296
ISBN 0-691-04213-6